The Hockey News
CENTURY OF
HOCKEY

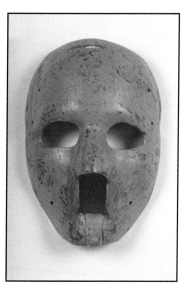

Merry Happy Trissmas! (2001)

Love,
Getti

The Hockey News

CENTURY OF HOCKEY

A Season-by-Season Celebration

FOREWORD BY BOBBY ORR

TRIBUTE BY BOB McKENZIE

EDITED BY STEVE DRYDEN

M&S

Cloth edition published 2000
Trade paperback edition published 2001

National Library of Canada Cataloguing in Publication Data

Main entry under title:
  Century of hockey

Includes index.
ISBN 0-7710-4179-9 (bound).—ISBN 0-7710-4180-2 (pbk.)

1. Hockey – History. 2. National Hockey League – History. I. Dryden, Steve,
1957-

GV846.5.C46   2000   796.962'64'09   C00-931246-3

We acknowledge the financial support of the Government of Canada through
the Book Publishing Industry Development Program for our publishing
activities. We further acknowledge the support of the Canada Council for
the Arts and the Ontario Arts Council for our publishing program.

Research by Denis Gibbons
Design by Matt Blackett and Jamie Hodgson, *The Hockey News*
Typeset by *The Hockey News* and M&S, Toronto
Printed and bound in Canada

Photo overleaf: Toronto Maple Leafs' star goalie Johnny Bower
goes head to head with Montreal Canadiens' superstar Jean Beliveau.
(Frank Prazak/HHOF)

McClelland & Stewart Ltd.
The Canadian Publishers
481 University Avenue
Toronto, Ontario
M5G 2E9
www.mcclelland.com

1   2   3   4   5   05   04   03   02   01

CONTENTS

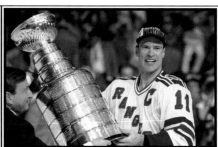

Foreword

By Bobby Orr

There is so much you can say about the game of hockey–past, present and future–but there are only two things I know for certain.

One, I was honored to have the opportunity to play the game, that it was good to me and I wouldn't trade any of it for anything.

Two, no one ever tried to change the way I played the game. And for that I am thankful, because if they had, I would not have been as effective.

I was what I was–an offense-minded player. I loved to take chances.

One example is the goal I scored to win our first Stanley Cup in Boston. People remember the picture of me flying through the air after the goal was scored. But what they might not recall is that I took a big chance, that if the puck had gone by me on the boards, it would have been a 2-on-1 the other way from the St. Louis blueline to our goal.

But that's the way I played.

Even though I was a defenseman, I didn't like to sit back. I was having fun. From the time I put on skates as a kid, that's how I played. As a kid, I never thought much about what kind of player I was. Looking back on it now, though, I realize I always could skate. I always was fast and that's how I liked to play.

Minor hockey, junior hockey, pro hockey, I never changed. I just played. It certainly wasn't a style the pros liked or were used to.

It's not what a coach would like. But the Bruins, to their credit, never tried to change my style.

They had me for four years in Oshawa and didn't try to make me something I wasn't. The only thing they ever said to me was, 'Try to be careful.' I think they understood that the hardest thing in the world for me would have been to change the way I played.

Mind you, in my second year in the National Hockey League they tried to play me up front as a forward. They

watched me for awhile and said, 'You're terrible, get back there.' And that was fine with me.

I was lucky. I always had teammates who understood the way I played, that I liked to take chances and they would cover up for me.

I would like for every kid who plays the game to have what I had–a chance to be myself, to do what comes naturally. I'm not sure that happens as often as it should.

I look back on the career I had and I wouldn't change any of it. A lot of people talk about the goals I scored or the records I set, but I'll be honest, what I remember most about my career was playing the games, winning the Stanley Cup, the Canada Cup. That's what sticks out.

For me, it was all about playing.

Unfortunately, I played a style that made me susceptible to injury. Hockey's a tough sport, it's a hitting sport, and the way I played the game, my style, meant I got hit more and hurt more.

I'm not even sure how many times I had operations on my knee. I think it's 13 or 14, including some after retirement. When it got to the point that, because of the injuries, I couldn't play the game the way I liked to play it, I had to retire. If I couldn't play my style, I couldn't go on being something I wasn't.

Regrets? Not one. My career was a dream come true. I was a kid from Parry Sound, Ont., who used to see players like George Armstrong hoist the Cup over their head. And I got to do that, too.

Oh, I wish I could have played longer. I guess I could sit back and wonder what could have been, but I honestly don't do that. I knew going in I wasn't going to be a 20-year player. My style wouldn't allow for it.

I still probably should have had seven or eight more years, but I'm not complaining. I have no right to complain.

The game was very good to me. It's a great game and I'm forever thankful I got to play it, the way I liked to play it.

Full Speed Ahead

By Bob McKenzie

Phil Esposito scored 717 goals, 778 if you count playoffs, during his 18-year NHL career. There's one goal he'll never forget and he didn't even score it.

"It's the most amazing thing I ever saw Bobby Orr do and I saw him do lots of amazing things," Esposito said. "We were playing the Oakland Seals. I was out killing a penalty with Eddie Westfall.

"Bobby got the puck and he just took off on his own. The Seals were chasing him all the over ice. They knocked off his glove, but they couldn't get the puck off him. I skated by our bench and Gerry Cheevers asked me if I wanted to read the racing form. I might as well have because I wasn't doing anything on the ice except watching Bobby.

"He just kept going, round and round with the puck. While he was skating with the puck, he bent down and picked up the glove he had lost. Then he took off and scored a short-handed goal. It was unbelievable, just unbelievable."

Orr was asked about that one.

"Where I picked up my glove?" Orr said.

He giggled and that was it.

Esposito's story only reinforces what every hockey fan over the age of, say, 35–those fortunate enough to see Orr in his prime–and Bobby Clarke have known for a long time.

That Orr was something special, unique when he broke in as an NHL rookie in 1966 and unique even now, 21 years after his injury-ravaged left knee cut him down in his prime.

"Remember what it was like to play kids' hockey and there always was one kid who was so much better than everyone else?" said Clarke, the former Philadelphia Flyer captain who waged war with Orr in the early 1970s. "Well, that's what it was like playing against Bobby Orr—he was so much better than everyone else. It was like he was too good for the NHL."

❑ ❑ ❑ ❑

Too good for the NHL? The mere suggestion boggles the mind.

Orr's statistics and collection of honors do not begin to tell the story of the man who changed the way the game was played, but they are a starting point.

The shy kid with the brushcut from Parry Sound, Ont., arrived to play with the Oshawa Generals in 1962 as a 14-year-old. He starred there for four years. In his final season of junior, he averaged two points per game and led the Generals to a Memorial Cup appearance.

He joined a bad Bruin team for the 1966-67 season–the last of the Original Six-Era–and though Boston missed the playoffs for the seventh consecutive season that year, the 18-year-old phenom made his presence felt immediately.

He won the Calder Trophy as NHL rookie of the year, and he was named, along with Tim Horton, to the NHL's second all-star team. What followed was utter domination.

Beginning with his second NHL season, there were eight consecutive first-team all-star selections, and eight consecutive Norris Trophies. Orr, and please do try to remember he was a defenseman, won the Hart Trophy as NHL MVP three consecutive years, from 1970 through 1972. He won the Art Ross Trophy as the league's leading scorer in 1970 and 1975.

He recorded six straight seasons of 100 points or more, with goal totals that ranged from 29 at the low end to, at the time, an NHL record 46 goals. Even today, only Paul Coffey's

mark of 48 goals eclipses Orr's 46 in 1975. His 102 assists in 1971 stand as an NHL record for defensemen. So, too, do his 139 points that same year. Of the top five point totals ever accumulated in one season by a defenseman, Orr owns three.

And if you would like to get the hair on the back of his neck all bristled up, ask him if those numbers were perhaps a little higher than they might otherwise have been because

of NHL expansion from six to 12 teams for the 1967-68 season.

"How many teams are there now, 30?" Orr asked.

Touché.

Along with Phil Esposito, Orr was the catalyst for the Bruins ending a 29-year drought and winning the Cup in 1970, and claiming it again in 1972. Both times, Orr was awarded the Conn Smythe Trophy as playoff MVP.

Oh, and did we mention that much of what he accomplished was done in excruciating pain, the result of countless injuries, and corresponding surgeries, to a wonky left knee? "Bobby Orr was better on one leg," said former Toronto Maple Leaf captain Darryl Sittler, "than anybody else was on two."

If you were blessed to see Orr play, the statistical recitation and list of awards only underscores what you already know–he was one of a kind. Until Orr came along, a defenseman was just that—a *man* who played *defense* almost exclusively. Orr broke the mold. He was a rambling, gambling rover who regularly skated beyond all limitations.

"That's the way I always played," Orr said. "I didn't like to sit back. I was having fun. From the time I was a kid, that's how I played...The hardest thing in the world for me would have been to change my style."

Thankfully, no one ever tried to do that. Not that there was any chance of it, any more than there was of shutting down Orr when he had a head of steam and a mind to make things happen. It's difficult to paint a picture of how Orr played the game. At least it is if you're trying to explain it to someone who hasn't witnessed the majesty of his game, either live or on tape. Words simply don't cut it. But we can try.

This isn't the story of Orr's life. It's not about his ill-fated relationship with disgraced agent Alan Eagleson or the loss of his wealth, which he has regained many times over. It's not about leaving the Bruins for the Chicago Black Hawks or his difficulty coping with a retirement that came far too early. And it's not about what he thinks of the game today or his foray into the player agent business.

While every one of those are intriguing aspects of Orr's life story–which, incidentally, he said will never find its way into any book–this is a celebration of Orr's ability as a player.

Because with Orr, playing was always the thing.

❏ ❏ ❏ ❏

No discussion of Bobby Orr, the player, could begin with anything but how he skated.

"No matter how fast anyone else was, Bobby always had an extra gear," said legendary NHL coach Scott Bowman. "No one ever seemed to gain on him. He would just keep kicking it into the next gear and opening up space."

"He had those big bow legs," added Sittler. "He was so strong on his skates, he had such a strong and powerful stride."

Phil Esposito won't ever forget the first time he saw Orr. It was in 1966-67, when Esposito was still with the Chicago Black Hawks and Orr was playing his first regular season game at the Chicago Stadium. "The Bruins were trying him at center," Esposito said. "We'd all heard so much about this kid who was supposed to be so great. I remember saying to someone, 'He's okay but just that.' Then they put him on the point during a power play and he picked up the puck behind the net and took off. I said to someone, 'Holy f—, can that guy motor.' "

If Orr has an aversion to cataloguing his greatest or most meaningful goals–and he most assuredly does–he has no such hang-ups talking about his skating.

"The one thing I could do was skate," Orr said. "Growing up, it was skate, skate, skate, skate...that's all I did. I was blessed with an ability to skate...People talk about pressure. I never felt any pressure until I couldn't do what I once could do and that was skate. When I could no longer skate like I could, that's when I started feeling pressure. That was the major reason I retired."

Orr's first two steps were explosive. Then he would, as Bowman and Sittler noted, just keep changing gears until he was into some sort of warp speed that left everyone standing still.

If Orr's quintessential quality was his speed, his overall strength and toughness, mental and physical, were right up there. Longtime Montreal *Gazette* hockey writer Red Fisher recalled his first look at a rookie Bobby Orr. A brawl broke out between the Bruins and Habs, Fisher said, with the rookie Bruin finding himself alongside noted Montreal pugilist Ted Harris.

Orr not only engaged the big Canadien defenseman in a battle, Fisher said, "he picked (Harris) up and slammed him back-first into the boards and onto the ice. After the game, I asked Harris, 'What do you think of the kid?' He said, 'Raunchy, isn't he?' "

At 6-foot, 197 pounds, Orr wasn't small. But he wasn't a behemoth either. He was, however, strong and tenacious. While his focus was slanted heavily in favor of generating offense, he made every effort to staple opponents into the boards and do battle in front of the net.

And fight?

"Oh, he fought and, boy, could he fight," Esposito said. "Actually, he fought too much, but he didn't want to show any weakness."

That, of course, was by design.

"Early in my career, they wanted to test the rookie," Orr said. "Did I want to fight? No, but in my mind I was thinking, 'I've got to go.' If you wouldn't go, they were going to be all over your butt all the time. In the beginning, there was quite a bit (of fighting). A lot was said and written about this kid coming up and they wanted to see what he was all about, if I would hang in. I consciously hung in there. I wanted them to leave me alone."

Fast and tough, Orr also had a flair for the dramatic or unusual. There was the memorable goal against Oakland (the shorthanded effort recounted by Esposito) and an unconventional wraparound against Atlanta when Orr played pied piper to an entire team of skaters. They all followed him behind one side of the net and he emerged out the other to score unopposed.

Many of his great plays came about because of his state of mind. That is, he loved to gamble. Even though he was a defenseman, he didn't mind being the last one out of the offensive zone or the first one out of the defensive zone. He would stay on the offensive blueline and try to pick off passes. No one did a better job of knocking pucks out of the air with his stick.

Much of what he did was framed by the fact he was a left-handed shot who played the right side. More often than not, he would race down the right wing with the puck and attempt to use his speed and strength to beat the defenseman wide. He would go into that wide, protect-the-puck stance, leading with his left knee, his left arm up to fend off the attacker and the right arm controlling his stick and the puck.

It was that left knee that took the beating. If it wasn't leading his reckless charges to the net, it was being dragged behind as he tried to finesse his way around the defender.

"I was trying to beat guys where I shouldn't have been beating them," Orr said. "I did dumb things. But I knew it would be coming. You can't get ready for a hit like that, but I would know it was coming. I was always dragging that left leg. That's where I would get in trouble."

And still he would drive the net. Watch the Orr highlight tapes and you lose count of how many times he ended up crashing into: a) the goalie; b) the net; c) the end boards; d) all of the above.

On those occasions when he would beat a defenseman wide and get a lane to the net, it was not unusual to see him shoot the puck with only one hand on his stick, at the top of the shaft. He'd put the puck on the backside of the blade and wrist a flip shot over the goalie. More than a few found their way into the back of the net.

Occasionally, he would take the path of least resistance, swoop behind the offensive net and curl all the way back up to his blueline posi-

Bobby Orr was an NHL all-star every full season of his career.

tion, from where he was so dangerous. There, he would survey the offensive zone as if it were his empire. He'd thread a pass or fire one of his patented half-slappers from the point.

His shot was unique. It was hard and it was heavy, but the wind-up was never above his waist and quite often no more than knee-high. Orr said he can't begin to count how many goals or assists he tallied by simply getting the puck to the net with the ultra-efficient wind-up.

"When you've got Phil Esposito in the front of the net screening or waiting for a loose puck, you didn't want to waste

time or get it blocked," Orr said. "It was pretty basic."

If there was an economy to his shooting, there was even more to his goal celebrations. His arms usually went up about as high as his slapshot wind-up. And only for a split second. Orr would strike quickly for a goal and if you blinked, you missed the celebration. More often than not, his face didn't show any emotion.

Another of his trademarks was shotblocking, especially when his goaltender was pulled and an enemy forward was bearing down on the empty net. He would make like a goalie–he used to put on the pads for fun during pre-practice hijinks in Oshawa–and make the save while turning the puck up ice for one final attack to get the equalizer.

Esposito said no player he has ever seen played the give-and-go better than Orr. That was, in part, because of his God-given ability to skate but also because of a burning desire to be in the middle of the action.

"For him to give up the puck and then not expect to get it back," Esposito said, "well, that just didn't happen."

As good a skater as Orr was, Esposito isn't convinced No. 4 was a great backwards skater.

"For one thing," Esposito said, "he didn't do it very often. Instead of skating backwards on a 1-on-1, Bobby would skate forward towards the player, turn and go shoulder-to-shoulder and angle him off."

Orr roared when told of Esposito's comments.

"I could skate backwards," Orr said, laughing. "But I would do what Phil said. That was my style. I wasn't one for sitting back and saying, 'Come on down.' It was more fun for me to play a different style. I didn't want to be a conventional defenseman. That's how I enjoyed playing the game."

Certainly, no one used the goalframe to his advantage more than Orr, especially when penalty-killing.

"If a team was stupid enough to send only one guy after Bobby when he was behind the net while killing a penalty, Bobby would just keep skating in circles around the goal," Esposito said. "We used to laugh about it, he was so good at it."

And before there was the 'Savardian Spinnerama,' popularized by pivoting Montreal Canadien defenseman Serge Savard,

Orr was breaking ground with a high-risk move while standing on the offensive blueline. The left-shot, right defenseman would pump like he was taking a shot, drawing the attacking player toward the puck, and then whirl to his backhand and explode out of his shooting stance toward the net.

"I got burned on a it a few times," Orr said, "but if (the attacking player) read the play, I would just dump a backhand shot into the corner."

And if there were any doubts about Orr being one of a kind, consider: he didn't wear socks in his skates; he didn't lace up his skates to the top; he used little or no tape on his stick; and he didn't wear shoulder pads, at least not in the conventional sense–Orr had plastic shoulder caps sewn onto the top of his suspenders.

Sittler said he thinks Orr's ability to do the spinnerama was rooted in how he laced his skates. "The players today have the laces done up to the top, real tight," Sittler said. "I'm not sure how he did it, but Bobby had so much agility. It was like his ankles were on hinges."

Unique doesn't begin to sum up Orr.

"All those things," Orr said, "that's just me. I can't explain why I did them other than that's what made me feel comfortable. I didn't like new equipment, I didn't like anything bulky or stiff. You have to feel comfortable and that's how I felt comfortable."

It is ironic–no, make that tragic–that a player so determined to find comfort was so often in discomfort. Even now, not a day goes by when Orr doesn't experience a painful reminder of why his glowing NHL career was limited to what amounted to nine seasons.

Oh, the record shows he played 12, but 1974-75–the year he led the league in assists (89) and points (135)–was his last full campaign. He was 27 years old at the time. Cut down in the prime of a career? Orr is the poster boy. He played just 36 games over the next three seasons–10 in Boston, 26 in Chicago–and took off the entire 1977-78 season before finally calling it quits in 1978-79. And it was all because of that left knee. The right knee is fine, perfect almost. There's one little scar, about the size of a bullet hole, where he had an arthroscopic procedure. The left, though, is a mess. It looks like a road map of downtown Boston, and if you've ever driven there, you get the picture. Roads, or in this case scars, intersecting at odd angles. The

Bobby Orr's Super Stats

Hometown Parry Sound, Ont.
Birthdate March 20, 1948
Regular Season & Playoff Statistics

Year	Team	GP	G	A	Pts.
'62-63	Oshawa	34	6	15	21
		—	—	—	—
'63-64	Oshawa	56	29	43	72
		6	0	7	7
'64-65	Oshawa	56	34	59	93
		6	0	6	6
'65-66	Oshawa	47	38	56	94
		17	9	19	28
'66-67	**Boston**	**61**	**13**	**28**	**41**
		—	—	—	—
'67-68	**Boston**	**46**	**11**	**20**	**31**
		4	0	2	2
'68-69	**Boston**	**67**	**21**	**43**	**64**
		10	1	7	8
'69-70	**Boston****	**76**	**33**	**87***	**120***
		14	9	11	20
'70-71	**Boston**	**78**	**37**	**102***	**139**
		7	5	7	12
'71-72	**Boston****	**76**	**37**	**80**	**117**
		15	5	19*	24*
'72-73	**Boston**	**63**	**29**	**72**	**101**
		5	1	1	2
'73-74	**Boston**	**74**	**32**	**90***	**122**
		16	4	14*	18
'74-75	**Boston**	**80**	**46**	**89***	**135***
		3	1	5	6
'75-76	**Boston**	**10**	**5**	**13**	**18**
		—	—	—	—
'76-77	**Chicago**	**20**	**4**	**19**	**23**
		—	—	—	—
'77-78	**Chicago**	Did Not Play			
'78-79	**Chicago**	**6**	**2**	**2**	**4**
		—	—	—	—
NHL Totals		**657**	**270**	**645**	**915**
		74	26	66	92

Honors	No.	Year(s)
Calder	1	'67
Norris	8	'68, '69, '70, '71, '72, '73, '74, '75
Hart	3	'70,'71,'72
Art Ross	2	'70, '75
Conn Smythe	2	'70, '72
1st All-Star	8	'68, '69, '70, '71, '72, '73, '74, '75
2nd All-Star	1	'67

*League-leading   **Stanley Cup

kneecap itself seems permanently swollen, hard and shiny.

"The ligaments are actually fine, they're intact," Orr said, surveying the carnage. "It's the cartilage that was the problem. There's none left. And they had to go in to get out bone chips and flakes."

The long and the short of it is that Orr can't fully bend his left knee, not even when he sits down. It goes about halfway, at a 45-degree angle, and locks up. That, he said, is not as painful as it is uncomfortable, especially when it comes time to stand up. That's when a limp or gait is most pronounced with Orr. It takes him a few strides to unhitch the locked knee.

It was suggested to him that he owns the most famous knee in all of sports. Orr pondered that for a moment before replying: "No, Joe Namath."

If you are looking for a detailed breakdown of his battles with wounded knee, Orr is the wrong guy to ask. He "thinks" there have been "13 or 14" operations on the left knee. Some of them, fewer than half, he said, were done after he was retired. The others, he said, "kind of run together." The first serious problems, he said, arose in his second NHL season. And he doesn't need a calendar or a good memory to know that his knee woes cost him the opportunity to participate in the 1972 Canada-Soviet Summit Series, an event which, to this day, he treasures as if he played in it.

"At the end of the 1972 playoffs, I had surgery," Orr said of his second Cup-winning year. "I don't remember a lot about it, only that it was bothering me for a long time. I thought I could hang in, play in the finals. But I had to have surgery when it was over. I was sore–the early surgeries were not easy to come back from."

Although he couldn't play in the historic Summit Series, Orr was there every step of the way, a member of the team in every way except on the ice. Asked for his most memorable moments as a player, he identified the '72 series as one of them.

"I was with them," Orr said. "I don't know if there's been a better team in sport than that one. I don't think anyone can fully understand what that team went through. I didn't like not being able to play, but it was an experience. What that team did, what those players did against that Soviet team, to have to win three of four in Moscow and then lose the first one there...to have to deal with the conditions there. To this day, I don't think I've ever been part of anything like that team did under those conditions."

It was Orr's burning desire to play for Canada that prompted him to participate in the 1976 Canada Cup tournament. It has been said he played the tournament on one leg. He was coming off a season in which he was limited to 10 games with the Bruins because of his knee problems. Some have suggested that his desire to play in that event was ill-conceived, that it was the last straw, what ultimately killed his career.

Not so, said Orr, who explained that he knew before the tournament his career was all but over.

"That's the reason I went to the Canada Cup," he said. "I knew I didn't have much longer. That series didn't do it. I knew I was close (to retirement) right there. I thought I could get the next season in, but not much after that. I said, 'Let's give it a go,' and I'm glad I did. I knew looking at (the talent on) that team, I wouldn't have to do as much. I wouldn't have traded it for anything. I'd never really represented my country."

Orr's effort and performance in that tournament rank high in the annals of the game. He was named MVP, but aside from those on the team, no one could imagine what it took for him to play in those games. Clarke said, to this day he hasn't seen anything like what Orr did in 1976.

"He would hardly be able to skate on the morning of the game," Clarke said. "And he would hardly be able to walk in the afternoon. I would say to him, 'You can't play, you don't have to do this.' And then, at night, he would be the best player on one of the greatest teams that's ever been assembled. He was the best player in every game; he was the best player in the tournament. He couldn't skate like he used to, but he could still go."

The legend stretches out on a sofa–his ravaged left knee bearing the scars of "13 or 14" surgical procedures.

Orr suspected the 1976 Canada Cup would be his last hurrah. But that it took almost three years before he decided to retire speaks to how much he loved the game.

"When I was younger, I was like everyone else," Orr said. "I thought I was indestructable. I thought I could come back quickly. I soon started realizing that as the surgeries went on, they got harder and harder to come back from...I never felt pressure until I couldn't do what I could once do. That was because I couldn't skate. My lateral movement was terrible. I couldn't jump up into the play like I once did. That was the major reason I retired. I probably could have played a little longer by just sitting back, but it wasn't my game. It wasn't how I enjoyed playing."

Orr won't kid you–premature retirement was difficult. All he had ever known was hockey and hockey was being taken away from him.

"I made a mistake," Orr said. "I didn't have any interests beyond hockey. It was hockey, hockey, hockey and now, suddenly, I had to retire and get a real job. I probably moped around for a couple of years. I wasn't bitter, but there were difficult days. The reason I kept going at the end as long as I did, I wanted to make sure there was no coming back and there was no coming back for me. It was hard, it was confusing, they'd taken my skates away from me. But I soon figured out I could approach my business the same way as the game. There are no differences. You have teammates. You have to be disciplined. You have to work hard. There are no differences."

And though his achy knee provides a constant reminder of how his career ended, Orr tries to avoid thinking of what could have been if he hadn't been struck down in his prime.

"I wish I could have played longer," he said. "But I have no right to complain. The game was very good to me."

Not as good as he was to the game.

The Ice Age Begins

By Jason Paul

The name James George Aylwin Creighton doesn't roll off the tongues of most hockey fans. But it's a name all fans should remember. He has never received the acclaim of baseball's Abner Doubleday or basketball's Dr. James Naismith, but James Creighton is the closest person in hockey to belonging in that sports pioneer brotherhood.

Indeed, Creighton helped create the spark that produced the game of hockey in North America and is generally considered 'The Father of Hockey.'

Creighton took part in the first 'recognized' hockey game of record on March 3, 1875, at the indoor Victoria Rink in Montreal. There were nine players aside on a 200-by-85-foot ice surface. Spectators were warned to keep their heads up for the wooden puck because there were no boards. There were no nets, just two sticks in the ice eight feet apart and six feet tall–leaving it to a referee and goal judge to determine if a goal was scored. (No reports exist of video replay being used to rule on the legality of goals.) Players could not protect the goal or pass the puck forward.

That day's edition of the Montreal *Gazette* reported "a game of hockey will be played at the Victoria Skating Rink this evening between two nines chosen from among the members. Good fun may be expected, as some of the players are reputed to be exceedingly expert at the game. Some fears have been expressed on the part of intended spectators that accidents were likely to occur through the ball flying about in too lively a manner, to the imminent danger of lookers-on, but we understand that the game will be played with a flat circular piece of wood, thus preventing all danger of its leaving the surface of the ice."

James Creighton

Creighton captained his team to victory that day. He was not only a leading force in this historic game, but also a pioneer in taking ice hurley–based on an Irish stick-ball game–from the frozen lakes of Nova Scotia to an organized sport in Montreal when he moved there in 1872. This has led to the great debate among hockey historians: Where is the real birthplace of hockey?

In one corner is the city of the NHL's most glorified team, Montreal, and in the other a small town on the bank of the Avon River in Atlantic Canada, Windsor, N.S.

Kingston, Ont., home to the original Hockey Hall of Fame, has also been labeled the cradle of hockey, but the city's claim is more myth than reality.

Kingston, which sits halfway between Toronto and Montreal, was first called "the birthplace of hockey" by a local newspaper in 1903. Kingstonian James Thomas Sutherland–one of the trailblazers of the game–wrote several articles proclaiming hockey's origins there. "I think it is generally admitted and has been substantially proven on many occasions that the actual birthplace of organized hockey is the city of Kingston in 1888," Sutherland wrote in 1924.

One of his articles found its way into the 1927 New York Rangers' program, perpetuating a myth that would grow as large as Kingston native Don Cherry's collars.

Kingston did, though, become the gateway for hockey as the game made its way west across Canada. The first published report of a seven-aside match was in 1886. It took place on Kingston's frozen harbor–two years before the time Sutherland claimed the game was born.

That game was the start of hockey's longest-standing

Early 1800s	1872	1877	1887
Ice hurley, an early form of hockey, is played in Nova Scotia	*Halifax's James Creighton takes concept of hockey to Montreal*	*First published rules appear in Montreal Gazette*	*First league founded, Amateur Hockey Association of Canada*
1859	**1875**	**1883**	**1893**
Boston newspaper article praises 'winter sport' in Nova Scotia	*First 'recognized' hockey game is played in Montreal*	*Hockey's first tournament held at Montreal Winter Carnival*	*Lord Stanley of Preston donates Cup; won by Montreal A.A.A.*

rivalry, between Royal Military College of Canada and Queen's University–the first educational institution to challenge for the Stanley Cup in 1895.

In 1941, Sutherland initiated a farcical study, through the Canadian Amateur Hockey Association, to investigate the game's origins. The report was essentially Kingston propaganda and led to the creation of a hockey hall of fame, which was awarded to the city although the decision was based more on Kingston's location than its claim to the origins of the game.

Windsor, N.S., took over Kingston's challenge to Montreal as the birthplace of hockey during the latter part of the 20th century. A form of shinny or hurley on ice was played on Nova Scotia's lakes and rivers in the 1800s. Windsor's leading proponent, Garth Vaughan, proclaims that a form of ice hockey was being played around 1800. He bases his claim on the writings of author Thomas Chandler Haliburton, who was born in Windsor in 1796, and who attended nearby King's College School.

In 1844, Haliburton wrote about classmates playing "hurley on the long pond on the ice." The stories make no mention of the games being played on skates.

The only other documentation supporting Windsor's claim is from a Boston *Evening Gazette* article entitled 'Winter Sports in Nova Scotia' that ran in December, 1859. The report praised the game "with skates on feet and hurleys or hockey (sticks) in hand." Windsor is not mentioned in the article and it refers to a ball being used rather than a puck.

The early game in Nova Scotia was usually played with 10 to 20 players aside, but

A painting of Montreal's Victoria Rink, home of the first 'recognized' hockey game.

HHOF

Hockey's Oldest Debate

The definitive answer to the question, 'Where is the birthplace of hockey?' rests in the answer to another question, 'When does a sport become a sport?' It's agreed a primitive form of hockey was played in Nova Scotia and it's also agreed the game first became truly organized in Montreal. Supporters of Windsor, N.S., argue that these games of 'shinny' constitute the defining roots of hockey. The crucial stage of hockey evolution, however, came in 1872 when Nova Scotian James George Aylwin Creighton moved to Montreal. Creighton was the driving force behind the first organized game, played with a referee and rules, March 3, 1875, at Montreal's indoor Victoria Rink. From there, hockey's stature grew exponentially.

there were never any set rules and the nets were defined by two stones used as posts.

Creighton was just nine when the story was published. Thirteen years later, after developing skills as a figure skater, he moved to Montreal to become an engineer. Nova Scotia was a center for equipment manufacturing and high-class skates were made there as early as 1861. Creighton had sticks sent to Montreal in 1875.

It's widely held that he wrote the first published rules, which appeared in the Montreal *Gazette* Feb. 27, 1877, two years after the first game at Victoria Rink.

Five years later, Creighton moved to Ottawa to become a civil servant and, together with colleagues, formed a team–the Rideau Rebels–which included two sons of Lord Stanley of Preston (who would donate the Stanley Cup in 1893).

Hockey began to take hold in 1883 with the first hockey tournament at the Montreal Winter Carnival. Three teams–McGill, the Victorias and a third from Quebec City–played on the ice-covered St. Lawrence River with seven players aside.

The following year, five teams participated and in 1885 it became a six-team tournament–including five clubs from Montreal (the Victorias, the Crystals, McGill, the Montreal Football Club, and the Montreal Amateur Athletic Association–better known as the Montreal A.A.A.) and one from Ottawa.

This led to a winter-long tournament the following year and in 1887 an official league called the Amateur Hockey Association of Canada was formed. In 1892-93, the Montreal A.A.A. was awarded the first Stanley Cup.

Creighton never did have his name engraved on hockey's holy grail, but his name has an even more prominent place in the history of the game in North America.

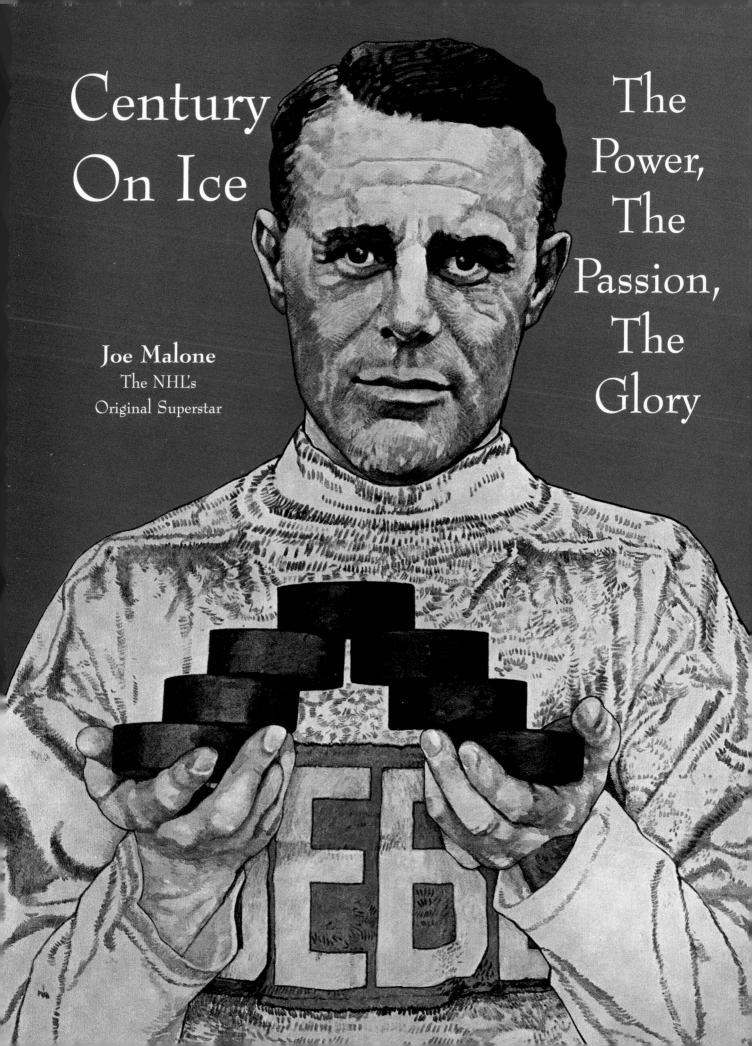

Century
On Ice

The
Power,
The
Passion,
The
Glory

Joe Malone
The NHL's
Original Superstar

The story of elite-level hockey in North America before formation of the National Hockey League in 1917 falls into four main periods over the first two decades of the century:
1. 1900-04: End of the Amateur Era. 2. 1905-09: Birth of Professionalism.
3. 1910-13: Pro Leagues Take Control of Stanley Cup. 4. 1914-17: Pro Hockey Expands.
The history of 'Century on Ice' is the story of these distinct periods,
and the 83 years that follow in the NHL.

HHOF

Lord Stanley of Preston donates the Stanley Cup in 1893. It becomes hockey's most cherished possession.

End Of The Amateur Era 1900-04

No. 1 STORY Net gain for hockey

The second-year Canadian Amateur Hockey League opens the 1899-1900 season with a new feature–netting strung between the goal posts. Supported by an iron crossbar and with white cotton cord instead of darker hemp, the new nets make it easier for goal umpires to spot the puck. They are an instant hit, especially with Montreal Amateur Athletic Association goalie Fred Munro, who smacks his head on the crossbar in his first game.

2. Stanley Cup quest considered tiresome

Teams facing continuous Stanley Cup challenges claim the matches are tiresome and consider dropping out because it's hampering their ability to remain competitive in their own leagues. "The Cup is far from beneficial to the game, it is detrimental to it," insists Montreal A.A.A. captain Dickie Boon in 1903, whose squad loses the Cup to Ottawa after fending off Winnipeg the previous month. Eventually, such talk subsides.

3. Amateur league introduces goal line

When the CAHL refuses to allow new members, a rival league is formed in December, 1903. The Federal Amateur League begins play with four teams–the Montreal Wanderers, Montreal Nationals, Ottawa and Cornwall. The league adopts a goal line to help goal umpires. The champion Wanderers face the CAHL's Ottawa Silver Seven for the Stanley Cup, but the Wanderers quit the series over incompetent refereeing. The league folds after one more year.

1905-09 Birth Of Professionalism

No. 1 STORY 'One-Eyed' McGee Silver Star

Center-rover Frank McGee leads the Ottawa Silver Seven team to nine straight defenses of the Stanley Cup (1903-06). He scores 63 goals in 22 Cup games, including a record 14 in a 23-2 win over Dawson City, Yukon on Jan. 16, 1905. The star loses his left eye during a game in 1900, giving rise to a famous nickname: 'One-Eyed' Frank McGee. All seven players were given a silver nugget after their first Cup, hence the name.

2. First pro loop attracts star players

The Michigan-based International League, hockey's first pro loop, starts in 1905. Stars Cyclone Taylor, Joe Hall and Newsy Lalonde go south for the money. Realizing the threat to Stanley Cup play, trustees change the rules which forbid professionals. On Dec. 27, 1906, Riley Hern, Hod Stuart, Pud Glass, Ernie Johnson and Jack Marshall of the Montreal Wanderers are the first pros to play for the Stanley Cup.

3. Death on ice leads to charges

Cornwall's Owen McCourt is struck in the head during a March 6, 1907, Federal Amateur League game with Ottawa and dies the next day. A coroner's inquest rules McCourt's death results from a "blow from the hockey stick of (Ottawa's) Charles Masson." The player faces manslaughter charges, but Masson is acquitted following the trial when testimony reveals more than one stick hit McCourt.

Early Century Non-NHL All-Stars 1900-20

Hockey at the turn of the century features six skaters–the five familiar position players and a rover. The NHA pioneers the five-skater game in 1911-12 when it eliminates the position. Other leagues continue to ice a rover. Nobody is better at it than Pacific Coast Hockey Association star Cyclone Taylor, who also plays defense. The Vancouver Millionaires' legend is considered the best player of the pre-NHL era. Taylor remains in the PCHA during the NHL's formative years. Here's the best of the pre- and non-NHLers.

THN's First Team

G **Hugh Lehman**, Vancouver
D **Hod Stuart**, Mon. Wanderers
D **Lester Patrick**, Mon. Wanderers
R **Cyclone Taylor**, Vancouver
LW **Tommy Phillips**, Kenora (Ont.)
C **Frank McGee**, Ottawa
RW **Didier Pitre**, Mon. Canadiens

HHOF

Frank McGee, far right second row, starred for the 1905 Stanley Cup-winning Ottawa Silver Seven.

1910-13 Pro Leagues Take Control Of Stanley Cup

No. 1 STORY Canadiens join new NHA

Shunned by the newly formed Canadian Hockey Association, the National Hockey Association is formed Dec. 2, 1909 with teams in Renfrew, Ont., Haileybury, Ont., Cobalt, Ont., and two in Montreal–the Wanderers and a team of French-speaking players called the Canadiens. The NHA lures most of the game's best players and the Ottawa Senators and Montreal Shamrocks also join from the CHA which folds Jan. 15, 1910.

2. Salary cap controls spending

Renfrew owner Ambrose O'Brien opens the vault to sign several stars, including Ottawa's Cyclone Taylor to a $5,250 contract for a 12-game season. Only baseball's Ty Cobb is paid more to play pro sports in 1909-10. Rising salaries nearly drive the league out of business, and the following season a cap of $5,000 per team is introduced. Players threaten to unionize and plan their own league, before capitulating when they can't get ice time.

3. NHA drops rover for six-man units

In 1910, NHA rulemakers alter the structure of a game from two 30-minute halves to three 20-minute periods. The following year, the rover position is dropped and six-man hockey is introduced, featuring a goalie, two defensemen and three forwards. Uniform numbers are also added to easily identify the players on each team. By 1913, the league's pro competition comes from the Pacific Coast Association and Maritime Pro League.

No. 1 STORY Hockey goes coast-to-coast

The Pacific Coast Association, founded Dec. 7, 1911, by Frank and Lester Patrick, lures stars Newsy Lalonde and Cyclone Taylor westward, but doesn't achieve major league status until 1914 when Stanley Cup trustees invite it to challenge for the trophy. The new loop features the first Canadian arena with artificial ice,in Vancouver. Taylor's Millionaires win the PCHA's first Cup in 1915 over Ottawa in their 10,000-seat arena.

2. Legends lost in WWI

The enormity of World War I leads to players joining the war effort. Among those who lose their lives are Frank McGee, Hobey Baker and Scotty Davidson. Baker is the best of early American players, starring at Princeton. (The award that goes to the best player in U.S. college hockey will be named in Baker's honor.) The 228th Battalion enters a team in the NHA in 1916-17, but is shipped overseas in February.

3. Americans enter Cup battle

Portland enters the PCHA in 1914, becoming the first American team eligible to compete for the Stanley Cup. The Rosebuds do so in 1915-16, losing to Didier Pitre's Montreal Canadiens of the NHA. One season later, the PCHA's second-year Seattle Metropolitans, managed by Pete Muldoon, beat the Habs to become the first American club to lift the mug. Bernie Morris scores a team-high 14 times in the four-game final.

Stanley Cup Champions

The Stanley Cup is donated by Lord Stanley of Preston, governor-general of Canada, in 1893 for presentation to the country's amateur hockey champions. In the early years, teams issue challenges for the Cup and reigning champs face multiple challenges in single seasons. As a result, some years have more than one Cup champion. Beginning in 1914, the National Hockey Association and Pacific Coast Hockey Association champions meet for the Cup. The NHL takes full control of the Cup in 1926. Listed are North America's pre-eminent leagues over the first two decades of the century and Stanley Cup champions before formation of the NHL in 1917-18.

Top leagues before formation of the NHL

1899-1905	Canadian Amateur Hockey League (CAHL)
1904-1906	Federal Amateur Hockey League (FAHL)
1905-1907	International (Pro) Hockey League (IHL)
1906-1909	Eastern Canada Hockey Association (ECHA)
1909-1917	National Hockey Association (NHA)
1911-1924	Pacific Coast Hockey Association (PCHA)

Stanley Cup Winners

Year	Champion	Year	Champion
'99-00	Montreal Shamrocks	'07-08	Montreal Wanderers
'00-01	Winnipeg Victorias	'08-09	Montreal Wanderers
'01-02	Winnipeg Victorias		Ottawa Senators
	Montreal A.A.A.	'09-10	Ottawa Senators
'02-03	Montreal A.A.A		Montreal Wanderers
	Ottawa Silver Seven	'10-11	Ottawa Senators
'03-04	Ottawa Silver Seven	'11-12	Quebec Bulldogs
'04-05	Ottawa Silver Seven	'12-13	Quebec Bulldogs
'05-06	Ottawa Silver Seven	'13-14	Toronto Blueshirts
	Montreal Wanderers	'14-15	Vancouver Millionaires
'06-07	Kenora (Ont.) Thistles	'15-16	Montreal Canadiens
	Montreal Wanderers	'16-17	Seattle Metropolitans

Hobey Baker

HHOF

THN's Century Legend

Here are short forms and trophies that appear in 83 NHL season-by-season profiles and the '40 Greatest Seasons' feature.

Abbreviations
Skaters: GP games, **G** goals, **A** assists, **P** points, **Pts.** points, **PIM** penalty minutes, **GPG** goals per game, **APG** assists per game, **PPG** points per game
Goalies: W wins, **L** losses, **T** ties, **SO** shutouts, **GAA** goals-against average **Misc.: No.** number **Pct.** per cent, **Yr.** Year, * league-leading total **Positions: G** goalie, **D** defenseman, **LW** left winger, **C** center, **RW** right winger, **R** rover

NHL Trophies
Art Ross leading scorer, introduced 1918
Calder best rookie, 1933
Conn Smythe playoff MVP, 1965
Hart MVP, 1924
Lady Byng most gentlemanly player, 1925
Masterton perseverance, 1968
Norris best defenseman, 1954
Selke best defensive forward, 1978
Vezina goalie on team with lowest goals-against average until 1981-82 at which time, NHL began awarding it to the best goalie

How Time Flies In The NHL: From The Ducks To The Jets

NHL Teams	Abbr.	Years
Anaheim Mighty Ducks	Ana.	'93-94
Atlanta Flames (to Cgy.)	Atl.	'72-73/'79-80
Atlanta Thrashers	Atl. T	'99-00
Boston Bruins	Bos.	'24-25
Buffalo Sabres	Buf.	'70-71
California-Oakland Seals (to Cle.)	Cal.	'67-68/'75-76
Calgary Flames (ex-Atl.)	Cgy.	'80-81
Carolina Hurricanes (ex-Hart.)	Car.	'97-98
Chicago Blackhawks	Chi.	'26-27
Cleveland Barons (ex-Cal.)*	Cle.	'76-77/'77-78
Colorado Avalanche (ex-Que.)	Col.	'95-96
Colorado Rockies (ex-KC, to NJ)	Col. R	'76-77/'81-82
Columbus Blue Jackets		'00-01
Dallas Stars (ex-Min.)	Dal.	'93-94
Detroit Cougars-Falcons-Wings**	Det.	'26-27
Edmonton Oilers	Edm.	'79-80
Florida Panthers	Fla.	'93-94
Hamilton Tigers	Ham.	'20-21/'24-25
Hartford Whalers (to Car.)	Hart.	'79-80/'96-97
Kansas City Scouts (to Col. R)	KC	'74-75/'75-76

Abbreviations for all NHL teams are listed, including first years of current teams, and first and last years of defunct and transferred teams, as indicated by 'to and ex-.'

NHL Teams	Abbr.	Years
Los Angeles Kings	LA	'67-68
Minnesota North Stars (to Dal.)	Min.	'67-68/'92-93
Minnesota Wild		'00-010
Montreal Canadiens	Mon.	'17-18
Montreal Maroons	Mon. M	'24-25/'37-38
Montreal Wanderers	Mon. W	'17-18/'17-18
Nashville Predators	Nas.	'98-99
New Jersey Devils (ex-Col. R)	NJ	'82-83
New York Islanders	NYI	'72-73
New York Rangers	NYR	'26-27
New York/Brooklyn Americans	NYA	'25-26/'41-42
Ottawa Senators (to St.L E)	Ott. S	'17-18/'33-34
Ottawa Senators	Ott.	'92-93

NHL Teams	Abbr.	Years
Philadelphia Flyers	Phi.	'67-68
Philadelphia Quakers (ex-Pit. P)	Phi. Q	'30-31/'30-31
Phoenix Coyotes (ex-Win.)	Pho.	'96-97
Pittsburgh Pirates (to Phi. Q)	Pit. P	'25-26/'29-30
Pittsburgh Penguins	Pit.	'67-68
Quebec Athletics	Que. A	'19-20/'19-20
Quebec Nordiques (to Col.)	Que.	'79-80/'94-95
San Jose Sharks	SJ	'91-92
St. Louis Blues	St.L	'67-68
St. Louis Eagles (ex-Ott. S)	St.L E	'34-35/'34-35
Tampa Bay Lightning	TB	'92-93
Toronto Arenas-St. Pats-Leafs***	Tor.	'17-18
Vancouver Canucks	Van.	'70-71
Washington Capitals	Was.	'74-75
Winnipeg Jets (to Pho.)	Win.	'79-80/'95-96

*Cleveland merges with Minnesota in '78-79
**Cougars '26-27/'29-30, Falcons '30-31/'31-32, Red Wings '32-33
***Arenas '17-18/'18-19, St. Patricks '19-20/'25-26, Maple Leafs '26-27

1917-18

Stanley Cup: Toronto Arenas T

Cyclone Taylor leads the PCHA in goals with 32 in 18 games in 1917-18.

NO. 1 STORY: NHL starts first season with four teams

Two weeks after the National Hockey Association disbands a new pro loop, the National Hockey League, is formed during a meeting Nov. 26, 1917, at Montreal's Windsor Hotel. Four NHA franchises–the Ottawa Senators, Quebec Bulldogs, Montreal Wanderers and Montreal Canadiens–survive with a fifth, the Toronto Arenas, being added. Quebec immediately announces it is taking a leave of absence, leaving the new league with four teams. Frank Calder is named president and the NHL's 22-game schedule gets under way Dec. 19.

2. Canadiens' and Wanderers' home burns down

A raging fire, Jan. 2, destroys the 6,000-seat Westmount Arena, home to both of Montreal's NHL teams, the Canadiens and the Wanderers. Two days later the Wanderers, citing losses of $30,000, withdraw from the league after only six games. The Canadiens elect to continue, scrounging up new equipment from other teams and moving into the tiny 3,250-seat Jubilee Rink.

3. Goalies allowed to drop to ice to make saves

The first major rule change in NHL history goes on the books, Jan. 9, when the league removes the stipulation that assesses a minor penalty to any goalie who leaves his feet to stop the puck. Netminders–especially Ottawa's Clint Benedict–had become adept at making their sprawling saves look like accidents. "You could fake losing your balance and put the officials on the spot," Benedict admits. "Did I fall or did I intentionally go down?"

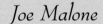

▶ **IMPACT PERSON**

Joe Malone

The NHL's first scoring star sparkles on opening night at Ottawa scoring five goals, which remains a Montreal Canadiens' record for a road game. Malone has two other five-goal games–no other player has ever registered more than one in an NHL season. His 44 goals in 20 games stands as the NHL single-season mark until 1944-45 when Rocket Richard scores 50 in 50.

HHOF

HHOF

Fast First Period

The Ottawa Senators and Montreal Canadiens begin their Feb. 16 game at a frenetic pace, skating through the first period in an actual elapsed time of 21 minutes and 52 seconds.

HOCKEY LISTS OF THE CENTURY Making Instant History

Joe Malone sets the bar impossibly high in year one of the NHL when he averages 2.20 goals per game (GPG), the best-ever such mark. He has 44 goals in 20 games. Wayne Gretzky's 87 goals in 74 games (1983-84) is the best Modern Era mark (1.18).

Early Era (Pre-'43-44)	GPG	Modern Era (Post-'43-44)	GPG
1. **Joe Malone**, Mon. ('17-18)	2.20	1. **Wayne Gretzky**, Edm. ('83-84)	1.18
2. **Cy Denneny**, Ott. ('17-18)	1.80	2. **Wayne Gretzky**, Edm. ('81-82)	1.15
3. **Newsy Lalonde**, Mon. ('17-18)	1.64	– **Mario Lemieux**, Pit. ('92-93)	1.15
4. **Joe Malone**, Mon. ('19-20)	1.63	4. **Mario Lemieux**, Pit. ('88-89)	1.12
5. **Newsy Lalonde**, Mon. ('19-20)	1.61	5. **Brett Hull**, St. L. ('90-91)	1.10

Chalk Talk

"As far as I am concerned, they can stand on their head(s)."

NHL president Frank Calder, announcing goalies can leave their feet to stop a puck

Newsy Lalonde, Montreal Canadiens

HHOF

1918-19

Stanley Cup: Not Awarded

No. 1 STORY: Influenza epidemic wipes out Cup final

For the first and only time, the Stanley Cup final is cancelled, April 1, with the Montreal Canadiens and the Pacific Coast Association's Seattle Metropolitans deadlocked at 2-2-1 in the series. Seattle declines to accept the title by default as six Canadiens–Joe Hall, Newsy Lalonde, Louis Berlinquette, Billy Couture, Jack McDonald and manager George Kennedy–are hospitalized with the Spanish influenza virus, part of an epidemic that sweeps across the world. Hall dies five days later in Seattle's Columbus Sanitarium.

2. Toronto team folds forcing end to regular season

The defending Stanley Cup-champion Toronto Arenas leave the NHL a two-team outfit when they withdraw from play Feb. 20. NHL officials halt the regular season and order Montreal and Ottawa to play a best-of-seven series for the league title. The dormant Toronto franchise is purchased Nov. 26, 1919, by a group headed by Fred Hambly. After originally calling their new team the Tecumsehs, the new owners switch the name to St. Patricks.

3. Malone misses most of season

As proof the NHL is still a major league in its infancy Joe Malone, who led the NHL with 44 goals in 1917-18, plays just eight games for Montreal. "I had hooked on to a good job in Quebec City which promised a secure future, something hockey in those days couldn't," Malone explains later. His salary in 1917-18 was $1,000.

▶ IMPACT PERSON

Joe Hall

"A fellow is just as old as he feels and right now, I feel I am good for at least 10 more years of hockey," proclaims the Montreal Canadiens' defenseman at season's start. By the end of the campaign, Hall, 36, is dead, a victim of the Spanish flu epidemic. Nicknamed 'Bad' Joe Hall because of his rough play, he's the NHL's penalty minutes leader in its first two seasons.

Imperial Oil - Turofsky/HHOF

Stripes and Stars

Odie Cleghorn, who officiated in Game 4 of the 1918 Stanley Cup final, plays for the Montreal Canadiens in the 1919 playoffs and scores eight goals in 10 games.

HOCKEY LISTS OF THE CENTURY Top Goalies Of All Time

Georges Vezina, who plays in the NHL from 1917 through 1925 and has a trophy named in his honor, is ranked 12th best NHL goalie of all-time in 1998 by The Hockey News. Not listed among the greats is Dominik Hasek, who had not yet played enough dominant seasons when this ranking was determined. Goalies are listed with most prominent teams.

1. **Terry Sawchuk**, Det. ('49-50 – '69-70)
2. **Jacques Plante**, Mon. ('52-53 – '72-73)
3. **Glenn Hall**, Chi. ('52-53 – '70-71)
4. **Ken Dryden**, Mon. ('70-71–'78-79)
5. **Bill Durnan**, Mon. ('43-44 – '49-50)
6. **Patrick Roy**, Mon. ('85-86 – present)
7. **G. Hainsworth**, Mon. ('26-27 – '36-37)
8. **Turk Broda**, Tor. ('36-37 – '51-52)
9. **Bernie Parent**, Phi. ('65-66 – '78-79)
10. **Frank Brimsek**, Bos. ('38-39 – '49-50)

Chalk Talk

"This has been the most peculiar series in the history of the sport."

PCHA president Frank Patrick on the 1919 Stanley Cup final

1919-20

Stanley Cup: Ottawa Senators

No. 1 STORY: Quebec bullish in first NHL season

After a two-season sabbatical from pro hockey, Quebec enters the NHL. Although the team is called the Athletics, people still refer to it as the Bulldogs–Quebec's nickname in the old National Hockey Association. But even with the help of Joe Malone's league-leading 39 goals, Quebec sets NHL futility marks for the fewest wins (four) and highest goals-against average (7.38), and fails to win a game on the road. Quebec allows five or more goals 19 times in 24 games, surrendering double-digits five times.

2. Canadiens fire 16 past Quebec

A 16-3 rout of the Athletics in Quebec City, March 3, puts the Montreal Canadiens into the NHL record book for the most goals scored in one game. Filling the net is nothing new for the Canadiens. Two months earlier, the Habs celebrated the opening of the new Mount Royal Arena, Jan. 10, by outscoring the Toronto St. Patricks 14-7. Newsy Lalonde's six goals and the combined goal total of both teams established an NHL record.

3. Wild man of the West shakes up NHL

One of the NHL's early bad boys, Cully Wilson leads the league in penalty minutes with 86 in 23 games in his first season. His presence is an indication of the frontier attitude which permeates the NHL; he is signed by the Toronto St. Patricks after being banned from the Pacific Coast Association when his cross-check shatters the jaw of Vancouver's Mickey MacKay. Wilson scores 20 goals and mellows in later seasons when he discovers horticulture.

▶ **IMPACT PERSON**

James Rice/HHOF

Joe Malone

The Quebec Athletic forward scores seven times in a 10-6 win over the Toronto St. Pats, Jan. 31, setting an NHL record which is still on the books. An eighth goal is disallowed on an offside call by referee Cooper Smeaton. Toronto switches goalies after Mike Mitchell is beaten four times in the first two periods, but Malone fires three pucks past Howard Lockhart in the last 10 minutes.

HHOF

Four Score And…

Habs' defenseman Harry Cameron scores four goals against Quebec to become the only blueliner to do that twice. His first four-goal game was Dec. 26, 1917 with Toronto against his future team.

HOCKEY LISTS OF THE CENTURY Dynamic Duo

Joe Malone and Newsy Lalonde are the only players in NHL history to score more than 100 career goals and average more than a goal a game. They had strikingly similar careers over the first 25 years of the century, averaging virtually the same number of goals per game (1.35 vs. 1.36) in competition outside the NHL. Here are their NHL and cumulative records (italicized) from other major leagues, including games, goals and goals per game. NHL seasons are listed.

Player	NHL	Seasons	GP	G	GPG	Yrs.	GP	G	GPG
Newsy Lalonde, Mon., NYA	5	'17-18–'21-22	99	124	1.25	*15*	*239*	*325*	*1.36*
Joe Malone, Mon., Que., Ham.	7	'17-18–'23-24	125	143	1.14	*9*	*148*	*200*	*1.35*

Chalk Talk

"The thing I recall most vividly is that it was bitterly cold."

Joe Malone's memory of the night of his record seven-goal game

Reg Noble teams with Babe Dye to give Toronto a powerful scoring combo.

1920-21

Stanley Cup: Ottawa Senators

No. 1 STORY: NHL tries to break up Ottawa juggernaut

Looking to balance competition in the league, NHL president Frank Calder awards the rights to Ottawa right winger Punch Broadbent and defenseman Sprague Cleghorn, both future Hall of Famers, to the fledgling Hamilton Tigers, Dec. 30. The Senators protest vehemently and both players refuse to report to the Tigers, eventually finding their way back to Ottawa to help the Senators become the first NHL team to repeat as Stanley Cup champions.

2. Senators leave ice over officiating

Angered by what they feel is one-sided officiating by referee Cooper Smeaton, the Senators leave the ice with 5:13 to play in their Jan. 26 game against the Montreal Canadiens. With no opponent on the ice, Newsy Lalonde and Amos Arbour score uncontested goals and Smeaton awards the Habs a 5-3 victory. Smeaton resigns over the incident, but is convinced to return before the end of the season. NHL president Frank Calder fines the Senators $500 for their actions.

3. Aging Canadiens barred from driving automobiles

Alarmed by his club's lack of stamina, Montreal manager Leo Dandurand bars his players from driving their newfangled automobiles, believing it gives them cramps in their hands and legs. It's more likely the physical ailments are a reflection of Montreal's average age: 30.9 years, Montreal is the oldest team in the league.

▶ IMPACT PERSON

Babe Dye

Loaned to the Hamilton Tigers to start the season, the hard-shooting sniper lasts just one game with the club. Dye scores two goals for Hamilton and is reclaimed immediately by the Toronto St. Patricks. He leads the NHL with 35 goals in 24 games and has an 11-game goal-scoring streak. Dye, whose real name is Cecil, is nicknamed 'Babe' because he also plays professional baseball.

One And Only

The Hamilton Tigers become the only NHL team to post a shutout in their debut, a 5-0 win over the Montreal Canadiens Dec. 22. It's the only shutout of goalie Howard 'Holes' Lockhart's NHL career.

HOCKEY LISTS OF THE CENTURY May They Rest In Peace

Do you believe in reincarnation? The Ottawa Senators do. The Senators are the only one of 11 franchises to return to life after pushing up daisies in the NHL graveyard. The original Senators last from 1917-18 through 1933-34 before going belly up. They return in 1992-93. Listed are defunct NHL teams and their first and last seasons.

1. **Montreal Wanderers**, ('17-18–'17-18)
2. **Quebec Athletics**, ('19-20–'19-20)
3. **Hamilton Tigers**, ('20-21–'24-25)
4. **Montreal Maroons**, ('24-25–'37-38)
5. **NY/Brooklyn Americans**, ('25-26–'41-42)
6. **Pittsburgh Pirates**, ('25-26–'29-30)
7. **Philadelphia Quakers**, ('30-31–'30-31)
8. **St. Louis Eagles**, ('34-35–'34-35)
9. **Oakland/California Seals**, ('67-68–'75-76)
10. **Cleveland Barons**, ('76-77–'77-78)

Chalk Talk

"A referee is always paid and receives the same salary, regardless what team wins."

NHL referee-in-chief Cooper Smeaton, who resigns briefly following criticism of his work by the Ottawa Senators

1921-22

Stanley Cup: Toronto St. Pats STPATS

Sprague Cleghorn, Montreal Canadiens

No. 1 STORY: 1. Streaking Broadbent sets goal mark

Christmas Eve turns out to be special for Ottawa Senator Harry 'Punch' Broadbent. The right winger scores once in a 10-0 rout of the Montreal Canadiens, beginning his NHL-record 16-game goal-scoring streak, a mark which still stands. Broadbent scores 27 goals during the streak and has nine multi-goal games. He goes on to lead the NHL in goals (32), assists (14) and points (46), netting at least one point in 21 of the Senators' 24 games.

2. St. Patricks and Senators record first tie in NHL history

Following four NHL seasons with no tie games, the streak ends Feb. 11. After battling through 20 minutes of overtime, the Toronto St. Patricks and Ottawa Senators finish in a 4-4 deadlock–the first tie in NHL history. John Ross Roach makes 78 saves for Toronto, while the Senators' Clint Benedict stops 63 shots. St. Patricks' defenseman Harry Cameron is credited with the NHL's first game-tying goal.

3. Two-man wrecking crew fined by league

Brothers Sprague and Odie Cleghorn, in their first NHL season together with the Canadiens, go on a rampage during a 4-2 Habs' loss in Ottawa Feb. 1. They put three Senators–Frank Nighbor (broken arm), Cy Denneny (leg injury) and Eddie Gerard (head injury)–out of the game. Both brothers are assessed major penalties and $30 fines, and referee Lou Marsh tacks on a match penalty to Sprague's transgressions. The brothers finish the season one-two in scoring and penalty minutes for the Canadiens.

▶ IMPACT PERSON

Punch Broadbent

A battlefield hero, who spent three of his prime playing years in the trenches of World War I, Broadbent sets an NHL record yet to be equalled when he scores in 16 straight games for the Ottawa Senators. But his most heroic deeds are performed in battle. He was awarded the Military Medal and recommended for a Commission For Bravery in World War I.

Money Talks

Toronto St. Patricks' goaltender Jake Forbes holds out for a $2,500 salary and becomes the first NHLer to sit out an entire season in a contract dispute. His contract is sold to Hamilton after the season.

HOCKEY LISTS OF THE CENTURY Streaking To Immortality

Dave Lumley has the good fortune to play on one of the Edmonton Oilers' powerhouses. The 1981-82 Oilers are so good they put Lumley, a career 98-goal-scorer, in the record books. Fifteen of those goals come during a 12-game scoring streak, the fifth-highest ever. Lumley sticks out on a list of great scorers and their record scoring streaks.

Player	No.	Player	No.
1. **Punch Broadbent**, Ott. '21-22	16	5. **Cy Denneny**, Ott. '17-18	12
2. **Joe Malone**, Mon. '17-18*	14	– **Dave Lumley**, Edm. '81-82	12
3. **Newsy Lalonde**, Mon. '20-21	13	– **Mario Lemieux**, Pit. '92-93	12
– **Charlie Simmer**, L.A. '79-80	13	*Malone has record 35 goals during streak	

Chalk Talk

"Those Cleghorns are a disgrace to the league and the game of hockey."

Referee Lou Marsh on the Montreal Canadiens' rambunctious Odie and Sprague Cleghorn

HHOF

HHOF

HOCKEY LISTS OF THE CENTURY
Greatest Voices In NHL History

Foster Hewitt pioneers hockey broadcasting, starting a proud tradition. Here are our favorite voices (including Russian Nikolai Ozerov who broadcast games rinkside), primary time periods of work and teams whose games they called most prominently.

1. **Foster Hewitt**
Toronto   1920s-'60s
2. **Danny Gallivan**
Montreal   1950s-'80s
3. **Rene Lecavalier**
Montreal   1950s-'80s
4. **Dan Kelly**
St. Louis   1960s-'90s
5. **Dick Irvin**
Montreal   1960s-present
6. **Mike Lange**
Pittsburgh   1970s-present
7. **Fred Cusick**
Boston   1950s-'90s
8. **Lloyd Pettit**
Chicago   1960s-'70s
9. **Jim Robson**
Vancouver   1960s-'80s
10. **Nikolai Ozerov**
Soviet Union   1970s

Chalk Talk

"If it had been left up to me, it would have been my first and last broadcast."

Foster Hewitt's recollection of his radio play-by-play debut

Hall of Fame broadcaster Foster Hewitt

No. 1 STORY: Game aired over radio for first time

Pete Parker, not Foster Hewitt, performs hockey's first radio broadcast, describing an Edmonton-Regina playoff game in the Western Canada League, March 14. Hewitt calls his first game eight days later, using a telephone line linked to station CFCA from a cramped four-foot by four-foot broadcast booth. A reporter for the Toronto *Star*, Hewitt does play-by-play of an Ontario Hockey Association game at Toronto's Mutual Street Arena between Parkdale and Kitchener. Moving to Toronto Maple Leafs' broadcasts in the 1930s, he becomes the most famous voice in hockey.

2. Canadiens trade legend Lalonde for unknown

Montreal Canadiens' manager Leo Dandurand stuns the hockey world when he trades captain and two-time NHL scoring champion Newsy Lalonde, Sept. 18, to the Saskatoon Sheiks of the Western Canada League for $3,500 and the rights to an unproven amateur named Aurel Joliat. The move is panned–until Joliat finishes eighth in NHL scoring as a rookie, launching a Hall of Fame career which sees him play 16 seasons for the Habs.

3. Dandurand suspends his best blueliners

Canadiens' defensemen Sprague Cleghorn and Billy Coutu are suspended by Montreal manager Leo Dandurand after both receive match penalties for illegal hits against the Ottawa Senators during the first game of the playoffs. Minus their starting blueline duo, the Habs lose the two-game, total-goals series 3-2 and Ottawa advances to its third Stanley Cup final in four seasons.

▶ **IMPACT PERSON**

Aurel Joliat

Just 21, the 5-foot-7, 136-pound Ottawa native, later dubbed the 'Mighty Atom,' makes a smashing debut with Montreal, producing 13 goals and 22 points in 24 games. The next year Joliat teams with Howie Morenz to lead the Habs to a Stanley Cup. A decade later, Joliat wins the Hart Trophy.

1923-24

Stanley Cup: Montreal Canadiens

No. 1 STORY: Dye pursues field of dreams

Toronto sniper Cecil 'Babe' Dye, the NHL's leading scorer in 1922-23, shocks the team before the season when he announces he is retiring to pursue a career in pro baseball. Dye, who reaches the AAA level as a ballplayer, later changes his mind and returns to the St. Patricks' lineup in December, which gives him enough time to produce 17 goals and finish fourth in the scoring race.

2. Denneny leading scorer in low-scoring season

Ottawa Senators' left winger Cy Denneny wins his only scoring title with the worst winning totals in NHL history. He finishes with 22 goals and a lonely assist. Denneny is the only player to crack the 20-goal mark and average more than a point per game with 23 in 21 games. The league goals-per-game average of 5.3 is nearly half of what it was in 1917-18 (10.1). Following the season the NHL implements the anti-defense rule, which prohibits teams from keeping more than one player (other than the goalie) in the defensive zone when the puck is not there.

3. Nighbor first Hart Trophy winner

The NHL introduces its first individual award, the Hart Trophy, for "the player adjudged to be the most valuable to his team." Ottawa Senators' playmaking center Frank Nighbor is the first winner. Nighbor and Toronto Maple Leaf Teeder Kennedy (1954-55) are the only forwards to win the Hart without finishing among the top 10 scorers. In 1924-25, Nighbor is named the first winner of the Lady Byng Trophy.

▶ **IMPACT PERSON**

Howie Morenz

Slipping into Toronto's backyard to sign a slick center from the Stratford (Ont.) Indians proves to be one of the best moves in the storied history of the Montreal Canadiens. 'The Stratford Streak' teams with Billy Boucher and Aurel Joliat to form the 'Speedball Line'–the NHL's most dangerous attacking unit. Morenz finishes eighth in NHL scoring as a rookie.

Frank Nighbor, Ottawa Senators

HHOF

HHOF

Food For Thought

Ottawa's train is snow-bound overnight en route to Montreal for a Jan. 19 game. A hungry Cy Denneny goes looking for food–and falls down a well. Rescued by teammates, Denneny is not injured.

HOCKEY LISTS OF THE CENTURY Cy Denneny Vs. Cy Young

Hockey players with significantly more goals than assists are called Cy Young candidates because their goal-assist totals resemble win-loss records of star baseball pitchers. The original Cy Young candidate was the appropriately named Cy Denneny, the Ottawa Senators' sniper who played when assists were awarded sparingly. Here's a comparison of Denneny's best Cy Young years vs. the legendary pitcher's best years.

Denneny	G	A	Young	W	L	Denneny	G	A	Young	W	L
'17-18	36	10	1892	36	11	'24-25	27	15	1899	26	14
'20-21	34	5	1895	33	10	'23-24	22	1	1903	28	9
'21-22	27	12	1896	29	14	'25-26	24	12	1908	21	11

Chalk Talk

"I'll never forget walking downtown and seeing an illuminated sign which said, 'Billy Boucher 2, Frank Boucher 1.'"
Vancouver's Frank Boucher after he and brother Billy of the Habs scored all the goals in a game

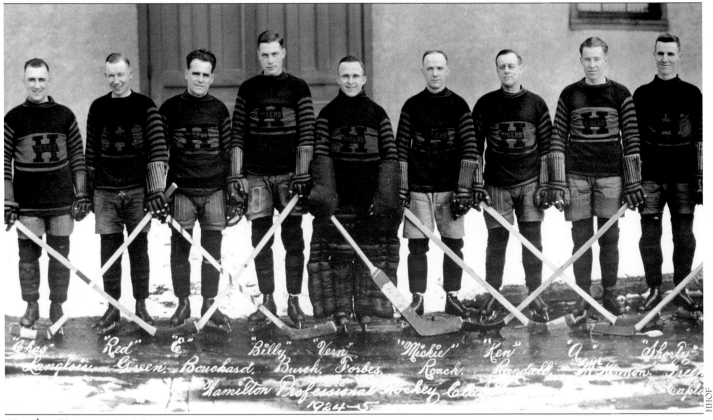

Hamilton Tigers, 1924-25

HOCKEY LISTS OF THE CENTURY
Pivots Usually Center Of Attention

Hamilton Tigers' center Billy Burch wins the Hart Trophy as league MVP in 1924-25; he is the second straight center–Frank Nighbor was the first a year earlier–to earn the honor, a harbinger of things to come. Centers dominate the selection process; 41 of 77 winners have been pivots. Here are the winners by position.

Position	Hart	Pct.
Centers	41	53%
Right Wingers	13	17%
Defensemen	13	17%
Goalies	6	8%
Left Wingers	4	5%

No. 1 STORY: Hamilton players strike before NHL final

After finishing first and qualifying for the playoffs for the only time in franchise history, the Hamilton Tigers stun the hockey world by going on strike prior to the NHL final with the Montreal Canadiens. Players take issue with not receiving a pay increase when the NHL increases its schedule from 24 to 30 games to start the season. The players allege a $200 bonus had been promised, but Hamilton owner Percy Thompson denies it and NHL president Frank Calder suspends the entire team March 9, awarding the title to the Habs. It will be another 67 years before the second league strike occurs–in April, 1992.

2. Bruins and Maroons join NHL

The NHL crosses the border when it awards its first American franchise Oct. 11 to Boston. The Bruins are selected along with a second team for Montreal–the Maroons. At the same time, it is announced that Pittsburgh and New York have been granted franchises for the start of the 1925-26 campaign. Franchise fees are $15,000, with $11,000 of the Maroons' payment going to the Canadiens for infringement of their territorial rights, the first such payment but not the last in league history.

3. Montreal Forum opens its doors

Billy Boucher opens the Canadiens' sparkling new $1-million Forum in style Nov. 26, firing a hat trick, including the first goal of the game, as 9,000 fans watch the Habs blow out the Toronto St. Patricks 7-1. A month later, on Dec. 27, the largest crowd in NHL history–11,000 fans–packs the building to watch the Canadiens and Montreal Maroons battle to a 1-1- tie.

Shorty Green

Hamilton's captain leads his Tiger teammates on strike prior to the playoffs over an unpaid bonus. "The boys are unanimous in what they consider their just dues, hence the reason for the stand we have taken," Green says. The team is suspended and Hamilton loses its team; the roster is sold to the New York Americans for $75,000.

1925-26

Stanley Cup: Montreal Maroons M

Georges Vezina, Montreal Canadiens

No. 1 STORY: Americans open at Madison Square Garden

The NHL comes to the Big Apple and it's a big success. An NHL-record crowd of 17,000 at Madison Square Garden Dec. 15 watches the Montreal Canadiens defeat the New York Americans 3-1. The boxing promoters at MSG quickly find themselves losing the battle to hockey. "I can make bigger money with less worry and fewer risks out of hockey than I have been getting out of boxing," says Garden promoter Tex Rickard.

2. Salaries skyrocket league-wide

The growing popularity of hockey is evidenced in the rapid expansion of the NHL, going from four to seven teams in two seasons, and in growing player salaries. A $35,000-per-team salary cap is introduced to slow the upward trend. Among the top earners are the Pittsburgh Pirates' Lionel Conacher ($7,500), Montreal Maroons' Dunc Munro ($7,500), New York Americans' Billy Burch ($6,500) and Joe Simpson ($6,000), Toronto Maple Leafs' Hap Day ($6,000) and Boston Bruins' Sprague Cleghorn ($5,000).

3. Vezina's longevity streak ends tragically

Montreal goalie Georges Vezina hasn't missed a game in 15 years when he appears for the season opener against Pittsburgh Nov. 28 despite a temperature of 102 Fahrenheit. He collapses in net during the opening period and backup Al Lacroix takes over in goal to start the second. Vezina is diagnosed with tuberculosis and has to retire. He dies March 26. The Vezina Trophy, which goes to the NHL's best goalie, is named in his honor.

▶ IMPACT PERSON

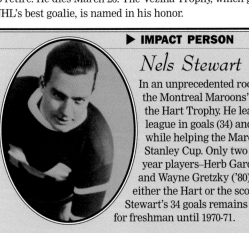

Nels Stewart

In an unprecedented rookie season, the Montreal Maroons' center wins the Hart Trophy. He leads the league in goals (34) and points (42) while helping the Maroons to the Stanley Cup. Only two other first year players–Herb Gardiner ('27) and Wayne Gretzky ('80)–have won either the Hart or the scoring title. Stewart's 34 goals remains a standard for freshman until 1970-71.

James Rice/HHOF

HHOF

Gimme A Break

Pittsburgh coach Odie Cleghorn changes the way the game is played by rotating three set forward lines. Previously, teams iced a starting six and players came off only when in need of a rest.

HOCKEY LISTS OF THE CENTURY NHL's Expanding Universe

Here's the full history of expansion, including nicknames of defunct teams, and franchise shifts (in parentheses).

'24-25 Montreal Maroons, Boston	'79-80 Edmonton, Hartford (Carolina),
'25-26 Pittsburgh Pirates, New York Americans	Quebec (Colorado), Winnipeg (Phoenix)
'26-27 New York Rangers, Chicago, Detroit	'91-92 San Jose
'67-68 Los Angeles, Minnesota (Dallas), California	'92-93 Ottawa, Tampa Bay
Seals, Philadelphia, Pittsburgh, St. Louis	'93-94 Anaheim, Florida
'70-71 Buffalo, Vancouver	'98-99 Nashville
'72-73 Atlanta (Calgary), New York Islanders	'99-00 Atlanta
'74-75 Kansas City (New Jersey), Washington	'00-01 Columbus, Minnesota

Bill Cook, New York Rangers

1926-27

Stanley Cup: Ottawa Senators

No. 1 STORY: Detroit, Chicago, Rangers awarded franchises

The NHL loses its competition when Frank Patrick, president of the rival Western Hockey League, sells the contracts of league players May 4, 1926, to the NHL for $258,000. Three new teams are added–the Detroit Cougars, Chicago Black Hawks and New York Rangers–and the 10-team league is divided into two divisions, Canadian and American. The new players have an immediate impact–Rangers' winger Bill Cook is the NHL scoring leader, while Montreal Canadiens' teammates, goalie George Hainsworth (Vezina Trophy) and defenseman Herb Gardiner (Hart Trophy), cop the major awards.

2. St. Patricks turn over new Leaf in Toronto

As Philadelphia entrepreneurs prepare to buy the Toronto St. Patricks and move the club, Toronto hockey man Conn Smythe assembles a 16-member ownership group which purchases the club Feb. 14 for $160,000. The team is renamed the Maple Leafs and they switch their green and white colors for blue and white, launching what would become Canada's team.

3. Green's career ends after near-fatal hit

The NHL comes close to its first on-ice fatality, when New York Americans' forward Shorty Green suffers a kidney injury Feb. 27 after absorbing a clean open-ice hit from 225-pound New York Ranger defenseman Taffy Abel. Green undergoes surgery March 3 to remove the damaged kidney and, at one point, is administered last rites. Green recovers, but never plays again.

▶ IMPACT PERSON

Art Ross

One of the game's great innovators, Ross will create a new model for the net, which the NHL adopts the following season. Pucks, which used to bounce out of the tight twine, now stay in the webbing. He also redesigns the puck by getting rid of its sharp edges. Now in his third season as coach in Boston, Ross will build the Bruins into a powerhouse, winning a Stanley Cup in 1928-29.

Motown No Town

With no suitable arena available in Detroit, the fledgling Cougars play all 22 of their home games during the season across the border in Canada at Border Cities Arena in Windsor, Ont.

HOCKEY LISTS OF THE CENTURY 1st Decade All-Stars

Clint Benedict backstops the Ottawa Senators to three Stanley Cups in the NHL's first decade (1917-18 through 1926-27). Toronto's Babe Dye is the league's offensive star.

The Hockey News' First Team		The Hockey News' Second Team	
G	**Clint Benedict**, Ott. *First wore mask*	G	**Georges Vezina**, Mon. *Cool in clutch*
D	**Sprague Cleghorn**, Mon. *Tough guy*	D	**Harry Cameron**, Tor. *Curved shots*
D	**George Boucher**, Ott. *Blueline sniper*	D	**Eddie Gerard**, Ott. *Sens' captain*
F	**Joe Malone**, Mon. *First scoring champ*	F	**Cy Denneny**, Ott. *Consistent scorer*
F	**Newsy Lalonde**, Mon. *Fit and fiery*	F	**Reg Noble**, Tor. *St. Pats' great*
F	**Babe Dye**, Tor. *Heavy shooter*	F	**Frank Nighbor**, Ott. *Stylish center*

Chalk Talk

"He drilled through the defense, extracted Hainsworth from the net and filled it with rubber."

Associated Press account of a goal by New York Rangers' Stan Brown, a hockey-playing dentist

1927-28

Stanley Cup: New York Rangers

No. 1 STORY: Manager Patrick rescues Rangers during final

When Nels Stewart's shot strikes New York Rangers' goalie Lorne Chabot in the eye during the second period of Game 2 of the Stanley Cup final, it looks as if the Cup belongs to the Montreal Maroons. Montreal leads the best-of-five series 1-0 and the Rangers have no backup. New York asks to use Ottawa's Alex Connell and minor-leaguer Hugh McCormick, but are turned down, so manager Lester Patrick, 44, dons the pads. He stops 17 of 18 shots and the Rangers win 2-1 in overtime. Farmhand Joe Miller takes over next game as the Rangers win the Cup in Game 5.

2. Referee, former coach advocate use of helmets

After Chicago Black Hawks' forward Dick Irvin suffers a fractured skull, two people promote the wearing of helmets. Referee Lou Marsh suggests fibre helmets similar to those worn by horse jockeys. Former Chicago coach Barney Stanley designs a pith and fibre helmet and presents it at an NHL governors' meeting, but to no avail.

3. Calder will allow no color barrier in NHL

The Boston Black Panthers are hockey's first all-African American team. While these players are well below the calibre of players on teams competing for the Stanley Cup, NHL president Frank Calder insists that unlike baseball, which has a distinct color barrier, all players are welcome to play in his league. "Pro hockey has no ruling against the colored man, nor is it likely to ever draw the line," Calder says.

▶ IMPACT PERSON

Alex Connell

A 4-0 win over the Toronto Maple Leafs Jan. 31 launches Connell on an NHL-record streak of six consecutive shutouts, lasting 461 minutes and 29 seconds. Sylvio Mantha of the Montreal Canadiens beats the Ottawa Senators' goalie Jan. 28. It will be almost a month before Connell is beaten again when Duke Keats of the Chicago Black Hawks scores Feb. 22.

HHOF

HHOF

Duke Gets His Due

Detroit Cougars' center Duke Keats incurs an indefinite suspension Nov. 26 when he swings his stick at a heckling fan in Chicago. Keats is reinstated Dec. 15 and traded one day later to the Black Hawks.

HOCKEY LISTS OF THE CENTURY The First Family

No family has dominated hockey history like the Patricks, the sport's First Family.

1900s-20s	**Joseph Patrick**		
	Finances Canada's first two artificial ice surfaces		
1900-40s	**Lester** (Joseph's son)	**Frank** (Joseph's son)	
	Player, Rangers' coach, manager, icon	player, Pacific Coast president	
1930s-70s	**Muzz** (Lester's son)	**Lynn** (Lester's son)	
	Rangers' coach, manager	NHL player, coach, executive	
Current	**Dick** (Muzz's son)	**Craig** (Lynn's son)	**Glenn** (Lynn's son)
	Capitals' president	Penguins' GM-president	AHL head coach

Chalk Talk

"He might get better results if he coached them from the mezzanine with a shotgun."
New York Times' writer John Kieran's advice to coach Shorty Green of the woeful New York Americans

Roy Worters, New York Americans

1928-29

Stanley Cup: Boston Bruins

No. 1 STORY: Year of the shutout

NHL netminders produce a record 120 shutouts in 220 games, holding shooters to a record-low 2.9 goals per game. Leading the way is Vezina Trophy-winner George Hainsworth of the Montreal Canadiens, whose 22 shutouts and 0.92 goals-against average are records that will endure all century. Seven other netminders, including Hart Trophy-winner Roy Worters of the New York Americans (with 13 shutouts), hit double digits in zeroes.

2. Black Hawks sleepwalk through scoring drought

Eight straight games. No goals. A Chicago Black Hawk finally scores a goal when Vic Ripley pots one three minutes into the third period of a 2-1 win March 2 over the Montreal Maroons, ending an NHL-record scoreless streak at 601 minutes and 41 seconds–a drought that spans 28 days. Chicago scores 33 goals in 44 games, setting an NHL standard for futility, as does the Hawks' 0.75 goals-per-game average and the 20 times they are blanked.

3. Retired Winkler gets name engraved on Stanley Cup

After winning the Stanley Cup, the Boston Bruins have former goalie Hal Winkler's name inscribed on it, even though he retired before the season when he was replaced by rookie Tiny Thompson. Winkler and Detroit defenseman Vladimir Konstantinov, who suffers career-ending head injuries the summer before the Red Wings' 1997-98 Cup victory, are the only players to have their names on the Cup without playing that season.

▶ IMPACT PERSON

George Hainsworth

Hainsworth, who replaces the legendary Georges Vezina in the Canadiens' goal, wins the Vezina in each of his first three NHL seasons, completing his hat-trick with 22 shutouts and a 0.92 GAA in 1928-29, records which haven't been equalled. Hainsworth is apologetic about his lack of flamboyance. "I can't jump on easy shots and make them look hard," he says.

Forward Thinking

Proposed rule changes, designed to increase scoring, are used in a March 17 game as the Rangers edge Pittsburgh 4-3. Players are permitted to kick the puck and forward passing is allowed in all three zones.

HOCKEY LISTS OF THE CENTURY Heroes of Zeroes

Perfection for puckstoppers is a shutout. George Hainsworth sets the all-time record in 1928-29 with 22 shutouts in 44 games. Listed are the three shutout numbers you have to know if you're a true fan, including Terry Sawchuk's career record–a mark surely never to be equalled. Patrick Roy is the leader among active goalies with 48 at the end of the 1999-2000 season, and is tied with Clint Benedict for career playoff shutouts with 15.

No.	All-Time Achievement
15	Modern Era single-season shutout record, Tony Esposito, Chi. ('69-70)
22	Early Era single-season record, George Hainsworth, Mon. ('28-29)
103	Career record, Terry Sawchuk, Det., Bos., Tor., L.A., NYR ('49-50 – '69-70)

Chalk Talk

"You learn things in other sports which come in mighty handy in hockey." *New York Americans' defenseman and multi-sport athlete Lionel Conacher on the advantages of playing football, baseball and other sports.*

1929-30

Stanley Cup: Montreal Canadiens

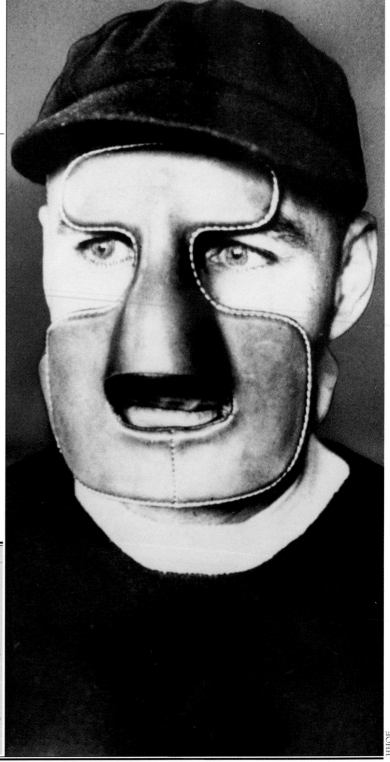

Clint Benedict, Montreal Maroons

No. 1 STORY: New rules produce goal rush

Alarmed by a steady decrease in scoring, which led to a record-low average of 2.9 goals per game in 1928-29, the NHL introduces rule changes which allow forward passing in all three zones, but not over either blueline. The impact is enormous. The goals-per-game average jumps to 5.9, while shutouts drop from 120 to just 26. A month into the season, NHL governors add an offside rule to prohibit attacking players from crossing the opponent's blueline before the puck.

2. Weiland smashes Morenz's scoring record

Cooney Weiland of the Boston Bruins doesn't just break the points record, he shatters it. The slick center's 73 points are 22 more than Howie Morenz's old mark (51) and won't be topped for 11 seasons. Weiland (43) and linemate Dit Clapper (41) lead the NHL goal parade and the Bruins to an incredible 38-5-1 record. Boston establishes several NHL records, including most points (77), wins (38), goals (179), winning streak (14 games) and highest winning percentage (.875), yet fail to win the Stanley Cup.

3. Benedict NHL's first masked man

Montreal Maroons' goalie Clint Benedict suffers a broken nose in a Jan. 8 game after being struck by a shot from Montreal Canadiens' Howie Morenz. When he returns to the lineup against the New York Americans Feb. 20, Benedict becomes the first NHL netminder to don facial protection. He wears a leather mask with a big nosepiece for one game, then discards it.

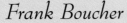

▶ **IMPACT PERSON**

Frank Boucher

The crafty New York Rangers' center doubles the NHL record for assists, setting up 36 goals. He continues his gentlemanly play, winning the Lady Byng Trophy a third straight time. He will win the award seven times between 1927-28 and 1934-35 and is finally given the trophy to keep. Despite a broken collarbone, Boucher plays in the 1930 playoffs, proving he is indeed tough.

HHOF

HHOF

Up, Up and Away

The New York Rangers become the first NHL team to travel by air when they hire the Curtis-Wright Corporation Dec. 13 to fly them to Toronto for a game the following day. The Rangers lose to the Maple Leafs 7-6.

HOCKEY LISTS OF THE CENTURY Evolution Of Scoring

1929-30 is a watershed year in NHL scoring. Combined goals by both teams rises from 2.9 in 1928-29 to 5.9. The three-goal increase is the highest in history from one season to the next. Here's the evolution of scoring by decades, including scoring leaders.

Yr.	GPG	Leader	Pts.	Yr.	GPG	Leader	Pts.
'17-18	10.1	Joe Malone, Mon.	48	'67-78	5.6	Stan Mikita, Chi.	87
'27-28	3.8	Howie Morenz, Mon.	51	'77-78	6.6	Guy Lafleur, Mon.	132
'37-38	5.1	Gordie Drillon, Tor.	52	'87-88	7.4	Mario Lemieux, Pit.	168
'47-48	5.9	Elmer Lach, Mon.	61	'97-98	5.3	Jaromir Jagr, Pit.	102
'57-58	5.6	Dickie Moore, Mon.	84	*Average GPG was 5.5 in '99-00			

Chalk Talk

"It was leather with a big nosepiece. The nosepiece proved the problem, because it obscured my vision."

Clint Benedict on his short-lived face mask

HOCKEY LISTS OF THE CENTURY
Howe, Bourque Top All-Stars

All-star teams are named for the first time in 1930-31. Listed are players with the most all-star selections by position. (First-team selections are in parentheses.)

Goalies	No.
Glenn Hall (7)	11
Frank Brimsek (2)	8
Jacques Plante (3)	7
Terry Sawchuk (3)	7
Defensemen	**No.**
Ray Bourque (12)	18
Doug Harvey (10)	11
Earl Seibert (4)	10
Bobby Orr (8)	9
Eddie Shore (7)	8
Red Kelly (6)	8
Left Wingers	
Bobby Hull (10)	12
Ted Lindsay (8)	9
Frank Mahovlich (3)	9
Centers	**No.**
Wayne Gretzky (8)	15
Jean Beliveau (6)	10
Stan Mikita (6)	8
Phil Esposito (6)	8
Right Wingers	**No.**
Gordie Howe (12)	21
Maurice Richard (8)	14
Mike Bossy (5)	8

Chalk Talk

"I know there are better teams in the league than the Quakers."

Manager Cooper Smeaton's understatement of the strength of the rest of the league compared to his 4-36-4 Philadelphia club

Tiny Thompson, Boston Bruins

No. 1 STORY: Smythe gambles on the King
Toronto Maple Leafs' manager Conn Smythe already has one Rare Jewel and uses it to acquire another. Smythe wins nearly $15,000 betting on Rare Jewel, a thoroughbred racehorse he owns, then borrows about $20,000 and sends defenseman Art Smith, forward Eric Pettinger and $35,000 to the Ottawa Senators Oct. 11 for star defenseman King Clancy. The charismatic blueliner becomes the leader of a Leafs' team which is the best in the 1930s.

2. Quakers win only four of 44 games
Coming off a dismal 5-36-3 season, the Pittsburgh Pirates franchise is transferred to Philadelphia and renamed the Quakers. Owned by former world lightweight boxing champ Benny Leonard, the Quakers are blanked in both of their first two games, en route to a pathetic 4-36-4 campaign and .136 winning percentage, the worst in NHL history.

3. Inaugural all-star teams legendary
Every player named to the first-ever first and second all-star teams is eventually elected to the Hockey Hall of Fame, an auspicious beginning for the all-star team concept. On the first team are goalie Charlie Gardiner (Chicago Black Hawks), defensemen Eddie Shore (Boston Bruins) and King Clancy (Toronto), left winger Aurel Joliat (Montreal Canadiens), center Howie Morenz (Montreal), right winger Bill Cook (New York Rangers) and coach Lester Patrick (Rangers). On the second team are goalie Tiny Thompson (Boston), defensemen Sylvio Mantha (Montreal) and Ching Johnson (Rangers), left winger Bun Cook (Rangers), Frank Boucher (Rangers), right winger Dit Clapper (Boston) and coach Dick Irvin (Chicago).

The Toronto Maple Leafs strut their stuff in preparation for the 1931-32 season.

▶ IMPACT PERSON

Conn Smythe

When the Toronto Maple Leafs beat the New York Rangers in the Cup final, Conn Smythe's fingerprints are all over the place–on his Leafs, on Maple Leaf Gardens and even on the Rangers. He was New York's first manager and signed six current players. Smythe's setback? The Canadiens spurn a $75,000 offer for Howie Morenz.

No. 1 STORY: Toronto throws Gardens party

Toronto manager Conn Smythe is laughed at when he reveals plans to build Maple Leaf Gardens during the Great Depression, but it's Smythe who has the last laugh when the doors open Nov. 12 and 13,233 pour through to watch the Chicago Black Hawks beat the Leafs 2-1. MLG is built in less than six months at a cost of $1.5 million. [Smythe finds creative ways to get the job finished, using Leaf players as security guards at the job site and convincing union workers to take 20 per cent of their pay in Gardens stock.]

2. Senators and Quakers bow out

For the first time since the 1918-19 campaign, the NHL has fewer teams than the previous season. The Philadelphia Quakers and Ottawa Senators both announce Sept. 26 that they will discontinue operations for the upcoming season. Philadelphia lost more than $100,000 in 1930-31, while the Senators, who will return to the NHL in 1932-33, dropped more than $50,000.

3. NHL cool to icing rule proposal

After the New York Americans ice the puck 61 times during a 3-2 win Dec. 8 at Boston, Bruins' owner Charles Adams demands the NHL introduce a rule calling for a faceoff in the defending team's zone when it elects to shoot the puck the length of the ice to relieve pressure. When his pleas fall on deaf ears, Boston makes a mockery of its next game against the Americans, icing the puck 87 times in a 0-0 tie Jan. 3 at New York. Despite these tactics, the icing rule will not be adopted by the NHL until the 1937-38 season.

HOCKEY LISTS OF THE CENTURY
Rise And Fall Of Great Arenas

Maple Leaf Gardens is the last of the Original Six buildings to open and the last to close.

Opening	Closing
Montreal Forum	
Nov. 29, '24	March 11, '96
Madison Square Garden*	
Dec. 15, '25	Feb. 11, '68
Detroit Olympia	
Nov. 22, '27	Dec. 15, '79
Boston Garden	
Nov. 20, '28	May 14, '95
Chicago Stadium	
Dec. 16, '29	April 28, '94
Maple Leaf Gardens	
Nov. 12, '31	Feb. 13, '99

*New MSG built at different location

King Clancy, Toronto Maple Leafs

1932-33

Stanley Cup: New York Rangers

No. 1 STORY: Detroit drops Falcons for Red Wings

Things were bad in Detroit. The club had gone into receivership and was so hard up it once carved a spare goalie out of plywood because there were no funds to sign a human. They even changed names from Cougars to Falcons in 1930. But in September the team is sold to Chicago grain millionaire James Norris. A member of the Montreal Amateur Athletic Association–the Winged Wheelers–Norris renames Detroit the Red Wings, feeling a winged wheel is a natural logo for a team representing the Motor City.

2. Doraty's goal ends playoff marathon

With Toronto and Boston scoreless after 100 minutes of overtime in the final game of their best-of-five semifinal April 3-4, drastic measures are considered. Maple Leafs' manager Conn Smythe and Bruins' manager Art Ross suggest resuming the game the next day, but are rejected by NHL president Frank Calder. So are suggestions to remove both goalies or flip a coin. Early in the sixth overtime period, Toronto's Ken Doraty beats Boston goalie Tiny Thompson, ending what was then the NHL's longest game at 1:50 a.m., after 104:46 of overtime. Three years later the record will be broken in a game between Detroit and the Montreal Maroons.

3. Future referee-in-chief wins first rookie award

Detroit forward Carl Voss wins the first Rookie Award–which is renamed the Calder Trophy in 1936-37. It's a rare achievement for Voss, who plays for eight teams in eight seasons, but gains Hall of Fame status as an official after serving as NHL referee-in-chief.

▶ **IMPACT PERSON**

Eddie Shore

'The Edmonton Express' scores a career-high 35 points to become the first defenseman to win the Hart Trophy as MVP. It's the first of four Harts he will earn–only five other blueliners have won the award. Rugged, skilled and charismatic, Shore would skate out to his position to the tune of 'Hail To The Chief,' wearing a matador's cape, then hand it to a waiting valet.

Last of Day Oners

Reg Noble, the last of the original NHLers, plays his final season, splitting the campaign between the Detroit Red Wings and Montreal Maroons. Noble broke in with the Toronto Arenas in 1917-18.

HOCKEY LISTS OF THE CENTURY Career Launching Pads

Carl Voss, who splits the season between two teams, is the first Calder Trophy winner in 1932-33. The center is traded from the New York Rangers to Detroit in December. Here's a list of the 10 best Calder winners ever.

Player, Season	Player, Season
1. **Bobby Orr**, Bos. ('66-67)	6. **Denis Potvin**, NYI ('73-74)
2. **Mario Lemieux**, Pit. ('84-85)	7. **Mike Bossy**, NYI ('77-78)
3. **Terry Sawchuk**, Det. ('50-51)	8. **Ken Dryden**, Mon. ('71-72)
4. **Ray Bourque**, Bos. ('79-80)	9. **Frank Mahovlich**, Tor. ('57-58)
5. **Glenn Hall**, Det. ('55-56)	10. **Bryan Trottier**, NYI ('75-76)

Chalk Talk

"Stay around after the game and we'll see how tough you are."

Toronto's King Clancy's suggestion to a heckling Boston fan, who he later discovers to be heavyweight champ Jack Sharkey

Imperial Oil – Turofsky/HHOF

HHOF

35

1933-34

Stanley Cup: Chicago Black Hawks

Ace Bailey, left, and Eddie Shore shake hands at a game staged to raise money for Bailey.

Imperial Oil – Turofsky/HHOF

▶ IMPACT PERSON

Charlie Gardiner

Gardiner had kept a weak Chicago Black Hawks' squad afloat for several years. His work finally pays off as he captains and backstops Chicago to its first Cup. Gardiner allows one goal or fewer in five of eight playoff games. Triumph turns to tragedy after the season when Gardiner dies of a brain hemorrhage June 13 in Winnipeg.

HHOF

No. 1 STORY: Bailey nearly killed in Shore attack

Boston and Toronto always have heated battles, but none can match the frightening Dec. 12 contest at Boston Garden. In the first period, Maple Leaf King Clancy dumps Bruin Eddie Shore and heads up ice with the puck. Ace Bailey drops back to cover Clancy's defense spot while Shore, regaining his feet, mistakes Bailey for Clancy and rams him from behind. Bailey's head hits the ice. Rushed to a nearby hospital, Bailey is listed in critical condition with multiple concussions. His death notice is mistakenly printed in the next morning's Boston papers. Bailey recovers, but never plays again. Shore is suspended for 16 games.

2. Benefit game staves off Bailey lawsuit

While Bailey considers suing Shore over his career-ending injury, the NHL offers a solution–a benefit game between the Leafs and a group of NHL all-stars Feb. 14, with proceeds going to Bailey. Played at Maple Leaf Gardens and won 7-3 by Toronto, the game raises $20,900 for Bailey, who shakes hands with Shore, a member of the all-stars, before the game. "I know it was an accident," says Bailey, who gets into coaching and later joins the staff of off-ice officials at MLG.

3. Coronation Day for the King

Maple Leaf Gardens is decorated in green and orange and filled with Irish music as the Leafs salute King Clancy on St. Patrick's Day. The Irishman parades in, seated on a throne wearing a crown. He doffs his robe to reveal a green jersey with a shamrock instead of a maple leaf and he wears it for the first period of a 3-2 win over the Rangers.

HOCKEY LISTS OF THE CENTURY

Nicknames: Volume I

Hockey nicknames come in all shapes and sizes. Our favorites fall in two categories: those inspired by origin and those just plain inspired. Below are our five favorite geography-related nicknames and on pg. 37 are five more colorful choices. Our favorite city nickname is 'Dipsy-Doodle-Dandy from Delisle,' given to puckhandling whiz Max Bentley of Delisle, Sask.

All-Time Nicknames I

1. **'Dipsy Doodle Dandy'**
   Max Bentley (1940s-50s)
   Excellent puckhandler
2. **'Stratford Streak'**
   Howie Morenz (1920s-30s)
   Exceptional skater
3. **'Chicoutimi Cucumber'**
   Georges Vezina (1920s)
   Cool under fire
4. **'Edmonton Express'**
   Eddie Shore (1920s-30s)
   Unstoppable force
5. **'Motor City Smitty'**
   Brad Smith (1980s)
   It rhymes

Chalk Talk

"Put me back in the game. They need me."

Ace Bailey's plea to Maple Leafs' assistant GM Frank Selke after suffering critical brain injuries Dec. 12 at Boston Garden

Howie Morenz, Chicago Black Hawks

HHOF

1934-35

Stanley Cup: Montreal Maroons M

No. 1 STORY: Morenz among big names dealt

A hard salary cap of $62,500 per team and $7,000 per player forces NHL clubs to make difficult decisions about veteran players. Goalie Lorne Chabot goes from the Montreal Canadiens to the Chicago Black Hawks, while defenseman Lionel Conacher and goalie Alex Connell wind up with the Montreal Maroons. But the most shocking move comes when the Habs ship legendary center Howie Morenz to Chicago. The NHL's career scoring leader with 392 points, 'The Stratford Streak' had won two scoring titles, three Hart Trophies and three Stanley Cups with the Habs, but had finished out of the league's top 10 scorers since 1932-33.

2. Sens leave Ottawa and land in St. Louis as Eagles

Following three last-place finishes and a one-year hiatus, the struggling Ottawa Senators–winners of four Stanley Cups–move to St. Louis, where the team is renamed the Eagles. Two years earlier, the NHL had turned down a request for an expansion franchise from the Missouri city because of the extensive travel. The team's fortunes don't improve as the Eagles finish last at 11-31-6 and fold following the season.

3. Goalies prevail in first year of penalty shot

A new wrinkle is added when the NHL introduces the penalty shot. It is taken from within a 10-foot circle that is 38 feet from the goalie and is awarded when an attacking player is fouled while "in a good scoring position." Goalies are the victors, though, stopping 25 of 29 shots.

▶ IMPACT PERSON

Charlie Conacher

Playing on the right side of the Toronto Maple Leafs' 'Kid Line' with center Joe Primeau and left winger Busher Jackson, Conacher defends his scoring title with 57 points, including a career-high 36 goals. He proves his versatility in a 5-3 win over the Canadiens March 16 with a hat trick and three minutes of shutout goaltending when George Hainsworth leaves to get a cut over his eye stitched.

Imperial Oil – Turofsky/HHOF

Debut Of No. 99

Long before Wayne Gretzky makes the number famous, Joe Lamb, Desse Roche and Leo Bourgault all wear jersey No. 99 at different times for the Montreal Canadiens during the season.

HOCKEY LISTS OF THE CENTURY Nicknames: Volume II

Goalies have inspired more great nicknames than any other position, to wit: Andre 'Red Light' Racicot (early 1990s), Steve 'The Puck Goes Inski' Buzinski (1942-43) and Andy 'The Glasgow Gobbler' Aitkenhead (1930s). Here are five more of our favorites.

All-Time Nicknames II

1. Frank **'Ulcers'** McCool	1940s	*Drinks milk to settle stomach*
2. Roland **'Rollie The Goalie'** Melanson	1980s	*Nickname just rolls off the tongue*
3. Frank **'Mr. Zero'** Brimsek	1940s	*Records series of shutouts in debut*
4. Tony **'O'** Esposito	1970s	*Earns Modern Era record 15 'Ohs'*
5. Nikolai **'The Bulin Wall'** Khabibulin	1990s	*Russian never crumbles in net*

Chalk Talk

"Chicago is receiving one of the greatest stars the National Hockey League has ever seen."

Montreal manager Leo Dandurand after trading Howie Morenz to the Black Hawks

1935-36

Stanley Cup: Detroit Red Wings

No. 1 STORY: Bruneteau ends longest playoff game

His name is Mud; his legend eternal. In his first Stanley Cup game, Detroit rookie Modere 'Mud' Bruneteau beats Maroons' goalie Lorne Chabot with the only goal after 176:30 of playing time, ending the longest game in Cup history March 24-25. It breaks the mark set by Boston and Toronto in the 1932-33 playoffs by 11 minutes and 14 seconds. Wings' goalie Normie Smith, also in his first Cup game, blocks 89 shots and doesn't let in a goal for an NHL-record 248:32 until Game 3 as Detroit wins its first title.

2. Canadiens' owners tempted by Cleveland

The Cleveland Canadiens? It nearly happens. With the Depression hampering attendance at NHL games in Montreal, Canadiens' owners Leo Dandurand and Joe Cattarinich, who lost $40,000 the previous season, consider a proposal to sell to Cleveland interests which would move the team there. Montreal entrepreneurs Ernie Savard, Maurice Forget and Louis Gelinas save the day, purchasing the team Sept. 17 for $165,000.

3. NHL takes over Americans and doomed Eagles

Faced with a financial crisis, the NHL purchases the St. Louis Eagles and New York Americans Sept. 28. President Frank Calder announces the league will operate the Amerks and names Red Dutton manager. The Eagles request a leave of absence, but the NHL folds the franchise, selling the players to the other clubs. The biggest catch is future scoring champ Bill Cowley, who goes to Boston.

▶ IMPACT PERSON

Marty Barry

A chance meeting between Detroit Red Wings' coach-GM Jack Adams and Boston Bruins' coach Frank Patrick at the 1935 final leads to a deal sending Cooney Weiland to Boston for center Marty Barry. Adams puts Barry between Larry Aurie and Herbie Lewis on hockey's best line for two years. Barry places second in NHL scoring and the trio leads Detroit to its first Stanley Cup.

More Late Hours

Four players are part of hockey's two longest games–Lorne Chabot ('33 Leafs, '36 Maroons), Bob Gracie ('33 Leafs, '36 Maroons), Marty Barry ('33 Bruins, '36 Wings), and Joe Lamb ('33 Bruins, '36 Maroons).

HOCKEY LISTS OF THE CENTURY Working Overtime

Mud Bruneteau's place in hockey lore is assured when he ends the longest game in Stanley Cup history. The longest since is Philadelphia's 2-1 win over Pittsburgh in 2000, which Keith Primeau ends after more than 92 minutes of OT. Here are the five longest ever.

Date	OT	Score	Winning Goal	Winning Goalie
March 24, '36	116:30	Detroit 1 Maroons 0	Mud Bruneteau	Normie Smith
April 3, '33	104:46	Toronto 1 Boston 0	Ken Doraty	Lorne Chabot
May 4, '00	92:01	Philadelphia 2 Pittsburgh 1	Keith Primeau	Brian Boucher
April 24, '96	79:15	Pittsburgh 3 Washington 2	Petr Nedved	Ken Wregget
March 23, '43	70:18	Toronto 3 Detroit 2	Jack McLean	Turk Broda

Chalk Talk

"He never could referee and never will be able to."

Boston's Eddie Shore, who is assessed a misconduct after banking a shot off the backside of referee Odie Cleghorn in a playoff game at Toronto

James Rice/HHOF

1936-37

Stanley Cup: Detroit Red Wings

No. 1 STORY: Morenz's death stuns hockey world

Picked up by the Montreal Canadiens and reunited with old line-mates Aurel Joliat and Johnny Gagnon, Howie Morenz finds new life in his 34-year-old legs. But his return is suddenly halted Jan. 28 at the Montreal Forum after he suffers four broken bones in his left leg and ankle when slammed into the boards by Chicago Black Hawks' defenseman Earl Seibert. Morenz suffers a nervous break-down while in the hospital; then on March 8 he dies as a result of a pulmonary embolism. Thousands file past Morenz's body, which lies in state at center ice of the Forum, and up to 200,000 line the streets of Montreal to watch the funeral procession.

2. 'Kraut Line' leads new wave of future stars

Veteran stars King Clancy, Joe Primeau, Roy Worters, Alex Connell, George Hainsworth and Lorne Chabot all hang up their blades before, during or after the campaign. Offsetting the losses is an outstanding crop of rookies that includes Toronto's Turk Broda, Syl Apps and Gordie Drillon, and Boston's 'Kraut Line' of Milt Schmidt, Woody Dumart and Bobby Bauer.

3. Chicago's all-American experiment fizzles

Bent on icing an all-American team, Chicago owner Major Frederic McLaughlin instructs coach Clem Loughlin to experi-ment with a lineup including nine U.S.-born players for the Black Hawks' final five league games. "I intend to throw off the tradi-tional Canadian influence over this game," McLaughlin says. But Chicago wins only one of its last five games.

▶ IMPACT PERSON

Ebbie Goodfellow

A center when he joined the Detroit franchise in 1929, Goodfellow fin-ished second in the 1930-31 NHL scoring race. He switched to defense when Detroit acquired Marty Barry in 1935 and the tran-sition helps the Red Wings to back-to-back Stanley Cups. Goodfellow was a second all-star team choice on defense in 1935-36 and earns first team status in 1936-37.

HHOF

20-20 Club Founder

Appropriately named, Montreal Maroons' for-ward Russ Blinco makes a spectacle of himself and becomes the first NHL player to appear in a game wearing glasses.

HOCKEY LISTS OF THE CENTURY 2nd Decade All-Stars

Ill-fated Montreal center Howie Morenz and Boston defenseman Eddie Shore each win three Hart Trophies during the NHL's second decade (1927-28 through 1936-37).

The Hockey News' First Team		**The Hockey News' Second Team**	
G	**G. Hainsworth**, Mon. *Shutout king*	G	**Charlie Gardiner**, Chi. *Dominant*
D	**Eddie Shore**, Bos. *Basher with flair*	D	**Ching Johnson**, NYR *Defensive star*
D	**King Clancy**, Tor. *Irish icon*	D	**Babe Siebert**, Mon. M. *Strong checker*
LW	**Aurel Joliat**, Mon. *Diminutive dandy*	LW	**Busher Jackson**, Tor. *Fun-loving star*
C	**Howie Morenz**, Mon. *Jet on skates*	C	**Frank Boucher**, NYR *Slick passer*
RW	**Bill Cook**, NYR *Super scorer*	RW	**Charlie Conacher**, Tor. *'Big Bomber'*

Chalk Talk

"I think more boys wanted to be like him than any other player in the league."

New York Rangers' coach Lester Patrick on the impact of Howie Morenz

1937-38

Stanley Cup: Chicago Black Hawks

No. 1 STORY: Hawks scramble for goalie in final

Alfie Moore comes to Maple Leaf Gardens before Game 1 of the Stanley Cup final looking for tickets and ends up on the hot seat. The minor-league netminder suits up and backstops Chicago to a 3-1 win over Toronto after Black Hawks' goalie Mike Karakas is unable to play with a broken toe. Moore is paid $300 for the only playoff victory of his NHL career. It's a brief gasp of glory as NHL president Frank Calder rules Moore ineligible for the remainder of the series, since he's not under contract to Chicago. Karakas returns later in the series to lead the Hawks to the Cup.

2. 'Old Poison' first to score 300 goals

At 36, Nels Stewart shows no signs of slowing down. The man who shared the NHL goal-scoring crown with 23 goals in 1936-37 follows up with 19 for the New York Americans. 'Old Poison,' so-called because of the way he stings the opposition, beats New York Rangers' goalie Dave Kerr March 17 to become the first NHL player to reach the 300-goal plateau. Stewart retires in 1940 with 324 career goals, which isn't surpassed until 1952 by Rocket Richard.

3. Red Wings go from best to worst

Two-time defending-champion Detroit Red Wings drop to the basement of the American Division and miss the playoffs, winning just 12 games. The Wings had finished last in 1934-35, then first overall in both of their Stanley Cup seasons. No other team in history has missed the playoffs, won consecutive Stanley Cups, then missed the playoffs again. Coach-GM Jack Adams blames himself, claiming he kept the nucleus of his title-winning club together too long.

▶ IMPACT PERSON

Bill Stewart

A major-league baseball umpire, who impresses Chicago owner Major Frederic McLaughlin with his authority, Stewart is hired to coach the Black Hawks. He stands up for his club by getting into a punch-up with Toronto player 'Baldy' Cotton and manager Conn Smythe before Game 1 of the final. His squad wins the Cup, but he's fired 21 games into the next season.

Morenz Benefit

A total of $20,000 is raised for the family of deceased Montreal Canadiens' center Howie Morenz Nov. 2, as the NHL All-Stars edge a combined Habs-Maroons squad 6-5 at the Montreal Forum.

HOCKEY LISTS OF THE CENTURY All The Presidents' (And Commissioner's) Men

The NHL has been led by six men during its 82-year history. Each has faced good and bad times. Here are their legacies, including commissioner Gary Bettman's work in progress. His predecessors carried the title of president.

Years	Leader	The Good Times	The Bad Times
1917-43	Frank Calder	Leads struggling NHL during infancy	Suspends striking Tigers in '24-25 playoffs
1943-46	Red Dutton	Initiates post-WWII recovery	Suspends Babe Pratt for gambling
1946-77	Clarence Campbell	'67 expansion widens hockey presence	Richard suspension leads to riot in '55
1977-92	John Ziegler Jr.	Ends war with dismantled WHA	'92 player strike leads to his ouster
1992-93	Gil Stein	Excels in promotion...of himself	Tries to orchestrate Hall of Fame election
1993-	Gary Bettman	Professionalizes league front office	'94 lockout doesn't solve salary problem

HHOF

HHOF

1938-39

Stanley Cup: Boston Bruins

No. 1 STORY: 'Sudden Death' Hill strikes three times

A 10-goal scorer during the regular season, Boston's Mel Hill explodes for six in 12 playoff games. The timing of his goals is amazing. He scores a record three overtime goals in a seven-game semifinal win over the New York Rangers. Two of them come in triple OT, including the Game 7 winner on a pass from teammate Bill Cowley. Hill never scores another overtime goal, but will forever be remembered as 'Sudden Death' Hill.

2. League bids farewell to Montreal Maroons

Stanley Cup champions just three seasons earlier, the Montreal Maroons posted an NHL-worst 12-30-6 mark in 1937-38. In the summer of 1938, citing financial hardship, the Maroons take a leave of absence from the league, but will never return. Maroons' players are divvied up among the seven remaining teams and the two-division format is dropped. Six of the seven clubs qualify for the post-season.

3. Blake scoring champ and Hart winner for dismal Habs

The Montreal Canadiens get their foot in the door of the Stanley Cup playoffs, thanks mainly to their big Toe. Despite the Habs finishing sixth with a record of 15-24-9, left winger Toe Blake leads the NHL in scoring with 47 points and is presented with the Hart Trophy as league MVP in his third season. It's the fourth Hart/scoring title double in NHL history. All have been turned by Montreal players: the Canadiens' Howie Morenz (1927-28, 1930-31), the Maroons' Nels Stewart (1925-26) and Blake.

▶ IMPACT PERSON

Frank Brimsek

Boston Bruins' fans cry foul when four-time Vezina Trophy-winner Tiny Thompson is traded to the Detroit Red Wings and replaced by rookie Frank Brimsek. But jeers turn to cheers as Brimsek posts six shutouts in his first eight starts. He wins the Calder and Vezina Trophies, is a first-team all-star and helps the Bruins to the Stanley Cup, four single-season feats matched by no other NHL goalie.

Hairy Proposition

Rangers Muzz Patrick and Art Coulter become the first known bearded players, cashing in on a $500 bet with coach Lester Patrick. Growing whiskers and bad beards later becomes an NHL tradition during the playoffs.

HOCKEY LISTS OF THE CENTURY Under-Appreciated Greats

Frank Brimsek earns the nickname, 'Mr. Zero,' and the Calder Trophy in his rookie season, bringing acclaim to a position that has received curiously little in relation to its importance. Twelve of 68 Calder winners have been goalies. Only six regular season MVPs (Hart Trophy) have been goalies. Proper appreciation has come during the playoffs; 11 goalies (31 per cent of winners) have won the Conn Smythe Trophy as MVP.

Trophy	Winners	Pct.	Noteworthy
Hart	6/77	8%	Dominik Hasek's Hart ('96-97) ends 35-year goalie drought
Calder	12/68	18%	Mike Karakas only winner ('35-36) not to have impact career
Smythe	11/36	31%	Two goalies have won twice, Bernie Parent and Patrick Roy

Chalk Talk

"Trying to get him to make the first move is like pushing over the Washington Monument."

Rangers' coach Lester Patrick on Boston goalie Frank Brimsek

1939-40

Stanley Cup: New York Rangers

Red Horner, Toronto Maple Leafs

No. 1 STORY: Bruins trade Shore to New York Americans

Four-time Hart Trophy-winner Eddie Shore and Boston Bruins' manager Art Ross are at odds at the start of the season when Shore, 37, purchases the Springfield Indians of the International-American League and asks to play for that club. Shore and Ross agree that he will play all of Boston's home and playoff games, but Ross decides, instead, to trade Shore to the New York Americans Jan. 25 for forward Eddie Wiseman and $5,000. The Americans agree to allow Shore to play for both teams, but he retires from the NHL at the end of the season.

2. Habs suffer through humiliating season

The season starts tragically when Babe Siebert, the Montreal Canadiens' new coach, drowns Aug. 25 before coaching a game. Under new coach Pit Lepine, the Habs finish last and equal club futility marks for fewest wins (10) and home wins (five), endure club-record seven-game losing and 15-game winless skids at the Forum and record their lowest-ever winning percentage (.260).

3. American clubs dominate individual awards

Players from American-based clubs clean up the league's individual awards. Boston's Milt Schmidt wins the scoring title, while teammate Bobby Bauer earns the Lady Byng. Ebbie Goodfellow of the Detroit Red Wings wins the Hart, Dave Kerr of the New York Rangers, the Vezina, and teammate Kilby MacDonald, the Calder. The Toronto Maple Leafs' Red Horner leads the NHL in penalty minutes for a record eighth straight season.

▶ IMPACT PERSON

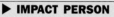
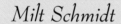

Milt Schmidt

Schmidt, center of Boston's famed 'Kraut Line,' tops the NHL in assists (30) and points (52), with linemates Woody Dumart and Bobby Bauer (43 points apiece) right behind him. It's the first time linemates rank 1-2-3 in NHL scoring, and one of only four times in history. Schmidt is a first team all-star, while his linemates make the second team.

Live, From New York

A 6-2 win by the New York Rangers over the Montreal Canadiens Feb. 25 at Madison Square Garden is also seen by viewers of New York television station WZXBS, making it the first NHL game to be televised.

HOCKEY LISTS OF THE CENTURY Top Lines Of All-Time I

'The Kraut Line' is hockey's best unit in 1939-40 and No. 10 among the best forward lines ever, as chosen by The Hockey News. The top five appear on this page; the next five on pg. 43. One non-NHL line earns recognition, the famed Soviet 'KLM' unit.

Name	Team	Era	LW, C, RW
1. 'Production'	Det.	1940s-50s	Ted Lindsay, Sid Abel, Gordie Howe
2. 'Punch'	Mon.	1940s	Toe Blake, Elmer Lach, Rocket Richard
3. 'KLM'	Soviet	1980s	Vladimir Krutov, Igor Larionov, Sergei Makarov
4. 'Trio Grande'	NYI	1980s	Clark Gillies, Bryan Trottier, Mike Bossy
5. 'Kid'	Tor.	1930s	Busher Jackson, Joe Primeau, Charlie Conacher

Chalk Talk

"I never thought I would ever leave my favorite city, but I'd pretty well worn out my tonsils trying to get a settlement from Art Ross and the Boston Bruins."

Eddie Shore's reaction to his trade from Boston to the New York Americans

Imperial Oil - Turofsky/HHOF

'The Kraut Line': Bobby Bauer, Milt Schmidt, Woody Dumart

HOCKEY LISTS OF THE CENTURY

Top 10 Lines Of All-Time: II

The best of the rest.

Name	Era
Team, LW, C, RW	
6. No Name	1970s
Mon.: Steve Shutt, Jacques Lemaire, Guy Lafleur	
7. 'Dogs of War'	1970s
Bos.: Ken Hodge, Phil Esposito, Wayne Cashman	
8. 'GAG'	1960s-70s
NYR: Vic Hadfield, Jean Ratelle, Rod Gilbert	
9. 'French Connection'*	
Buf.: Rick Martin, Gil Perreault, Rene Robert	
10. 'Kraut'	1930s
Bos.: Woody Dumart, Milt Schmidt, Bobby Bauer	
*1970s	

No. 1 STORY: Streaking Bruins win Stanley Cup

Boston is almost unstoppable en route to its fourth straight first-place finish and third Stanley Cup. The team has an NHL-record 23-game unbeaten streak (15-0-8) which lasts two months. The Bruins also go 15 games at home without losing and have their astonishing 49-game unbeaten streak (13-0-36) in regular season overtime halted by a 3-2 loss at Chicago Dec. 8–a streak that dates back six years to Dec. 13, 1934. The Bruins won't win the Cup again for another 29 seasons until 1970.

2. Habs grab Irvin from Leafs to take over at helm

The Montreal Canadiens scoop up veteran coach Dick Irvin, who resigns in Toronto. Irvin has guided eight teams to the Stanley Cup final in the last decade. Although Montreal's 16-26-6 record in Irvin's first season gives no indication of things to come, he will turn a dormant Canadiens' franchise into a league powerhouse. Montreal will reach the final eight times with Irvin as coach, winning three Cups.

3. LoPresti pelted with 83 shots

Chicago Black Hawks' goalie Sam LoPresti is the target in a Boston Garden shooting gallery, facing 83 shots in a 3-2 loss March 4. LoPresti blocks 42 over the first 25 minutes before Roy Conacher scores. Milt Schmidt connects on the 59th shot and Eddie Wiseman beats LoPresti for the winner with 2:31 left. LoPresti's 80 saves are a record, but not his most remarkable feat. Two years later during World War II, his U.S. Navy ship is torpedoed by a German U-boat February, 1943. He and shipmates float in a lifeboat for 41 days until they are rescued.

Bill Cowley

Cowley is always there to lend a helping hand. The Boston Bruins' center earns a record 45 assists–shattering Joe Primeau's mark by eight–to become the first player to record more assists in a season than any other player has points. Cowley wins the scoring title by 18 with 62 points and the Hart Trophy as league MVP.

HHOF

1941-42

Stanley Cup: Toronto Maple Leafs

No. 1 STORY: Leafs stage amazing comeback

It's a comeback for the ages. Toronto is down 3-0 to Detroit in the Stanley Cup final and struggling with the Red Wings' dump-and-chase style. Maple Leafs' coach Hap Day benches veterans Gordie Drillon and Bucko McDonald in favor of youngsters Don Metz and Ernie Dickens. Before Game 4, Day reads a letter from a 14-year-old girl who believes they will come back. No team has ever rallied from such a deficit. Day's new line of center Syl Apps between the Metz brothers, Nick and Don, nets the game-winner in three straight Toronto victories to tie the series. A Canadian-record crowd of 16,128 packs Maple Leaf Gardens for Game 7 to witness hockey history as Toronto wins 3-1 to capture the Cup.

2. Hockey stars join war effort

The Dec. 9, 1941 game at Boston Garden between the Bruins and Chicago Black Hawks is delayed as 10,000 fans listen to U.S. President Franklin Delano Roosevelt's declaration of war following the Dec. 7 Japanese attack on Pearl Harbor. Toronto manager Conn Smythe enlists and urges all of his players to do likewise. Boston's entire 'Kraut Line' of Milt Schmidt, Woody Dumart and Bobby Bauer joins the Royal Canadian Air Force.

3. Rangers finish first for last time in 50 years

The 29-17-2 New York Rangers finish atop the standings for the first time in franchise history, heights they won't reach again for 50 years. The Rangers are led by scoring champion Bryan Hextall (56 points). No Ranger since has won the Art Ross Trophy.

▶ **IMPACT PERSON**

Hap Day

A star player with the Maple Leafs and a well-educated man with a degree in pharmacy, Day took over as coach of Toronto in 1940. He establishes his reputation with the 1942 Cup rally. Day's ability to adjust to Detroit's strategy allows Toronto to come back from its 3-0 deficit. He becomes the third NHLer to captain and coach a champion. He was captain of the 1931-32 Cup champs.

Imperial Oil – Turofsky/HHOF

Imperial Oil – Turofsky/HHOF

American Invasion

It's speculated (incorrectly) American teams will play in Canada in 1942-43 due to passport issues. Among the supposed changes in venue: Chicago to Montreal, the Rangers to Toronto, the Americans to Ottawa, and Boston to Hamilton, Ont.

WHEN THE WORLD WENT TO WAR

Many hockey players answer a higher calling during WWII. Three are among the millions who lose their lives. The memories of each is honored. The International League names its championship trophy in memory of Joe Turner, an amateur goalie who plays one

IN MEMORIAM
Red Tilson
1924-1944
Red Garrett
1924-1944
Joe Turner
1919-1945

Honoring Our Dead

NHL game with Detroit. The Ontario League names its MVP award after Red Tilson, a junior star and Toronto prospect. The American League names its rookie award after Red Garrett, who plays 23 games with the New York Rangers in 1942-43.

Chalk Talk

"Don't worry about us–we'll take them four straight."

Toronto center Billy Taylor's surprisingly accurate prediction after Toronto falls behind 3-0 in the Stanley Cup final

All In The Family

Max, Doug and Reggie Bentley form the first all-brothers line in NHL history on New Year's Day and produce two goals, including the winner, as the Chicago Black Hawks edge the New York Rangers 6-5. Reggie plays just 11 career NHL games.

HOCKEY LISTS OF THE CENTURY

All The Facts On Brother Acts

The Bentleys make headlines in 1942-43 as the latest brother act in NHL history. There have been many memorable NHL combinations. Here are our five favorites.

Name & Claim to Fame

1. **Richard** *Maurice, Henri* 'Rocket' is one of the game's most important players; 'Pocket Rocket' sets record for most Stanley Cups (11).

2. **Esposito** *Phil, Tony* Phil is a record-setting scorer and Tony, a record-setting goalie.

3. **Sutter** *Brian, Darryl, Duane, Brent, Ron, Rich* No family has more NHL players.

4. **Boucher** *Frank, George, Billy, Bobby* They combine to win eight Stanley Cups 1920-33.

5. **Stastny** *Peter, Anton, Marian* Trailblazing Czechoslovak trio defect and have huge effect in Quebec.

Chalk Talk

"This is the hardest blow the game has felt. There couldn't have been a better president."

Montreal Canadiens' GM Tommy Gorman on the death of Frank Calder

Conn Smythe, 'The Major,' leads the way in urging players to enlist in the war effort.

No. 1 STORY: NHL continues despite severity of WWII

As World War II continues, 80 NHLers are serving in the armed services and rosters are reduced by one, to 14 players per team. There are concerns the season may be cancelled, but NHL president Frank Calder announces that the U.S. and Canadian governments feel hockey should continue "in the interest of public morale." His final major act as president comes Nov. 21 when he announces that the 10-minute overtime period has been scrapped because of wartime travel restrictions.

2. Loss of Brooklyn leaves NHL with Original Six

Brooklyn manager Red Dutton and NHL president Frank Calder are at odds in September as the NHL drops Dutton's Americans, which the league has operated since 1936. "The Brooklyn Americans haven't quit the NHL–we've been scuttled," says Dutton in protest. "We're out of the league because Madison Square Garden forced us out." The former New York Americans shared MSG with the Rangers, but are not offered dates for the season. The loss of the Amerks leaves the NHL with six teams, later dubbed the 'Original Six,' for the 25 seasons until expansion in 1967-68.

3. Dutton succeeds Calder as head of NHL

Frank Calder, 65, who has served as NHL president since its inception in 1917, suffers a heart attack Jan. 25 while holding a meeting in Toronto and dies 11 days later on Feb. 5. "Hockey will miss Frank Calder more than any of us realize right now," says Rangers' GM Lester Patrick. Former Brooklyn Americans' manager Red Dutton, who is filling in for Calder, is named interim president.

▶ IMPACT PERSON

Frank Calder

The flip of a coin brought the NHL its first president. Born in Scotland, Calder flipped a coin to pick whether he would emigrate to Canada or the U.S. It came up Canada. During his quarter-century in charge, he transformed the NHL from a tiny league based in Ontario and Quebec into one spanning much of North America.

The NHL's Modern Era

1943-44

Stanley Cup: Montreal Canadiens

Babe Pratt, Toronto Maple Leafs

No. 1 STORY: Center ice red line opens up game

In what is considered the beginning of hockey's Modern Era, the NHL changes the rules to open up the game. Previously, teams couldn't pass the puck across the blueline which allowed forecheckers to pin opponents in their own zone by ganging up on the puck-carrier. End-to-end hockey returns, though, when the league allows defending teams to pass across their bluelines and adds a red line at center ice to which they can pass the puck from within their end. Goals per game jump from 7.2 to 8.2, the league's highest total since 1920-21. "I'd say it was the biggest change hockey ever made and perhaps the best," says NHL referee and former all-star defenseman King Clancy.

2. Pratt sets defenseman scoring record

Toronto Maple Leafs' defenseman Babe Pratt is known as a high roller, but coach Hap Day senses Pratt is en route to something special and insists the playboy room with him the rest of the season. Pratt responds with 57 points, an NHL record for a blueliner, and is awarded the Hart Trophy. Two seasons later he is suspended for life for betting on hockey, but reinstated after nine games.

3. Depleted Rangers defeated and defeated and...

The New York Rangers have lost 28 men to the armed forces. With only six players back from the season before, coach Frank Boucher, 43, activates himself, but they get off to an NHL-worst 0-14-1 start and finish 6-39-5. The misery includes an NHL-record 15-0 loss to the Detroit Red Wings Jan. 23.

▶ IMPACT PERSON

Bill Durnan

Reluctant to turn pro, Durnan finally makes his NHL debut at 27 and is an immediate success, backstopping Montreal to an excellent 38-5-7 record and victory over Toronto in the Stanley Cup final. He wins the Vezina Trophy and earns first all-star team status–honors he receives six times each over the next seven seasons, an unprecedented run.

Imperial Oil – Turofsky/HHOF

Imperial Oil – Turofsky/HHOF

Nothing Doing

Chicago's Mike Karakas and Toronto's Paul Bibeault post shutouts and Bill Chadwick referees as the Black Hawks and Maple Leafs skate through the only scoreless, penalty-free game in NHL history Feb. 20, 1944.

HOCKEY LISTS OF THE CENTURY Radical Rule Changes

In the final season of the century–1999-2000–the NHL introduces 4-on-4 play in regular season overtime; it's the most significant manpower change since 1911-12, when the National Hockey Association went from seven players on the ice to six. Here are four other seminal NHL rule/enforcement changes.

Year	Rule Change
'29-30	Forward passes are allowed in all three zones, but not across bluelines.
'37-38	Icing is introduced, penalizing teams for dumping the puck down the ice.
'43-44	Game opens up with addition of the red line and passing over the blueline.
'91-92	Video replay introduced to help referees rule on legitimacy of goals.

Chalk Talk

"We've got no hockey players."

GM Lester Patrick's frank assessment of his woeful New York Rangers

Flying High

While flying a transport mission to Burma (Asia), Flight Sergeant J.L. Arnett of the Royal Canadian Air Force reports he is able to clearly pick up Foster Hewitt's broadcast of a Toronto–Chicago game on his airplane radio.

HOCKEY LISTS OF THE CENTURY
Fastest To 50 Goals In NHL History

Rocket Richard sets the hockey world ablaze in 1944-45 with 50 goals in 50 games. It remains the benchmark for scoring greatness. Eight players have scored 50 in 50 or fewer games a total of 13 times. They are Wayne Gretzky, Mario Lemieux, Cam Neely, Alexander Mogilny, Brett Hull, Richard, Mike Bossy and Jari Kurri. Listed is the game number in which each player scored his 50th; it's not necessarily his team's game number.

Name	Year	No.
Gretzky, Edm.	'81-82	39
Gretzky, Edm.	'83-84	42
Lemieux, Pit.	'88-89	44
Neely, Bos.	'93-94	44
Mogilny, Buf.	'92-93	46
Lemieux, Pit.	'92-93	48
Gretzky, Edm.	'84-85	49
Hull, St.L	'90-91	49
Richard, Mon.	'44-45	50
Bossy, NYI	'80-81	50
Kurri, Edm.	'84-85	50
Hull, St.L	'91-92	50
Lemieux, Pit.	'95-96	50

Chalk Talk

"He's going to be a real hockey player or I miss my guess."

Montreal defenseman Leo Lamoureux's assessment of Detroit rookie forward Ted Lindsay

Flash Hollett, Detroit Red Wings

No. 1 STORY: Rocket fires 50 goals in 50 games

The Montreal Canadiens are paced by right winger Rocket Richard, whose 50 goals in 50 games are an NHL single-season record. It breaks the mark of 44 set in 1917-18 by Joe Malone, who is on hand to congratulate Richard. The Canadien also sets an NHL single-season mark with eight points in one game Dec. 28 against the Detroit Red Wings, but the NHL scoring title goes to teammate and Hart Trophy-winner Elmer Lach, who collects 80 points, including a record 54 assists. The 'Punch Line' (Lach, Richard and Toe Blake), which finishes 1-2-3 in scoring, Vezina Trophy-winning goalie Bill Durnan, defenseman Butch Bouchard and coach Dick Irvin occupy six of the seven first all-star team spots, also a new NHL standard for one team.

2. McCool overcomes ulcers to beat Red Wings

Winner of the Calder Trophy as top rookie, Toronto Maple Leafs' goalie Frank McCool is known as 'Ulcers' because of an unsteady stomach. He often becomes sick during games because of nerves. During Game 7 of the Stanley Cup final against Detroit, he leaves the ice in pursuit of his medicine during a stoppage and returns to beat the Red Wings 2-1. His three consecutive shutouts to start the series remain a Stanley Cup record.

3. Hollett flashes his way to goal mark

Detroit's Flash Hollett makes history when he beats Toronto goalie Frank McCool March 17 to become the first NHL defenseman to post a 20-goal campaign, earning a spot on the first all-star team. Hollett's record will stand for 24 seasons until Bobby Orr scores 21 goals in 1968-69.

▶ IMPACT PERSON

Rocket Richard

The Rocket establishes himself as the NHL's pre-eminent scorer. He breaks Joe Malone's record of 44 goals by beating Toronto's Frank McCool Feb. 25 and puts his 50th puck past Boston's Harvey Bennett in the final game of the season March 18. No player will score 50 that quickly until Mike Bossy matches the feat in 1980-81.

1945-46   Stanley Cup: Montreal Canadiens

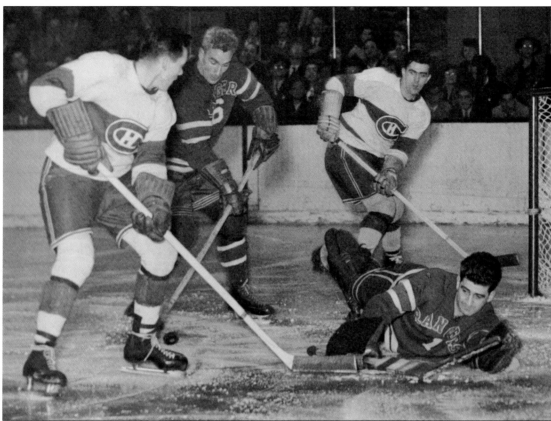

HHOF

Ranger goalie Charlie Rayner stops the Canadiens while Rocket Richard peers in from behind.

▶ IMPACT PERSON

Max Bentley

The 'Dipsy Doodle Dandy from Delisle' teams up with brother Doug and Bill Mosienko to form Chicago's potent 'Pony Line.' Center Max plays the role of pony express, winning the NHL scoring title with 61 points. He makes the first all-star team and is named winner of the Hart Trophy as the league's most valuable player.

Imperial Oil – Turofsky/HHOF

No. 1 STORY: League gets talent boost as WWII ends

The end of World War II brings many of the NHL's best players back into action. Among the returnees are the Boston Bruins' 'Kraut Line' of Milt Schmidt, Woody Dumart and Bobby Bauer and goalie Frank Brimsek, the Chicago Black Hawks' Bentley brothers (Doug and Max), New York Rangers' Patrick brothers (Lynn and Muzz), Detroit Red Wings' Sid Abel, along with Syl Apps and Turk Broda of the Toronto Maple Leafs. "The caliber of play is going to make the fans forget the war years," predicts NHL president Red Dutton.

2. Hockey Hall of Fame welcomes first members

The Hockey Hall of Fame is born when the NHL OKs a plan at its June, 1945 governors' meeting to honor the greats of the game. Boston GM Art Ross and former NHL stars Georges Vezina, Howie Morenz, Charlie Gardiner and Eddie Gerard are inaugural inductees, as are pre-NHLers Hod Stuart, Dan Bain, Hobey Baker, Russell Bowie, 'One-Eyed' Frank McGee, Tommy Phillips, Harvey Pulford and builder Lord Stanley Of Preston, who donated the Stanley Cup.

3. Rangers experiment with two-goalie system

Rangers' coach Frank Boucher tries a two-goalie system of Charlie Rayner and 'Sugar' Jim Henry. He alternates his goalies game by game, then tries shuttling them back and forth during the game every four to six minutes. "The system impressed me," says Montreal Canadiens' coach Dick Irvin. "I think we're coming into a time when goalies will be subbed as frequently as defensemen and forwards."

Brother Act

Max Bentley's scoring title follows his brother Doug's win in 1942-43, making them the first brothers to lead the NHL. Charlie and Roy Conacher tie the mark when Roy tops the league in 1948-49. Charlie had won the Ross in both 1933-34 and 1934-35.

HOCKEY LISTS OF THE CENTURY
NHL's All-Time Point Leaders

Unheralded Syd Howe retires after 1945-46 as the NHL's all-time leading scorer. Listed are all-team point totals, plus players' teams and last seasons. Elmer Lach and Rocket Richard are passed before their careers end. Lach finishes with 623 points, Richard 965.

Name	Pts.
Joe Malone, '23-24	100
Mon., Que., Ham.	
Cy Denneny, '28-29	331
Ott., Bos.	
Howie Morenz, '36-37	467
Mon., Chi., NYR	
Nels Stewart, '39-40	515
Mon., Mon. M., Bos., NYA	
Syd Howe, '45-46	528
Ott., Phi., Tor., St.L, Det.	
Bill Cowley, '46-47	548
St.L, Bos.	
Elmer Lach, '53-54	610
Mon.	
Rocket Richard, '59-60	946
Mon.	
Gordie Howe, '79-80	1,850
Det., Hart.	
W. Gretzky, '98-99	2,857
Edm., L.A., St.L, NYR	

Chalk Talk

"I never saw a Toronto team, either in my years as player or coach, which looked so bad."

Maple Leafs' coach Hap Day, whose club misses the playoffs after winning the Stanley Cup the previous season

1946-47

Stanley Cup: Toronto Maple Leafs

No. 1 STORY: Campbell named NHL president

Hoping to revive his inactive Brooklyn Americans' franchise, Red Dutton resigns as NHL president and touts Clarence Campbell as his successor. Campbell, named assistant to the president in June, is endorsed by NHL governors. A former NHL referee, a lawyer and Rhodes Scholar who was a lieutenant-colonel in the Canadian army during World War II, Campbell acted at the Nuremberg War Crimes trials before returning to Canada.

2. Detroit rookie Howe impresses all

At six feet and 201 pounds, Gordie Howe's physical attributes help him stand out, but it is the 18-year-old Detroit Red Wing rookie's play that will really set him apart and eventually earn him the nickname, 'Mr. Hockey.' Ambidextrous and naturally strong, Howe scores on Toronto Maple Leafs' goalie Turk Broda in his NHL debut, then runs Chicago Black Hawks' goalie Paul Bibeault in his third game, touching off a brawl. "He has a blow that can kill a man," Ab Howe says of his son's power.

3. Meeker, Taylor establish NHL records

Two enduring single-game records are set by Toronto right winger Howie Meeker and center Billy Taylor of Detroit. Playing at Chicago March 16, Taylor sets up seven goals in a 10-6 Red Wings' victory. Meeker, who wins the Calder Trophy over Gordie Howe, sets a rookie record Jan. 8 when he scores five goals on Paul Bibeault as the Maple Leafs whip the Black Hawks 10-4. While both records have since been equalled, neither has been surpassed.

▶ IMPACT PERSON

Dit Clapper

Emerging from retirement Nov. 27 for a game against the New York Rangers, the Boston Bruins' defenseman becomes the first NHL player to play in 20 seasons. But the six-time all-star retires from professional hockey for good Feb. 12 at the age of 40. His No. 5 jersey is retired by the Bruins and he receives immediate induction into the Hockey Hall of Fame.

Fighting Words

Frank Selke, who bolts Toronto to become GM of Montreal, says the Maple Leafs use wrestling tactics and suggests he'll suit up wrestler Yvon Robert. Leafs' GM Conn Smythe says then he'll dress Whipper Billy Watson.

HOCKEY LISTS OF THE CENTURY 3rd Decade All-Stars

Hard-hitting Earl Seibert earns seven straight all-star selections (including three first-team honors) during the NHL's third decade (1937-38 to 1946-47).

The Hockey News' First Team		The Hockey News' Second Team	
G	**Frank Brimsek**, Bos. *'Mr. Zero'*	G	**Turk Broda**, Tor. *Playoff gem*
D	**Earl Seibert**, Chi. *Heavy hitter*	D	**Babe Pratt**, Tor. *Wins Hart*
D	**Dit Clapper**, Bos. *Plays 20 years*	D	**Jack Stewart**, Chi. *Mean in corners*
LW	**Toe Blake**, Mon. *'Old Lamplighter'*	LW	**Doug Bentley**, Chi. *Small, but fast*
C	**Bill Cowley**, Bos. *Wizard with stick*	C	**Syl Apps**, Tor. *Supreme leader*
RW	**Rocket Richard**, Mon. *Nose for net*	RW	**Bryan Hextall**, NYR *Broadway star*

Chalk Talk

"He's the best prospect I've seen in 20 years."

Detroit Red Wings' coach Jack Adams, offering his opinion of rookie Gordie Howe

Imperial Oil – Turofsky/HHOF

Max Bentley, second from left, is a huge addition to Toronto after coming over from Chicago in a seven-player trade.

▶ IMPACT PERSON

Teeder Kennedy

Overshadowed at center by Toronto captain Syl Apps and two-time NHL scoring champion Max Bentley, Kennedy steps up in the playoffs, when he leads scorers in goals (eight) and points (14). Kennedy has a four-goal game against the Boston Bruins and scores twice in the Cup-clinching win in Detroit.

Frank Prazak/HHOF

No. 1 STORY: Bentley trade keeps Stanley Cup in Toronto

In what is called the biggest trade in NHL history, the Toronto Maple Leafs deal five players–Bob Goldham, Gaye Stewart, Bud Poile, Gus Bodnar and Ernie Dickens to the Chicago Black Hawks Nov. 4 for Cy Thomas and two-time NHL scoring champ Max Bentley. Maple Leafs' GM Conn Smythe insists Bentley is worth it because Toronto is getting the league's top scorer for center-ice duties. Together with Syl Apps and Teeder Kennedy, Bentley gives the Leafs unprecedented depth down the middle and helps them retain the Stanley Cup.

2. Gambling scandal rocks NHL

After a lengthy investigation, NHL president Clarence Campbell announces March 9 that Don Gallinger of the Boston Bruins and Billy Taylor of the New York Rangers are suspended indefinitely for "knowingly associating and communicating with James Tamer, a known criminal and gambler of Detroit." Campbell emphasizes that no other players were involved and that no attempt was made to fix a game. Gallinger acknowledges he spoke to Tamer, but insists he did not know of the man's background. "I never have been asked to bet on the outcome of a game," Taylor says.

3. Mosienko injured in first All-Star Game

A crowd of 14,138 fills Maple Leaf Gardens to watch the Stanley Cup-champion Maple Leafs drop a 4-3 decision to the NHL All-Stars Oct. 13 in the first official NHL All-Star Game. The game isn't a complete success–Chicago's Bill Mosienko sustains a broken right ankle when checked by Toronto's Jim Thomson.

HOCKEY LISTS OF THE CENTURY
The Hockey News Makes Debut

The first hockey-only publication goes on newsstands when The Hockey News publishes its first issue, Oct. 1. Here's a selection of stories from our first issue.
'Close but no cigar'
Cuban arena official wants to host NHL exhibition in Havana
'Veteran aims at record'
Toe Blake suits up one last year to break points mark; injury will stop him short
'Hershey's monument'
American League champs build 7,200-seat rink for town of 4,000

Bill Durnan, Montreal Canadiens

▶ IMPACT PERSON

Turk Broda

The 'Fat Man' is the epitome of a money goalie. This season marks the fourth time Broda backstops Toronto to the Cup and seventh time in 11 years he helps them reach the final. He loses just once in the 1949 playoffs. Broda posts a 1.57 goals-against average and allows more than two goals only once in nine games.

No. 1 STORY: Maple Leafs turn first Stanley Cup hat trick

It doesn't look like the Toronto Maple Leafs will repeat as Stanley Cup champs for a third time. Captain Syl Apps and Nick Metz retire before the season and Toronto stumbles through the regular season finishing fourth with a mediocre 22-25-13 record. "If the Leafs get in there sound, they'll take it all," says Toronto GM Conn Smythe just before the playoffs. He proves to be a prophet. Toronto ousts the Boston Bruins in five games and sweeps the Detroit Red Wings to become the first NHL team to three-peat.

2. Durnan lays goose eggs on opposition

Bill Durnan becomes a brick wall in the Montreal Canadiens' net, stopping everything he faces for 309 minutes and 21 seconds–a Modern Era record. After the Chicago Black Hawks' Roy Conacher beats him at 16:15 of the first period in a 3-1 Habs' win Feb. 24, Durnan whitewashes Detroit 2-0, blanks Toronto 1-0 and posts back-to-back shutouts against Boston before Black Hawk Gaye Stewart scores at 5:36 of the second period March 9 in a 2-2 tie to end the streak.

3. Rangers injured in auto accident

Six days prior to the start of the season, four New York Rangers are injured when their car crashes near Rouses Point, N.Y., en route to training camp at Saranac Lake. Buddy O'Connor, the 1947-48 Hart Trophy winner, suffers several broken ribs, Frank Eddolls has a knee tendon severed, Edgar Laprade is left with a broken nose and Bill Moe sustains head lacerations requiring stitches. A fifth player, Tony Leswick, escapes the mishap uninjured.

HOCKEY LISTS OF THE CENTURY
Captaining NHL Clean Team

Detroit Red Wings' Bill Quackenbush is the first defenseman to win the Lady Byng Trophy, playing all 60 games without a penalty minute in 1948-49. But he's a goon compared to left winger Val Fonteyne, who records five penalty-free seasons during the 1960s and 1970s. Here's the all-time NHL clean team.

Player, Era		
G	Mike Liut	'80s
D	B. Quackenbush	'40s-'50s
D	Red Kelly	'50s-'60s
LW	Val Fonteyne	'60s-'70s
C	Frank Boucher	'20s-'30s
RW	Mike Bossy	'80s

Imperial Oil – Turofsky/HHOF

Imperial Oil – Turofsky/HHOF

1949-50

Conn Smythe wages a 'Battle of the Bulge' with chubby goalie Turk Broda after the Leafs hit hard times.

▶ IMPACT PERSON

Sid Abel

A linchpin at center between Gordie Howe and Ted Lindsay, 'Old Bootnose' posts career bests of 34 goals, 35 assists and 69 points to finish behind Lindsay, who leads NHL scoring. Abel's winning goal in Game 6 of the Cup final against the New York Rangers saves Detroit from elimination as the Red Wings go on to win the Cup.

No. 1 STORY: Howe almost dies after on-ice mishap

The Detroit Red Wings not only lose Gordie Howe for the playoffs, they almost lose him for good. During a 5-0 Cup semifinal loss, Howe has Teeder Kennedy of the Toronto Maple Leafs lined up. "I saw Howe coming to check me," Kennedy says. "I stepped aside and he crashed headlong into the boards." Wings' coach Tommy Ivan claims Kennedy butt-ended or elbowed Howe, but NHL president Clarence Campbell, who is at the game, rules that out. Howe sustains a concussion, nose and cheekbone fractures and a lacerated right eyeball. Doctors drill through his skull to relieve pressure on the brain. Howe's family is rushed to his bedside, but he recovers to play next season.

2. Smythe tells Broda to cut the fat

With his team mired in a six-game winless skid Nov. 29, Toronto GM Conn Smythe decides his Leafs are fat cats and goalie Turk Broda is the poster boy for their complacency. "We are not running a fat man's team," Smythe says. "He is off the team until he shows some common sense." Smythe demands Broda get down to 190. Broda loses 10 pounds to meet Smythe's deadline, weighing in at 189 Dec. 1 and missing just one game.

3. Reardon bites tongue and lays off Gardner

Injured by Toronto's Cal Gardner in a game Jan. 1, 1949, Ken Reardon of the Montreal Canadiens has a long memory. "Even if I have to wait until the last game I ever play, Gardner is going to get it good and plenty," Reardon says. President Clarence Campbell forces Reardon to put up a $1,000 good-conduct bond. When he retires at the end of the 1949-50 season without harming Gardner, Reardon petitions for a refund and gets his money back.

Charlie's No Angel

After a 9-2 loss to Detroit, Chicago coach Charlie Conacher decks Lew Walter of the Detroit *Times*, claiming Walter slurred him. "I don't care whether it's a newspaperman or Joe Louis, nobody calls me that," Conacher says.

HOCKEY LISTS OF THE CENTURY
Penalty-Prone Point Leaders

No player has ever led the NHL in points and penalty minutes the same season, but Detroit's Ted Lindsay comes close in 1949-50 with 78 points and 141 PIMs, three minutes fewer than Toronto right winger Bill Ezinicki's league-leading total. Only 10 times in 83 seasons has the scoring leader had more than 100 penalty minutes. Stan Mikita, Jean Beliveau, Lindsay, Bobby Orr, Nels Stewart, Gordie Howe and Mario Lemieux make up the penalty-prone point kings. Listed is the year each wins the Ross and their penalty minutes.

Name	Yr.	PIM
Mikita, Chi.	'64-65	154
Mikita, Chi.	'63-64	146
Beliveau, Mon.	'55-56	143
Lindsay, Det.	'49-50	141
Orr, Bos.	'69-70	125
Stewart, Mon.	'25-26	119
Howe, Det.	'53-54	109
Orr, Bos.	'74-75	101
Howe, Det.	'62-63	100
Lemieux, Pit.	'88-89	100

Chalk Talk

"The Lord and 12 apostles couldn't have kept the Red Wings under control tonight."

Toronto Maple Leafs' GM Conn Smythe, after Detroit seeks retribution in the first game following Gordie Howe's injury

One of hockey's most famous pictures: Bill Barilko is caught falling to the ice after scoring the Cup-winning goal against Gerry McNeil.

HOCKEY LISTS OF THE CENTURY
Spine-Tingling Cup Clinchers

Bill Barilko's overtime Cup-winning goal in 1951, one of 14 in NHL history, is one of our picks as the three most memorable Cup winners ever.

1. **Bill Barilko**, '51, Toronto over Montreal in five. All five games go into OT.

2. **Pete Babando**, '50, Detroit over Rangers in seven. Wings are down 3-2 in series, then 3-1 in Game 6 and 2-0 in Game 7.

3. **Brett Hull**, '99, Dallas over Buffalo in six. Disputed goal ends second longest final game.

No. 1 STORY: Barilko's farewell goal wins Cup for Leafs

Toronto returns to the top in unique fashion after a one-year absence, alternating Turk Broda and Al Rollins in goal. Rollins, who plays in 40 of 70 regular season games, earns the Vezina Trophy. The Maple Leafs top the Montreal Canadiens in an exciting five-game final, with every game decided in overtime. Defenseman Bill Barilko nets the Cup winner at 2:53 of extra play. On Aug. 26, a plane carrying Barilko, 24, and pilot Dr. Henry Hudson disappears on a Northern Ontario fishing trip. Their remains aren't found until 1962, the same year the Leafs win their next Cup.

2. Howe stages amazing comeback

Rebounding from a near-fatal head injury in the 1950 playoffs, Detroit Red Wings' superstar Gordie Howe is a headache for NHL goalies. Wearing a helmet as a precautionary measure, Howe sets an NHL scoring record with 86 points while leading the league in goals (43) and assists (43). He's the first player to lead in all three categories since the Montreal Canadiens' Howie Morenz in 1927-28. It's a feat accomplished 13 times in NHL history.

3. Adams pulls trigger on record deal

Detroit GM Jack Adams makes a nine-player trade with the Chicago Black Hawks, the largest in NHL history. Goalie Harry Lumley, defensemen Jack Stewart and Al Dewsbury, and forwards Pete Babando and Don Morrison go to Chicago. In return, the Wings get goalie 'Sugar' Jim Henry, defenseman Bob Goldham, and forwards Metro Prystai and Gaye Stewart. Lumley has taken Detroit to the final four times since 1945, but Adams feels he has a ready replacement in Terry Sawchuk.

1951-52

Stanley Cup: Detroit Red Wings

Bill Mosienko, Chicago Black Hawks

▶ IMPACT PERSON

Terry Sawchuk

The Detroit goalie wins the Vezina Trophy during the regular season and performs even better during the playoffs with four shutouts and a 0.63 goals-against average as the Red Wings sweep to the Stanley Cup, recording eight straight wins over Toronto and Montreal. Sawchuk doesn't allow a goal on home ice during the playoffs.

No. 1 STORY: Mosienko bags NHL's quickest hat trick

Browsing through a record book late in the season, the Chicago Black Hawks' Bill Mosienko says, "It would be nice to have my name in there." On the last day of the season he arranges for it. With both teams already out of the playoffs, he puts three past New York Rangers' goalie Lorne Anderson March 23 in the third period, in a record 21 seconds. He scores at 6:09, 6:20 and 6:30. Mosienko almost adds a fourth moments later when he rings a shot off the post. The second-fastest NHL hat trick in history is later recorded by Jean Beliveau (44 seconds, 1955-56) and the team record is eventually set by Boston (20 seconds, 1970-71).

2. 'Kraut Line' reunited in fairy tale ending

The Boston Bruins honor the 'Kraut Line' before a game with Chicago March 18 and the line returns the favor. Bobby Bauer ends a four-season retirement to rejoin linemates Milt Schmidt and Woody Dumart and gets a goal and an assist in a 4-0 win. A magical moment comes when they set up Schmidt's 200th goal. Schmidt finishes with a goal and three assists, while Dumart has an assist as Boston clinches the final playoff spot.

3. Hawks forced to put 46-year-old in net

After 18 years, trainer Moe Roberts finds himself between the pipes again. When Chicago goalie Harry Lumley is injured during a game with the Detroit Red Wings Nov. 25, former NHL goalie Roberts takes over and plays a shutout period. At 46, he's the oldest player in NHL history. Roberts debuted in the NHL Dec. 8, 1925, for the Boston Bruins, posting 35 shutout minutes, and last played in 1933-34 for the New York Americans.

Baron Challenge

The American League-champion Cleveland Barons issue a Stanley Cup challenge to the NHL. They're turned down, as is the city's bid for an NHL expansion franchise.

HOCKEY LISTS OF THE CENTURY
Rookie Cards: Volume II

Bobby Orr not only revolutionizes the role of the defenseman in hockey, he helps popularize hockey cards in United States with publication of his rookie card in the scarce Topps' '66-67 set. His card is worth $2,500, more than half the price of the entire set ($4,000). Rocket Richard's '51-52 Parkhurst, his first card, is among the most popular cards for francophone collectors. Here are the remaining top 10 hockey rookie cards, continued from pg. 54. (All figures in U.S. dollars.)

6. **Bobby Orr**	$2,500	
Topps, '66-67	Bos.	
7. **King Clancy**	$2,000	
V145-1, '23-24	Ott.	
– **Eddie Shore**	$2,000	
V129, '33-34	Bos.	
9. **Rocket Richard**	$1,600	
Parkhurst, '51-52	Mon.	
10. **Aurel Joliat**	$1,300	
V145-1, '23-24	Mon.	

Source: Beckett Hockey Card Price Guide.

Chalk Talk

"The destiny of the bleu-blanc-rouge rests on the shoulders of a young French Canadian and he will get a shutout."

Montreal coach Dick Irvin's correct premonition about Jacques Plante's playoff debut

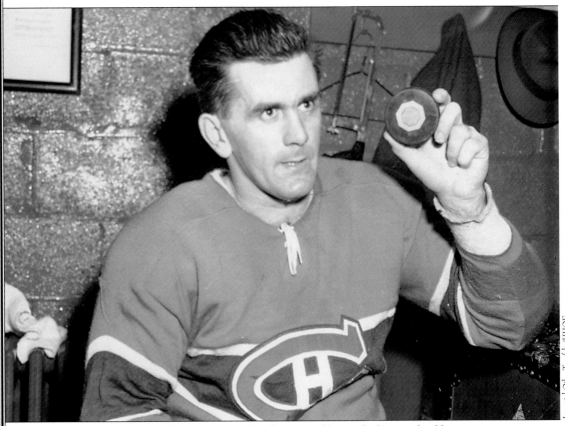

Rocket Richard moves past Nels Stewart on the all-time goal list with the 325th of his career.

No. 1 STORY: Rocket dethrones Stewart as scoring king

Ten years to the day that he scored his first NHL goal, the Montreal Canadiens' Rocket Richard beats Chicago Black Hawk goalie Al Rollins to become the league's all-time goal-scoring king. Richard's record 325th goal moves him past Nels Stewart. Canadiens' managing director Frank Selke announces the puck will be gold-plated and presented to Queen Elizabeth as a gift. Richard finishes with 28 goals, 21 behind Detroit's Gordie Howe, who just misses joining Richard in the exclusive 50-goal club by one.

2. Saturday night hockey debuts on TV

Following weeks of experimentation, NHL hockey hits TV in Canada for the first time. Montreal drops a 3-2 decision to Chicago Oct. 9 in the first televised game, a French-language broadcast with Rene Lecavalier calling the play-by-play. On Nov. 1, the first English-language telecast airs, with Foster Hewitt at the mike from midway through the second period as the Toronto Maple Leafs beat the Boston Bruins 3-2. Leafs' owner Conn Smythe fears that showing the entire game will cut into crowds at Maple Leaf Gardens.

3. Shake-up in Chicago makes Black Hawks Abel

Chicago acquires Sid Abel from Detroit July 22 and names him player-coach. Then on Sept. 11, the franchise is purchased by Arthur Wirtz , and Bruce and James D. Norris. The club ships all-star goalie Harry Lumley to Toronto for goalie Al Rollins, defenseman Gus Mortson, and forwards Cal Gardner and Ray Hannigan. The Hawks hold first place early in season and make the playoffs for the first time since 1946.

▶ IMPACT PERSON
Gordie Howe

Making a run at Rocket Richard's 50-goal season record, Howe goes into the final game of the regular season with 49 goals, but is held off the scoresheet by the Canadiens, who check vigorously to keep the Detroit winger from scoring. Nonetheless, Howe shatters his own NHL points record by nine with 95, winning both the Art Ross and Hart Trophies.

Stanley Cup: Detroit Red Wings

The 1954 World Championship Soviet Union team

HHOF

▶ IMPACT PERSON

Red Kelly

Kelly is the first winner of the James Norris Trophy as the NHL's top defenseman, named in honor of the former Red Wings' owner. The Detroit blue-liner finishes sixth in league scoring with 49 points and also wins the Lady Byng Trophy for the second consecutive season. He is the last defenseman to be named most gentlemanly player.

No. 1 STORY: Canadiens sign phenom Beliveau

With TV cameras on hand to record the moment and a financial advisor and tax specialist at his side to make sure he gets the best deal possible, Quebec Aces' superstar Jean Beliveau signs a five-year, $100,000 contract with the Montreal Canadiens. "It's the highest contract ever given any player–by a city block," proclaims Habs' managing director Frank Selke. A broken ankle limits Beliveau to 44 games and 34 points as a rookie. In short order, he will prove to be worth the investment.

2. Canadians absorb first setback to Soviets

It's raining and the outdoor ice in Stockholm turns to slush. But Soviet players, wearing old-fashioned gear at their first World Championship, use their soccer skills to kick the puck to teammates. They trounce the Toronto East York Lyndhursts 7-2, a senior team, to win the gold medal in the first match of a long-running cold war between the two countries. "The worst thing that ever happened to me was standing on the blueline in pouring rain and watching that Russian flag go up," said coach Greg Currie. "A lot of guys were crying. They felt they'd let Canada down."

3. Rocket told to put away poison pen

Writing a column Jan. 9 in the Montreal French-language weekly *Samedi-Dimanche*, Montreal star Rocket Richard blasts NHL president Clarence Campbell, labeling him a dictator. Richard is ordered to write an apology and deposit a $1,000 check as a good-conduct bond with the NHL and is instructed to refrain from sportswriting.

HOCKEY LISTS OF THE CENTURY
Soviets Impressive In Debut at Worlds

In its very first World Championship, the Soviet Union shocks Canada 7-2 to win the gold medal. Less than a decade later, in 1963, the Soviets begin a string of nine straight world titles. The Soviet Union/Russia leads the all-time standings with 23 gold medals.

Gold Medals	No.
1. Soviet Union/Russia	23
2. Canada	21
3. Czechoslovakia/Czech	9
4. Sweden	7
5. USA	2
6. Finland	1
Great Britain	1

1954-55

Unlucky Seven

Seven members of the Stanley Cup-champion Detroit Red Wings–John Wilson, Bill Dineen, Marcel Pronovost, Ted Lindsay, Alex Delvecchio, Vic Stasiuk and Red Kelly–will eventually become NHL head coaches, but none will coach a Cup winner.

HOCKEY LISTS OF THE CENTURY

Best Of Blueliners: Harvey & Orr

The Norris Trophy, for the best defenseman, was awarded for the first time in 1953-54, and it went to Red Kelly. But it's in 1954-55 that the best defenseman of the era takes ownership. Doug Harvey wins in 1954-55 and six of the next seven seasons. His record will be surpassed by Bobby Orr, who wins it eight times before chronic knee injuries force him to retire. Orr's dominance leads many to suggest the Norris should be renamed in his honor. Listed are all multiple winners of the Norris.

Player	No.
Bobby Orr, Bos.	8
D. Harvey, Mon., NYR	7
Ray Bourque, Bos.	5
Pierre Pilote, Chi.	3
Denis Potvin, NYI	3
Paul Coffey, Edm., Det.	3
Chris Chelios, Mon., Chi.	3
Larry Robinson, Mon.	2
Rod Langway, Was.	2
Brian Leetch, NYR	2

Chalk Talk

"They should have suspended him for life."

Detroit left winger Ted Lindsay's opinion of Rocket Richard's season-ending suspension

The Richard Riot

No. 1 STORY: Richard riot rocks Montreal

Reacting to a high stick from the Boston Bruins' Hal Laycoe in a March 13 game, the Montreal Canadiens' Rocket Richard attacks Laycoe with a stick three times and linesman Cliff Thompson with his fists, and is ejected. Following a hearing March 16, NHL president Clarence Campbell suspends Richard for the rest of the season, costing him a shot at what would have been his one and only scoring title. (Teammate Bernie Geoffrion surpasses Richard in points.) The next night, as Montreal plays Detroit, fans move towards Campbell's seats in the Forum, hurling insults and debris. Police attempt to restore order, but a tear gas bomb explodes, sending people rushing for the exits. The game is forfeited to Detroit, the crowd spills onto St. Catherine Street and rioting begins. When it's all over, the damage inflicted on local businesses is estimated in the hundreds of thousands of dollars.

2. Big changes at top of NHL ladder

Despite a Stanley Cup win in 1954, Tommy Ivan resigns as coach of Detroit to take a position as GM of the Chicago Black Hawks. While Ivan is about to launch a long career as an NHL executive, two others bring theirs to a close. GM Art Ross ends his 30-year association with the Boston Bruins and Conn Smythe retires as managing director of the Maple Leafs.

3. Zamboni makes clean sweep at Gardens

A new ice re-surfacing machine, the Zamboni, makes its NHL debut March 10 as Montreal battles Toronto at Maple Leaf Gardens. Although Zambonis quickly become standard equipment at NHL rinks, the fresh ice makes little difference this night. The game ends in a scoreless tie.

▶ **IMPACT PERSON**

Clarence Campbell

Proving to be a no-nonsense leader, Campbell suspends Rocket Richard for the season and then, refusing to be bullied, takes his usual seat for the fateful St. Patrick's Day game March 17 between Montreal and Detroit at the Forum. The NHL president ignores death threats that have been phoned in to the league's Montreal headquarters.

1955-56 Stanley Cup: Montreal Canadiens

The best team ever? The 1955-56 Canadiens. Front (left to right): D. St. Laurent, D. Harvey, K. Reardon (assistant GM), T. Blake (coach), E. Bouchard, W. Northey (president), F. Selke Sr. (GM), T. Johnson, J.G. Talbot. Middle: C. DesRoches (publicity director), D. Moore, H. Richard, M. Richard, J. Plante, B. Geoffrion, J. Beliveau, B. Olmstead, F. Selke Jr. (public relations). Back: G. Bettez (trainer), C. Provost, B. Turner, J. Leclair, K. Mosdell, F. Curry, D. Marshall, H. Dubois (trainer).

David Bier

▶ IMPACT PERSON

Toe Blake

Blake makes the transformation from star player to coach smoothly, guiding Montreal to an NHL-record 45 wins and a 100-point season, the club's first, in his debut behind the bench. When the Habs capture the Cup, Blake joins Eddie Gerard and Hap Day as the only NHLers to captain and coach teams that win the Cup.

No. 1 STORY: Wings trade Sawchuk in favor of rookie Hall

In a seven-week span after winning the Stanley Cup, Detroit Red Wings' GM Jack Adams dismantles his championship squad. He engineers a seven-player deal with the Chicago Black Hawks May 28, then stuns the hockey world by shipping star goalie Terry Sawchuk to Boston in a nine-player trade June 3, feeling rookie Glenn Hall is ready for the big time. When he's done, just nine players are left from the 1954-55 Cup squad. Detroit's record of seven consecutive first-place finishes is halted and so is the Wings' two-year reign as champions.

2. Blake takes helm of fab Habs

Legendary Montreal coach Dick Irvin moves to Chicago and former Canadiens' captain Toe Blake is named coach June 9. Jean Beliveau wins the Hart and Art Ross Trophies, Doug Harvey wins the Norris, Jacques Plante takes the Vezina, and rookies Claude Provost, Jean-Guy Talbot, Don Marshall, Bob Turner and the Rocket's younger brother, Henri, suit up as the Habs capture the Stanley Cup, the first of a record five straight.

3. Howe and Lindsay receive death threats

Anonymous calls to Toronto papers before a March 24 semifinal game between the Red Wings and Maple Leafs state Ted Lindsay and Gordie Howe will be shot if they play. GM Jack Adams suggests rookie Cummy Burton start the warmup wearing Lindsay's No. 7, and if all goes well, then put on Howe's No. 9. But Burton refuses. In the end, both men play and are not harmed. Howe scores once and Lindsay twice, including the game-winner, in a 5-4 Detroit overtime win.

HOCKEY LISTS OF THE CENTURY

Setting Standards For Sinning

New York Rangers' tough guy Lou Fontinato becomes the first NHLer to hit the 200-mark in penalty minutes in 1955-56. Record-holder Dave Schultz will more than double that total. Listed are benchmark single-season penalty minute totals.

Name	PIM
Joe Hall Mon., '17-18	100
Lou Fontinato NYR, '55-56	202
Dave Schultz Phi., '73-74	348
Dave Schultz Phi., '74-75	472

Jean Beliveau, Montreal Canadiens

No. 1 STORY: Lindsay attempts to organize players

A group of players, led by the Detroit Red Wings' Ted Lindsay, Montreal Canadiens' Doug Harvey, and Toronto Maple Leafs' Jim Thomson and Tod Sloan, begin the process of unionization, revealing plans to form a labor association. The idea does not sit well with Toronto's Conn Smythe, who labels his captain Thomson "a traitor and a quisling." Smythe trades Thomson and Sloan to Chicago. Detroit's Jack Adams also dislikes the idea and ships Lindsay and goalie Glenn Hall to Chicago.

2. Powerful Habs force power play rules

The potent power play of the Stanley Cup-champion Montreal Canadiens leads to a rule change when the NHL announces that players receiving minor penalties will return to the ice as soon as the opponent scores a goal. Previously, teams spent the full two minutes shorthanded, which was of great benefit to the talent-laden Habs, who often scored more than once during this span. Jean Beliveau scored three times in 44 seconds against the Boston Bruins Nov. 5, 1955.

3. Sawchuk walks out on Bruins

Suffering from infectious mononucleosis and saying, "I'm fed up, I'm quitting," Boston Bruins' goalie Terry Sawchuk walks away from the game Jan. 16. "My nerves are shot," he says. "I'm just edgy and nervous all the time." He sits out the remainder of the season, but returns next year, following a trade back to the Detroit Red Wings.

▶ IMPACT PERSON

Ted Lindsay

Early in the season, 'Terrible' Ted becomes the fourth NHLer to reach the 300-goal mark. Then he creates a stir Feb. 11, when he is elected the first president of the NHL Players' Association. All but one player, who is not named, puts up $100 to fund the association. "We're not looking for any trouble," Lindsay says. "We just want to make playing in the league more attractive."

Teeder's Back

With the Maple Leafs struggling to stay in the playoff race, Teeder Kennedy ends an 18-month retirement. He returns Jan. 6 after trimming down from 206 to 185 pounds. He scores 22 points in 30 games, but the Leafs miss the post-season.

HOCKEY LISTS OF THE CENTURY 4th Decade All-Stars

Rocket Richard is a first or second all-star all 10 seasons of the NHL's fourth decade (1947-48 through 1956-57). Richard and Gordie Howe split all first-team honors evenly.

The Hockey News' First Team			The Hockey News' Second Team		
G	**Terry Sawchuk**, Det.	*All-time best*	G	**Harry Lumley**, Tor.	*Shines with SO's*
D	**Doug Harvey**, Mon.	*Controls game*	D	**Bill Quackenbush**, Bos.	*Skilled 'D'*
D	**Red Kelly**, Det.	*Great hands*	D	**Bill Gadsby**, Chi.	*Great playmaker*
LW	**Ted Lindsay**, Det.	*Mean, talented*	LW	**Sid Smith**, Tor.	*Gentlemanly sniper*
C	**Jean Beliveau**, Mon.	*Elegant pivot*	C	**Ted Kennedy**, Tor.	*Fierce competitor*
RW	**Gordie Howe**, Det.	*All-around star*	RW	**Rocket Richard**, Mon.	*Nose for net*

Chalk Talk

"Actually, we don't have many grievances. We just felt we should have an organization of this kind."

Ted Lindsay on the formation of the NHLPA

1957-58

Stanley Cup: Montreal Canadiens

No. 1 STORY: NHLPA suffers setback

Exiled to the Chicago Black Hawks by the Detroit Red Wings, Ted Lindsay's hopes for a players' union take a hit when Labor Relations Board petitions fail and his old Red Wing teammates withdraw from the union because of a $3-million lawsuit filed by the NHLPA. The suit seeks a large piece of the TV pie and greater pension benefits. On Feb. 5, owners and players meet for the first time. The owners refuse to give the union official recognition, but make three concessions–increasing the minimum salary to $7,000, agreeing to match the players dollar-for-dollar in pension benefits and increasing the Stanley Cup-winning bonus $4,000 per player.

2. Black Hawks surrender Rocket's 500th goal

Fittingly, the Chicago Black Hawks are the victims as Rocket Richard becomes the first player in NHL history to score 500 goals. The historic marker comes at 13:52 of the first period of Montreal's 3-1 win Oct. 19, with Richard beating Glen Hall. The Black Hawks were also Richard's victims for Nos. 100, 200, 400 and 325, the tally which moved him past previous leader Nels Stewart.

3. O'Ree NHL's first black player

Boston's Willie O'Ree becomes the first black player in NHL history when he debuts Jan. 18 in the Bruins' 3-0 win at the Montreal Forum. O'Ree plays the next night in Boston against the Habs, then is returned to the minors. His NHL career concludes with 43 games in 1960-61 when he scores four goals and 14 points.

Willie O'Ree, Boston Bruins

James McCarthy/HHOF

▶ **IMPACT PERSON**

HHOF

Doug Harvey

Montreal's NHLPA rep, Harvey is one of the few union leaders who does not feel the wrath of management, simply because he is too valuable to the Canadiens' cause. Helping the Habs to their third straight title, Harvey earns first all-star status for the seventh consecutive season and wins the Norris Trophy as the NHL's top defenseman for the fourth season in a row.

Meek Leafs

Before the season starts, Maple Leafs' co-owner Stafford Smythe demotes Howie Meeker to publicity director, after just a few months as GM. It doesn't help as Toronto finishes last for the first time since 1918-19.

HOCKEY LISTS OF THE CENTURY All-Time Best Teams I

The Hockey News picks the 1955-56 Montreal Canadiens as the best NHL team ever; Frank Selke, GM of that team, says the 1959-60 Habs were better. We have put just one–our pick of course–on our top 10 list. On this page are Nos. 1-5; on pg. 61, Nos. 6-10.

Team	Year	Why
1. **Montreal**	'55-56	Lose only 17 games. Eleven players selected to Hall of Fame.
2. **Montreal**	'76-77	Set league record with 132 points. Ten players in Hall of Fame.
3. **Islanders**	'81-82	Win regular season title and third straight Stanley Cup.
4. **Edmonton**	'83-84	Win 57 games and set league record with 446 goals.
5. **Detroit**	'51-52	Finish first fourth straight year and are 8-0 in playoffs.

Chalk Talk

"Okay Louie, you've done a great job. Now be a good fellow and go to the penalty box."

New York coach Phil Watson's advice to Rangers' tough guy Lou Fontinato after he wreaks havoc during a brawl with the Montreal Canadiens

Howe About That

On 'Gordie Howe Night' in Detroit March 3, the 13-year veteran skates out before the game to receive a new car and discovers his parents, Ab and Catherine, in the back seat. They have come from Saskatchewan to see their first NHL game.

HOCKEY LISTS OF THE CENTURY

All-Time Best Teams II

Among teams rounding out our top 10 NHL teams of all time are a trio of clubs from the Boston Bruins.

Team	Yr.
6. **Boston**	'71-72

Why: Win 54 and lose only 13 during regular season, a club record. Go 12-3 in play-offs to win Cup.

7. **Toronto**	'47-48

Why: Finish first overall and go 8-1 in playoffs, allowing only 20 goals. Six players are Hall of Famers.

8. **Boston**	'38-39

Why: Allow only 76 goals in 48 games, an average of 1.6 per game. Eight players go on to Hall of Fame.

9. **Philadelphia**	'73-74

Why: Set post-expansion record by allowing only 164 goals while leading league with 1,750 penalty minutes.

10. **Boston**	'29-30

Why: Finish first overall for third straight year. Set league record with 14-game winning streak.

Chalk Talk

"The only crystal ball he's got is on his shoulders. What a beautiful head of skin."

Rangers' coach Phil Watson, mocking the predictions of Toronto coach Punch Imlach, who is bald

Bobby Hull, Chicago Black Hawks

No. 1 STORY: Imlach rallies Leafs to playoff spot

Toronto is seven points out of a playoff spot with nine days left in the season. Maple Leafs' coach Punch Imlach boasts he'll not only get his club into the playoffs, but also take them to the Stanley Cup final. While the Rangers stumble, the Leafs win four straight to move within a point of New York on the final day. The Rangers lose 4-2 to the Montreal Canadiens, while Toronto wins 6-4 against the Detroit Red Wings. The Leafs sideline the Boston Bruins in the semifinals before bowing to Montreal in the final.

2. Storey quits as NHL referee

Longtime referee Red Storey doesn't know it, but when he takes the ice April 4 for Game 6 of the Stanley Cup semifinal between Montreal and the Chicago Black Hawks, it will be his last game. Montreal wins 5-4 to oust Chicago and Black Hawks' coach Rudy Pilous raps the redhead, saying he "didn't have the guts" to call two late fouls by the Habs. A 25-minute protest, in which two fans attack Storey, follows Claude Provost's winning goal. The worst comes the next day, when NHL president Clarence Campbell claims Storey "froze." Storey resigns as a result of the comments.

3. Newcomers spark Chicago turnaround

With young stars Bobby Hull, Glenn Hall, Stan Mikita, Eddie Litzenberger, Eric Nesterenko and Pierre Pilote joining veterans Ted Lindsay, Tod Sloan and Dollard St. Laurent, long-dormant Chicago is suddenly a force to be reckoned with in the NHL. The Black Hawks finish third and their 69 points equal a club record, as Chicago makes the playoffs for the first time since 1952-53.

▶ **IMPACT PERSON**

Dickie Moore

Plagued by injuries early in his career, Moore emerges from the shadows of his illustrious teammates to win the scoring title in 1957-58. He repeats as Art Ross Trophy winner and his 96 points break Gordie Howe's six-year NHL record by one. Moore earns first all-star selections in 1957-58 and 1958-59 and plays on six Stanley Cup champions.

1959-60

Stanley Cup: Montreal Canadiens

No. 1 STORY: Fifth straight Cup for 'best-ever' Canadiens

Putting an exclamation point on their place in history, the Montreal Canadiens sweep to their record fifth consecutive Stanley Cup, taking care of the Chicago Black Hawks and Toronto Maple Leafs in eight straight games. "It's the best of all the great Canadiens' teams," says Montreal managing director Frank Selke. In its five-season reign as champion, Montreal never trails in a playoff series and is not pushed to a single Game 7. During the regular season, the Habs average more than 40 wins per campaign and cop 15 individual awards.

2. Masked marvel gives goalies new life

A day after Halloween, Jacques Plante dons a mask and changes the game forever. After being cut for seven stitches by an Andy Bathgate shot during a Nov. 1 game against the New York Rangers, Plante returns wearing a custom-made fiberglass mask he has been experimenting with in practice. He stops 29 of 30 shots in a 3-1 win. Montreal goes unbeaten in its first 11 games with its masked netminder. "If they let me wear it all the time, I can play until I'm 45," Plante says.

3. Kelly traded twice in five days

Unhappy with an article, which suggests he forced Red Kelly to play with a broken ankle, Detroit Red Wings' GM Jack Adams trades his all-star defenseman and forward Billy McNeill to the Rangers Feb. 5 for Bill Gadsby and Eddie Shack. Both Detroit players balk and announce their retirements, so the trade is rescinded. On Feb. 10, Adams then trades Kelly to Toronto for defenseman Marc Reaume. This time, Kelly approves the deal and reports to the Maple Leafs.

▶ **IMPACT PERSON**

Jacques Plante

Always an innovator, Plante's most significant contribution to the game–the goalie mask–is unveiled this season. He records all three of his regular season shutouts while wearing facial protection and, although his goals-against average is higher (2.58 to 2.33) while he is wearing the mask, he picks up his fifth consecutive Vezina Trophy on the NHL's best defensive team.

Hull Beats Bronco

Down one point in the scoring race heading into the last game of the season, Chicago's Bobby Hull overtakes Boston's Bronco Horvath with two points in a head-to-head matchup to win his first Art Ross Trophy with 81 points.

HOCKEY LISTS OF THE CENTURY All-Time WHL Team

Playmaking center Guyle Fielder wins the fifth of nine Western League (pro) scoring titles in 1959-60. Below is the all-time WHL team. Listed are primary teams (New Westminster, New West.), WHL years, games, goals, assists, points and penalty minutes.

G	**Lucien Dechene**	New West.	'48-'61	LW	**Gord Fashoway**	New West.	'50-'63	
	800 games, 390 wins, 47 shutouts				843 - 485 - 359 - 844 - 310			
D	**Connie Madigan**	Portland	'58-'74	C	**Guyle Fielder**	Seattle	'51-'73	
	806 - 97 - 406 - 503 - 1,846				1,425 - 416 - 1,430 - 1,846 - 491			
D	**Fred Hucul**	Calgary	'53-'67	RW	**Jackie McLeod**	Vancouver	'52-'60	
	711 - 151 - 425 - 576 - 646				472 - 246 - 265 - 511 - 384			

Chalk Talk

"It's the coming thing in the game. The time will come when they'll have an even better mask than Plante's and it will be standard equipment for goalies."
Montreal coach Toe Blake on Jacques Plante's new face mask

Frank Mahovlich, 'The Big M,' is upended in front of Terry Sawchuk.

Imperial Oil – Turofsky/HHOF

1960-61

Stanley Cup: Chicago Black Hawks

No. 1 STORY: Hawks end Canadiens' dynasty

It seems like a mismatch–the five-time Stanley Cup-champion Montreal Canadiens against a Chicago Black Hawks' team that hasn't won the Cup since 1937-38. But the Black Hawks pound the smaller, more skillful Canadiens into submission, then beat the Detroit Red Wings in the final.

2. Rocket calls it quits after 18 years

Montreal superstar Rocket Richard ends months of speculation when he announces his retirement Sept. 15 before the start of the 1960-61 season. "I guess I finally realized the game is getting too fast for me," says the 39-year-old Richard, whose 18-season career leaves him with 17 NHL records. He's the all-time leader in goals with 544, including a record 82 game-winners. Richard's additional 82 goals and six OT winners in the playoffs are also league marks. The Hockey Hall of Fame waives its three-year waiting period to admit Richard immediately.

3. 'Boom Boom', 'Big M' shoot for 50 goals

It looks certain the NHL will have its second 50-goal-scorer and it does–but not the guy everyone is watching. Toronto Maple Leafs' sniper Frank 'Big M' Mahovlich has 26 goals after 29 games and 41 by his 59th game. However, Mahovlich scores just seven times the rest of the season to finish with 48. Meanwhile, Montreal's Bernie 'Boom Boom' Geoffrion blasts past the 'Big M' with 22 goals in his last 21 games to reach the magical 50-goal plateau in 64 games.

▶ **IMPACT PERSON**

'Boom Boom' Geoffrion

Equalling the mark of Rocket Richard, Geoffrion becomes the second NHLer to record a 50-goal season when he puts the puck past Toronto's Cesare Maniago in a 5-2 Montreal victory March 16. He has two games left, but isn't able to surpass Richard's total. Geoffrion's league-high 95 points gives him the Art Ross Trophy and he also wins the Hart Trophy.

Frank Prazak/HHOF

Toeing The Line

Montreal coach Toe Blake receives a $2,000 fine, the largest in NHL history, for slugging referee Dalton McArthur after losing Game 3 of the Habs' Stanley Cup semifinal against Chicago on Murray Balfour's power play goal.

HOCKEY LISTS OF THE CENTURY Best In NCAA History

The Denver Pioneers post a 30-1-1 record in winning the 1960-61 Western Collegiate Hockey Association and National Collegiate Athletic Association titles. The Pioneers, led by Bill Masterton, are among the best teams ever in NCAA history. Sadly, Masterton will die in 1968 in the only on-ice fatality in NHL history.

League	Best Team, Key Player	Best Ever In League
Western Collegiate	Denver, '60-61, Bill Masterton	John Mayasich, Min., '52-'55
Central Collegiate	Bowling Green, '78-79, Ken Morrow	Brendan Morrison, Mich., '93-'97
Eastern Colleges	Cornell, '69-70, Ken Dryden	Ken Dryden, Cor., '66-'69
Hockey East	Maine, '92-93, Paul Kariya	Paul Kariya, Maine, '92-'94

Chalk Talk

"We've been playing nice, clean hockey too long. I'm tired of hearing the fans call our players yellow-bellies. This is going to change."

Montreal managing director Frank Selke, vowing the Habs will get tougher

1961-62

Stanley Cup: Toronto Maple Leafs

Rangers' defenseman Doug Harvey wins his seventh Norris Trophy.

Graphic Artists/HHOF

▶ IMPACT PERSON

Punch Imlach

Hired as Toronto's assistant GM in 1958, Imlach quickly took over as GM, then coach, and transformed the Maple Leafs into a contender. He guides them to appearances in the Stanley Cup final each of his first two seasons. In his fourth behind the bench, he takes the Leafs all the way to their first Cup victory in 11 years.

Imperial Oil – Turofsky/HHOF

No. 1 STORY: Leafs end 11-year Stanley Cup drought

A groin injury to 1960-61 Vezina Trophy-winner Johnny Bower thrusts Don Simmons, who backstopped the Boston Bruins to the Stanley Cup final in 1957 and 1958, into the spotlight. Simmons posts victories in Games 5 and 6 to bring the Toronto Maple Leafs the Cup in the last playoff action of his NHL career. With the series tied 2-2, the Leafs explode for an 8-4 victory over the Chicago Black Hawks at Maple Leaf Gardens, then get goals from Bob Nevin and Dick Duff in the final 10 minutes for a 2-1 win at Chicago Stadium. The Cup triumph is Toronto's first since 1951, marking the longest championship drought in franchise history.

2. Hull ties Bathgate in Art Ross race

For the first time in NHL history, there's a tie for the individual scoring title as the Chicago Black Hawks' Bobby Hull and New York Rangers' Andy Bathgate both finish with 84 points. Hull, the third 50-goal-scorer in NHL history, is awarded the Art Ross Trophy because he has more goals than Bathgate (50-28). Hull scores No. 50 on Gump Worsley in the March 25 season finale against the Rangers.

3. Habs trade All-Star Harvey to Rangers

Sticking to his plan to bring more toughness to the Canadiens, managing director Frank Selke trades six-time Norris Trophy-winner Doug Harvey to the Rangers for badman Lou Fontinato. Both fill the roles for which they have been acquired. Harvey, named player-coach in New York, earns the Norris again and helps the Rangers make the playoffs. Fontinato leads the league with 167 penalty minutes.

Remains Found

On June 6–seven weeks after the Leafs win their first title since 1951, when Bill Barilko scored the Cup winner and then was lost in a plane crash–the wreckage of Barilko's plane is found in dense Northern Ontario bush.

HOCKEY LISTS OF THE CENTURY
All-Time IHL Team

Gentlemanly Len Thornson wins the second of three consecutive International League MVP awards in 1961-62. Thornson claims seven MVP's in an 11-year span with the Fort Wayne Komets and is captain of THN's all-time IHL team. Listed are primary teams, IHL years, games, goals, assists, points and penalty minutes.

G **Glen Ramsay**
Cincinnati, '56-'74
1,053 games, 3.20 GAA

D **Moe Benoit**
Toledo, '60-'70
579 - 115 - 319 - 434 - 508

D **Bob McCammon**
Port Huron, '62-'73
736 - 141 - 397 - 538 - 250

LW **Scott Gruhl**
Fort Wayne, '79-'94
921 - 532 - 612 - 1,144 - 1,936

C **Len Thornson**
Fort Wayne, '56-'69
819 - 426 - 826 - 1,252 - 101

RW **Bryan McLay**
Muskegon, '57-'72
927 - 474 - 626 - 1,100 - 645

Chalk Talk

"On Toronto ice, we look like we left our skates at home and came with over-shoes."

Chicago coach Rudy Pilous, lamenting his club's 0-3 mark at Maple Leaf Gardens in the Stanley Cup final

Red's Day Job

Toronto's Red Kelly defeats future NHLPA boss Alan Eagleson for a seat in the House of Commons, joining Lionel Conacher, Bucko McDonald and Howie Meeker as the only NHLers to serve there. Frank Mahovlich later will be appointed to the Senate.

HOCKEY LISTS OF THE CENTURY
NHL Scoring Title Leaders

Gordie Howe continues to rewrite the record books in 1962-63, winning his sixth and final Art Ross Trophy. Howe remains among the point leaders until 1970-71, when his streak of 21-consecutive finishes in the top-10 finally comes to an end. Ten years later, Wayne Gretzky starts his record run, winning the first of 10 Art Ross Trophies. Only 19 players have more than one scoring title.

Name	No.
Wayne Gretzky	10
Edm., L.A., '80s-'90s	
Gordie Howe	6
Det., '50s-'60s	
Mario Lemieux	6
Pit., '80s-'90s	
Phil Esposito	5
Bos., '70s	
Stan Mikita	4
Chi., '60s	
Jaromir Jagr	4
Pit., '90s	
Guy Lafleur	3
Mon., '70s	

Chalk Talk

"No human being is worth $1 million–to buy or sell. I consider this to be a publicity stunt."

Toronto president Stafford Smythe, announcing that Chicago had not offered $1 million for Frank Mahovlich

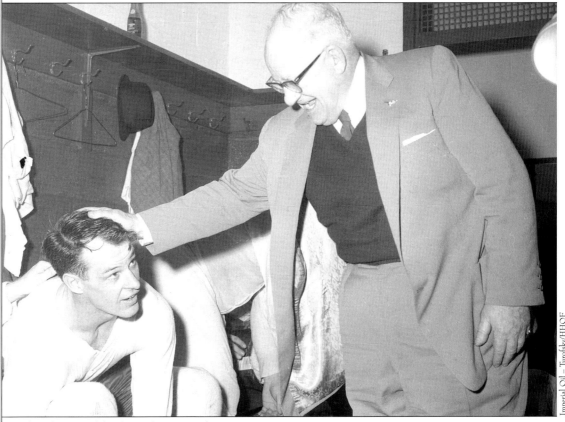

Jack Adams and his best player, Gordie Howe

No. 1 STORY: Hall halted at 502 straight games

He has not missed a game since the start of the 1955-56 season–seven whole years of activity–but Glenn Hall knows he's in trouble when he pinches a nerve in his back during a Nov. 6 practice. The Chicago Black Hawks' goalie dresses for the next game against the Boston Bruins, but after the first shot beats him, he gives way to Denis DeJordy. Hall can't play the next game, ending his consecutive game streak at 502–an NHL record for goalies. "I knew almost as soon as the game started that I couldn't finish," says Hall, who plays all 502 games and 49 more in the playoffs without the protection of a mask.

2. Adams leaves Red Wings after 35 years

A fixture in Detroit since he was hired as manager in the spring of 1927, Jack Adams retires as GM of the Red Wings April 25, 1962. He leaves behind a legacy of seven Stanley Cups. 'Jolly' Jack, 66, has another job lined up. He takes over as president of the newly organized Central Professional Hockey League.

3. First amateur draft held

Although one day it will become a major event on the NHL calendar, the first amateur draft is shrouded in secrecy. It's held behind closed doors on June 5 and the names of the 21 players selected are not revealed. Eligible to be drafted are 17-year-olds not currently playing with an NHL-sponsored amateur club. Eventually it's discovered that the Montreal Canadiens take Garry Monahan first overall, while Detroit grabs Peter Mahovlich with the second pick.

▶ **IMPACT PERSON**

Glenn Hall

The Chicago Black Hawks' goalie is known as much for vomiting before the game as he is for his record 502 consecutive games. "There are games when I haven't been as nervous as usual and I find I won't go after a shot as hard," Hall says. Hall wins the Vezina Trophy with a 2.55 GAA and earns his seventh all-star selection in eight years.

1963-64

Stanley Cup: Toronto Maple Leafs

Bob Baun, Toronto Maple Leafs

Imperial Oil – Turofsky/HHOF

No. 1 STORY: Howe, Sawchuk share historic day

Two magical moments occur in the same game as the Detroit Red Wings blank the Montreal Canadiens 3-0 at the Olympia Nov. 10. Gordie Howe beats Montreal goalie Charlie Hodge for his 545th career goal, moving him past former Hab Maurice Richard as the NHL's all-time leading goal-scorer. No one beats Red Wing netminder Terry Sawchuk, who stops 39 shots for his 94th career shutout, tying George Hainsworth's NHL record. Sawchuk breaks it Jan. 18 with a 36-save performance in a 2-0 win over the Canadiens.

2. Habs and Rangers make blockbuster deal

Montreal and New York pull off a completely unexpected seven-player deal June 4 which sees the Habs part with six-time Vezina Trophy-winner Jacques Plante, Don Marshall and Phil Goyette in return for goalie Gump Worsley and youngsters Dave Balon, Leon Rochefort and Len Ronson. "I'm getting the best goaltender in the business," says Rangers' coach Red Sullivan.

3. Courageous Baun Stanley Cup hero

With his team down 3-2 in games to Detroit in the Stanley Cup final, Toronto Maple Leafs' defenseman Bob Baun is carried from the ice on a stretcher after being hit in the right ankle by a Gordie Howe shot during Game 6. But Baun returns and is a hero when his shot beats Terry Sawchuk 1:40 into OT. Baun plays Game 7 as Toronto wraps up the title with a 4-0 win. Only after that game does he go for X-rays, which reveal he has a cracked bone.

▶ IMPACT PERSON

Andy Bathgate

Before Bathgate arrives in Toronto in a seven-player trade Feb. 22, the Maple Leafs are only three games over .500. But when he produces 18 points in the club's last 15 games, the Leafs lose just four times. Bathgate contributes 21 more points in 14 playoff games as Toronto wins the Cup. A Hart Trophy winner with the Rangers in 1958-59, he leads the NHL in assists this season with 68.

James McCarthy/HHOF

Scrap and Score

In his first NHL start Oct. 8 at Boston, Montreal's John Ferguson scraps with tough guy Ted Green 12 seconds into the game, the first step in establishing himself as the NHL's toughest player. Ferguson also scores two goals.

HOCKEY LISTS OF THE CENTURY Seminal Tough Guys

Some people call hockey "ballet on ice." None of those have ever seen John Ferguson play. Ferguson makes his NHL debut in 1963-64 and develops into the first impact physical role player, transforming the timid Canadiens into a powerhouse again. Ferguson quickly becomes the NHL heavyweight champion. Listed are the league's seminal tough guys by decade, starting with Sprague Cleghorn.

Player, Primary Team	Player, Primary Team	Player, Primary Team
'20s: **S. Cleghorn**, Mon.	'50s: **Gordie Howe**, Det.	'80s: **Dave Semenko**, Edm.
'30s: **Red Horner**, Tor.	'60s: **John Ferguson**, Mon.	'90s: **Bob Probert**, Det., Chi.
'40s: **Jack Stewart**, Det.	'70s: **Dave Schultz**, Phi.	Tie **Domi**, NYR, Win., Tor.

Chalk Talk

"He was the best goalkeeper I ever had, but he had become complacent…cocksure."

Montreal managing director Frank Selke's reason for trading Jacques Plante

Just Like Dad

Center Jimmy Peters Jr., 20, is called up from junior and centers Detroit's Gordie Howe, 36, and Ted Lindsay, 39, in a Nov. 11 game at Toronto. During the 1950s his dad, Jimmy Sr., played briefly between the two greats.

HOCKEY LISTS OF THE CENTURY
Poised Playoff Performers

The true measure of a player is how he performs in the playoffs. In 1965, Jean Beliveau becomes the first winner of a new honor, the Conn Smythe Trophy, which goes to the playoff MVP. The only higher honor in the playoffs is to have your name engraved on the Stanley Cup. Here are the players who have won the most Cups. Not surprisingly, six of the top seven are longtime Montreal Canadiens.

Player, Teams	No.
Henri Richard, Mon.	11
('56-'60, '65-'66, '68-'69, '71, '73)	
Jean Beliveau, Mon.	10
('56-'60, '65-'66, '68-'69, '71)	
Yvan Cournoyer, Mon.	10
('65-'66, '68-'69, '71, '73, '76-'79)	
Claude Provost, Mon.	9
('56-'60, '65-'66, '68-'69)	
Red Kelly, Det., Tor.	8
('50, '52, '54-'55, '62-'64, '67)	
Jacques Lemaire, Mon.	8
('68-'69, '71, '73, '76-'79)	
Maurice Richard, Mon.	8
('44, '46, '53, '56-'60)	

Chalk Talk

"I'm not looking for fights, but I'm not worried about them either. If anyone wants to fight me, I'll fight them back."

New York Rangers' Swedish rookie Ulf Sterner before his NHL debut

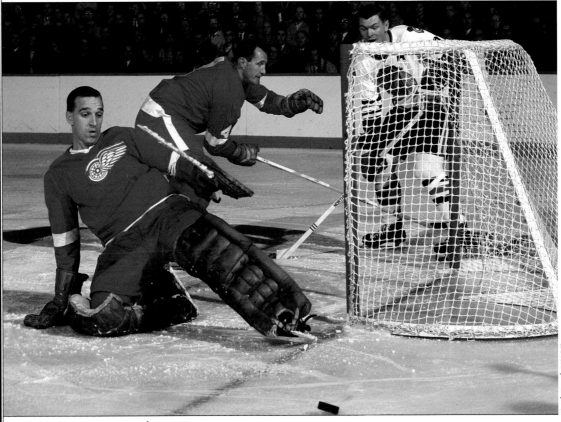

Frank Prazak/HHOF

Roger Crozier, Detroit Red Wings

No. 1 STORY: Lindsay stages remarkable comeback

Ending a four-season retirement, 39-year-old Ted Lindsay earns a spot with the Detroit Red Wings. 'Terrible' Ted produces a respectable 14 goals and 28 points in 69 games and shows he hasn't lost his edginess, doing battle with NHL president Clarence Campbell over $75 in fines he receives following a Jan. 2 game against Toronto. "I'm not going to sit for Campbell's kangaroo court," says Lindsay, who eventually apologizes and pays the fines.

2. Swede's debut precursor of European invasion

Swedish forward Ulf Sterner becomes the first European-trained NHLer, making his big-league debut with the Rangers Jan. 27 against Boston. Sterner, 24, discards his helmet and mouthguard in a bid to fit in with North American players. "I think maybe people would look at it and say: 'Swede, go home', " Sterner explains. He fails to pick up a point in four games before being farmed out to Baltimore of the American League, and returns to Sweden at the end of the season.

3. NHL opts for two-goalie system

Tired of waiting for spare goaltenders to don pads and warm up after an injury to the No. 1 man, NHL governors adopt a rule Feb. 2 which requires that two goalies be suited up for every game of the 1965 playoffs. It becomes a regular season practice in 1965-66. Meanwhile, replacing the legendary Terry Sawchuk, Detroit goalie Roger Crozier leads the NHL with 40 wins and six shutouts, wins the Calder Trophy and is the last goalie to play in all of his team's games (70).

▶ IMPACT PERSON

Pierre Pilote

Pilote breaks Babe Pratt's 21-year-old record for points by a defenseman. The crafty Chicago captain finishes with 59 points in 68 games; Pratt collected 57 points in 50 games for Toronto in 1943-44. Pilote wins his third straight Norris Trophy and earns the third of five consecutive berths on the first all-star team.

Graphic Artists/HHOF

1965-66

Stanley Cup: Montreal Canadiens

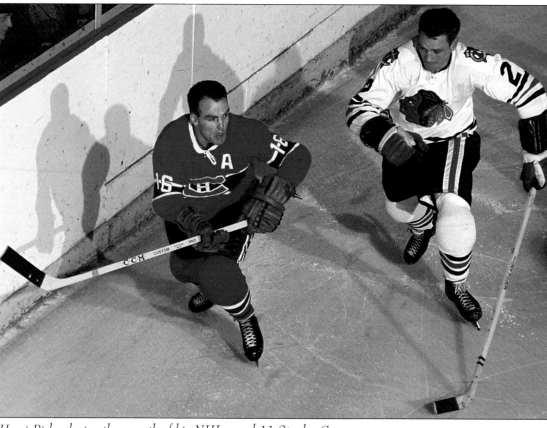

Frank Prazak/HHOF

Henri Richard wins the seventh of his NHL-record 11 Stanley Cups.

▶ IMPACT PERSON

Bobby Hull

Becoming the first NHLer to score more than 50 goals, Hull finishes the season with 54, 22 of which come on the power play. His 97 points set an NHL record and earn him the Art Ross Trophy for the second time. He also wins the Hart Trophy for the second straight season and is a first all-star selection for the fourth time in five seasons.

Frank Prazak/HHOF

No. 1 STORY: Golden Jet first to top 50 goals

It's just another typical Bobby Hull goal–except that it gives him more than any other player has scored in one season. With Chicago trailing the New York Rangers 2-1 in the third period March 12, the Black Hawks' star blows a slapshot by goalie Cesare Maniago on the power play for goal No. 51–breaking the record held by Rocket Richard, 'Boom Boom' Geoffrion and himself. "It was a thrill getting the goal, but the biggest thrill was that roar from the crowd," says Hull, who receives an eight-minute standing ovation.

2. NHL announces expansion plans

The NHL announces Feb. 9 it will double in size for the 1967-68 season, adding franchises in Philadelphia, Pittsburgh, Minnesota, Oakland, Los Angeles and St. Louis at a cost of $2 million each. St. Louis hasn't officially applied, but the St. Louis Arena is owned by Chicago owners Arthur Wirtz and Jim Norris, sparking cries of cronyism from Vancouver and Buffalo, two overlooked cities. Buffalo bidders, Seymour and Northrup Knox, say they are "bitterly disappointed." Cyril McLean, head of the Vancouver bid, calls the process "a cooked-up deal."

3. Adams first Lester Patrick Trophy winner

A Canadian, Jack Adams, is named first winner of the Lester Patrick Trophy for outstanding hockey service in the U.S. The former Detroit coach and GM guided the Red Wings from the verge of bankruptcy to their position as an NHL power. The award is introduced by the New York Rangers, for whom Patrick coached and managed.

Three's Company

Toronto coach Punch Imlach employs three goalies in a season-ending 3-3 tie at Detroit. Johnny Bower plays the first period, Terry Sawchuk takes over in the second and Bruce Gamble is in goal for the final 20 minutes.

HOCKEY LISTS OF THE CENTURY
Should It Be Named Bobby Hull Trophy?

Bobby Hull wins the fourth of a record seven goal-scoring titles in 1965-66, tickling the twine a record 54 times. Hull is the NHL's most dynamic scorer during the late 1950s and 1960s. Curiously, when the league introduces a trophy in 1998-99 for the leading goal-scorer, it's named in honor of Rocket Richard, who scores fewer goals than Hull (544-610) and leads the league in goals fewer times (five compared to seven). Listed are the players who have won the most goal-scoring titles.

Player	No.
Bobby Hull, Chi. ('50s-'60s)	7
Phil Esposito, Bos. ('70s)	6
Charlie Conacher, Tor. ('30s)	5
Rocket Richard, Mon. ('40s-'50s)	5
Gordie Howe, Det. ('50s-'60s)	5
Wayne Gretzky, Edm. ('80s)	5

Chalk Talk

"I feel like I'm now one echelon above the President of the United States."

Reaction of Jack Kent Cooke after he is awarded an expansion franchise for Los Angeles

Masked Man

Suffering from trachiatis, an inflammation of the breathing tube, Detroit's Paul Henderson wears a surgical mask while playing to keep cold air out of his lungs. Eventually, he's sent to Arizona to clear up the throat virus.

HOCKEY LISTS OF THE CENTURY

5th Decade All-Stars

Gordie Howe is a first or second all-star all 10 seasons of the NHL's fifth decade (1957-58 through 1966-67), remaining THN's top right winger.

THN's First Team

G **Glenn Hall**, Chi.
   'Mr. Goalie'
D **Pierre Pilote**, Chi.
   Superb at both ends
D **Doug Harvey**, Mon.
   Six-time Norris winner
LW **Bobby Hull**, Chi.
   Explosive scorer
C **Stan Mikita**, Chi.
   Slick playmaker
RW **Gordie Howe**, Det.
   'Mr. Hockey'

THN's Second Team

G **Jacques Plante**, Mon.
   Pioneering puckstopper
D **Marcel Pronovost**, Det.
   Graceful with puck
D **Bill Gadsby**, NYR
   20-year wonder
LW **Frank Mahovlich**, Tor.
   'Big M' big shooter
C **Jean Beliveau**, Mon.
   Ultimate captain
RW **Andy Bathgate**, NYR
   Sharpshooter, skater

Chalk Talk

"Some of them will retire and others will be lost in the expansion draft. But they're going out as champions and that's the way it should be."

Toronto coach Punch Imlach on his roster of grizzled veterans

Bobby Orr talks with coach Harry Sinden at the budding superstar's first Bruins' training camp.

No. 1 STORY: Orr's arrival signals dawn of new era

Defenseman Bobby Orr, 18, makes his NHL debut with Boston after signing a two-year, $75,000 contract with the Bruins. He does not disappoint. Orr finishes with 41 points in 61 games and is named the NHL's top rookie. "Bobby Orr was a star when they played the national anthem before his first game," says Boston coach Harry Sinden. Orr's skating and offensive talents expand the role of defensemen in the game, leading to a generation of imitators–none better than Paul Coffey two decades later.

2. Leafs oldest Stanley Cup winners in history

With Johnny Bower, Red Kelly and Allan Stanley all in their 40s and nine players in their 30s, the Toronto Maple Leafs look to be over the hill as they struggle to make the playoffs. But they stun the first-place Chicago Black Hawks in the semifinals, then down the Montreal Canadiens to take the Stanley Cup, despite an average age of 31.4 years, making the Leafs the oldest champs in NHL history. "Hockey is an old man's game in the head, where it matters," says Leaf coach Punch Imlach.

3. Black Hawks break 'Muldoon's Curse'

The mythical 'Muldoon's Curse' comes to an end March 12, as Chicago blanks Toronto 5-0 to clinch first place for the first time in franchise history. "Is the champagne cold?" asks Chicago's Stan Mikita. "It ought to be–it's been on ice for 40 years." Legend has it that Pete Muldoon, Chicago's first coach, cursed the team to never finish first after he was fired in 1927. The truth is the story was the product of writer Jim Coleman's fertile imagination.

▶ IMPACT PERSON

Stan Mikita

The Chicago center, who four times has garnered 100 penalty minutes in a season, is assessed just 12 this season, earning the Lady Byng Trophy. He also wins the Hart Trophy and collects a record 62 assists while equalling Bobby Hull's record of 97 points to win the Art Ross Trophy. He becomes the first NHLer to record this hardware hat trick.

1967-68

Stanley Cup: Montreal Canadiens

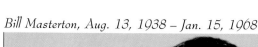
Bill Masterton, Aug. 13, 1938 – Jan. 15, 1968

No. 1 STORY: Original Six welcome six more

The largest single-season growth in NHL history takes place June 6, when six expansion franchises–the Los Angeles Kings, Minnesota North Stars, California Seals, Philadelphia Flyers, Pittsburgh Penguins and St. Louis Blues–stock their rosters. Each of the six established teams protects one goalie and 11 skaters. Among the players selected are three Vezina Trophy winners–first pick overall Terry Sawchuk, 37, (Los Angeles), Charlie Hodge, 33, (California) and Glenn Hall, 35, (St. Louis).

2. Masterton dies in on-ice collision

Hit by Oakland defensemen Larry Cahan and Ron Harris in a Jan. 13 game, Minnesota center Bill Masterton, 30, hits the back of his head on the ice, suffers massive brain injuries and dies two days later. It's the NHL's only on-ice fatality and many players don helmets as a result. The Bill Masterton Memorial Trophy for perseverance and sportsmanship is introduced and awarded for the first time to the Montreal Canadiens' Claude Provost.

3. Blockbuster trades rock the league

The Boston Bruins make the playoffs for the first time since 1958-59 after getting Phil Esposito, Ken Hodge and Fred Stanfield from the Chicago Black Hawks for Pit Martin, Gilles Marotte and Jack Norris. Esposito finishes second in NHL scoring. The Toronto Maple Leafs deal superstar Frank Mahovlich to the Detroit Red Wings, with Garry Unger, Pete Stemkowski and the retired Carl Brewer for Paul Henderson, Floyd Smith and Norm Ullman.

▶ **IMPACT PERSON**

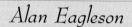

Alan Eagleson

A Toronto lawyer, Eagleson succeeds where the players failed in 1957, creating the NHL Players' Association, which is recognized as a bargaining group June 7 by NHL owners. Toronto center Bob Pulford is elected president. Eagleson gains the players' confidence after negotiating Bobby Orr's contract in 1966 and beginning meetings to discuss the NHLPA during the 1966-67 season.

Graphic Artists/HHOF

O-Pee-Chee Collection/HHOF

Extra-ORR-dinary

Just call it the N-Orr-is Trophy. Limited by a knee injury to 31 points in 46 games, Boston sophomore Bobby Orr is still voted the NHL's best defenseman. It's the first of eight straight Norris Trophies he will win.

HOCKEY LISTS OF THE CENTURY Original 12 Era Begins

The NHL stocks six new expansion teams from a selection of old and new players. Listed are the key details and players from the newly formed West Division's first year.

Team	Record	Goalie	Offensive Story of Year
Philadelphia	31-32-11	Bernie Parent	Leon Rochefort scores career-high 21 goals
Los Angeles	31-33-10	Wayne Rutledge	Bill Flett leads West's top offense (26 goals)
St. Louis	27-31-16	Glenn Hall	Red Berenson emerges as 'The Red Baron'
Minnesota	27-32-15	Cesare Maniago	Wayne Connelly is picked West player of year
Pittsburgh	27-34-13	Les Binkley	Andy Bathgate leads West scorers (59 points)
Oakland	15-42-17	Charlie Hodge	Bill Hicke leads West's worst offense (21 goals)

Chalk Talk

"I've never seen anybody go down that way. He was hit so hard that I'm sure he was unconscious before he fell."

Minnesota coach Wren Blair after the check which led to the death of Bill Masterton

No Brotherly Love

Montreal goalie Tony Esposito makes his first NHL start Dec. 5 at the Boston Garden in a 2-2 tie against the Bruins. Tony stops 33 shots, but both Boston goals are scored by his older brother Phil.

HOCKEY LISTS OF THE CENTURY
Major Stars In Major Junior

Bobby Clarke wins his second straight Western League scoring title in 1968-69, solidifying his status as the junior league's best forward ever. Here are the all-time best (by position) from the three major junior leagues.

Best Players by Position

Western League
G **Grant Fuhr**
Victoria   '79-'81
D **Barry Beck**
New Westminster   '73-'77
F **Bobby Clarke**
Flin Flon   '67-'69

Ontario League
G **Bernie Parent**
Niagara Falls   '63-'65
D **Bobby Orr**
Oshawa   '62-'66
F **Eric Lindros**
Oshawa   '89-'92

Quebec League
G **Tim Bernhardt**
Cornwall   '75-'78
D **Ray Bourque**
Sorel   '76-'79
F **Mario Lemieux**
Laval   '81-'84

Chalk Talk

"Some years, you plant 12 and five or six of them come up. Some years, you plant 12 and none come up. Tonight, everything was going in."

St. Louis star Red Berenson compares scoring a record six goals against Philadelphia to tree-planting

St. Louis' Red Berenson scores six goals against Philadelphia Nov. 7 to establish a Modern Era record.

No. 1 STORY: Espo, Hull, Howe surpass 100 points

It takes 51 years for an NHL player to score 100 points. Within a month the NHL has three. Boston Bruins' center Phil Esposito leads the way with two goals March 2 against Pittsburgh to hit the 100-point plateau and finishes with a record 126 points. Chicago Black Hawks' left winger Bobby Hull joins his former teammate 18 days later and later breaks his own goal record with 58 goals to go along with 107 points. Detroit Red Wings' right winger Gordie Howe scores his 100th point March 30, one day before his 41st birthday. The oldest player ever to hit triple digits, Howe winds up with a career-high 103 points.

2. Howe scores goal No. 700

In a 7-2 win Dec. 4 at Pittsburgh, Detroit's Gordie Howe fires a shot from the slot through the legs of Penguins' goalie Les Binkley for the 700th goal of his NHL career. Howe's only disappointment is that the record tally does not come on home ice. "They had (700) balloons ready for me in the rafters," he says.

3. Plante comes back to win seventh Vezina

Lured out of retirement by the St. Louis Blues, Jacques Plante teams with fellow veteran Glenn Hall to bring the Vezina Trophy to the second-season expansion franchise. It's the seventh time Plante's name goes on the award, more than any other goalie. Any trophy case for these two future Hall Of Famers would be quite full. They've combined for 10 Vezinas, one Hart, a Calder, a Conn Smythe Trophy and 17 first- or second-team all-star selections.

▶ **IMPACT PERSON**

Phil Esposito

Acquired in a 1967 blockbuster trade with Chicago, Esposito blossoms in Boston. His 77 assists and 126 points in 1968-69 are NHL records and 49 goals a club mark. He ranks among the NHL's top 10 scorers each of his eight full seasons as a Bruin, winning five Art Ross Trophies and earning six straight first all-star team berths.

1969-70 Stanley Cup: Boston Bruins Ⓑ

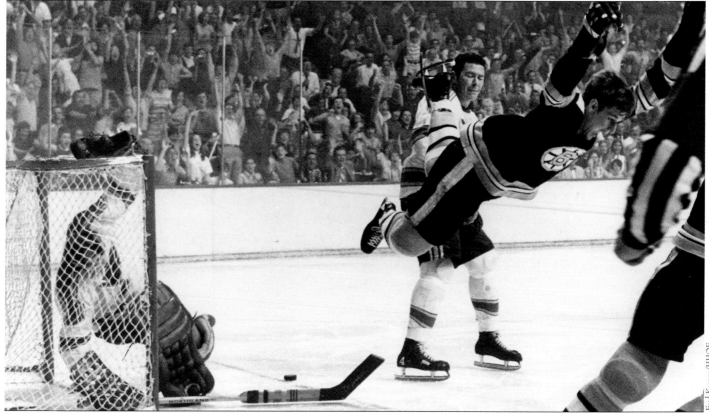

Bobby Orr flies through the air after beating Glenn Hall in overtime with the 1970 Stanley Cup-winning goal.

Fred Keenan/HHOF

▶ IMPACT PERSON

Bobby Orr

Orr sets records for defensemen, scoring 33 goals and 120 points to become the first blueliner to win the Art Ross Trophy; his 87 assists are more than any other player ever. Orr also wins the Hart, Norris and Conn Smythe, the only NHLer to win four major awards in a season. He finishes with the Cup-winning goal in overtime.

Graphic Artists/HHOF

No. 1 STORY: Orr and Tony 'O' rewrite record book

Boston Bruins' superstar Bobby Orr sets scoring marks for rearguards in all categories with 33-87-120 totals in becoming the first defenseman to win the Art Ross Trophy. Meanwhile Tony Esposito, claimed by the Chicago Black Hawks from the Montreal Canadiens, posts 15 shutouts, an NHL record for rookies and the highest number since the NHL introduced the red line in 1943. Tony 'O' wins both the Vezina and Calder Trophies.

2. Sawchuk dies following freak injury

An altercation on the lawn of their rented house between New York Rangers' teammates Terry Sawchuk and Ron Stewart April 29, leaves Sawchuk–the NHL's all-time leader in shutouts (103) and games by a goalie (971)–with a critical injury. He undergoes surgery to remove his gall bladder and then two more operations after complications arise. Shortly after the third one, Sawchuk, 40, dies of cardiac arrest. A grand jury investigation is held in Nassau County, N.Y., but no charges are laid against Stewart.

3. Maki fractures Green's skull

Boston's Ted Green and Wayne Maki of the St. Louis Blues engage in a vicious stick-swinging duel in a Sept. 21 exhibition game at Ottawa. Green first hits Maki with his stick, then the Blues' player retaliates by striking Green in the temple with his stick, fracturing Green's skull. Green undergoes five hours of surgery and misses the entire NHL season. Criminal charges are laid, but both players are exonerated. The NHL suspends Maki for 30 days and Green for 13 days.

One Of A Kind

A year after Ken Dryden graduates, the Cornell Big Red roll through the NCAA season with a perfect 29-0-0 record to win the ECAC title. All-NCAA defenseman Dan Lodboa scores a hat trick as Cornell downs Clarkson 6-4 in the NCAA final.

Chalk Talk

"Certainly on our club, I don't think there are too many guys who wear lace panties out there."

Boston's Ted Green, testifying to the toughness of NHL players during his assault trial

Nobody is more dangerous around the net than Boston superstar scorer Phil Esposito during the early 1970s.

Graphic Artists/HHOF

Pearson Awarded

Boston's Bobby Orr wins the Hart Trophy as MVP again, but Phil Esposito is awarded a new honor voted on by the players themselves–the Lester B. Pearson Award–a salute to the former Canadian prime minister.

Chalk Talk

"I might as well be blunt. He can't coach."

Sid Abel, assessing Detroit coach Ned Harkness shortly after Abel is fired as Red Wings' GM and replaced by Harkness

No. 1 STORY: Esposito and Orr lead Bruins' record assault

The Boston Bruins set 37 NHL standards in a record-breaking season, including new marks with 57 wins, 121 points and 399 goals. Leading the way is center Phil Esposito, who collects his 59th goal and 127th point against the Los Angeles Kings March 11, surpassing the old NHL records in both categories. He finishes the season with 76 goals and 152 points. The assist record is also broken as league MVP Bobby Orr becomes the first player to collect 100 helpers or more (102). All three individual marks will stand for a decade.

2. Sabres and Canucks make NHL a 14-team league

A spin of the wheel gives Buffalo first pick in the amateur draft and Sabres' coach-GM Punch Imlach grabs Montreal Jr. Canadiens' phenom Gilbert Perreault. Imlach vows the Sabres will be the first expansion team to win the Stanley Cup, but it's the Vancouver Canucks, the other first-year club, that makes a playoff run before fading in the second half of the season.

3. Rookie's dad killed in shootout over telecast

Roy Spencer, father of Toronto Maple Leafs' rookie Brian Spencer, excitedly awaits the chance to see his son play against Buffalo on *Hockey Night In Canada* Dec. 12. When he tunes in and instead sees a Vancouver-California game, Spencer grabs his gun and makes the 70-mile drive from his home in Fort James, B.C., to the CBC affiliate in Prince George, B.C. He enters the station and orders them at gunpoint to switch to the Toronto game. Police arrive and Spencer is killed in the ensuing shootout.

Ken Dryden

Called up late in the season, the rookie from Cornell University goes 6-0 with a 1.65 GAA for the Canadiens. Facing mighty Boston in the first round of the playoffs, Habs' coach Al MacNeil goes with Dryden. It works. Dryden beats the Bruins and takes Montreal all the way to the Stanley Cup, winning the Conn Smythe Trophy.

London Life – Portnoy/HHOF

1971-72

Stanley Cup: Boston Bruins

Gordie Howe, Detroit Red Wings

▶ IMPACT PERSON

Jean Ratelle

The only thing that can stop Ratelle is his teammate. The center for the Rangers' 'GAG Line' (goal-a-game) with Rod Gilbert and Vic Hadfield has his season ended when he suffers a broken ankle March 1 after being struck by teammate Dale Rolfe's shot. Ratelle plays only 63 games, but his 109 points shatters the Ranger single-season mark by 21.

No. 1 STORY: Legends Howe and Beliveau retire

Two all-time greats are missing when training camps open in September. Gordie Howe, 44, the NHL's career leader in goals (786), assists (1,023) and points (1,809), retires after a record 25 seasons with the Detroit Red Wings. "I could play one more year and I could play very badly," says Howe, who finds his way back to the NHL eight years later. Meanwhile, Jean Beliveau, a 500-goal scorer and 1,000-point man who has hoisted the Stanley Cup five times as the Montreal Canadiens' captain, also retires. "I think I took the right decision, because at 40 you have to get closer to your family," he says.

2. Orr lands landmark contract

Bobby Orr becomes hockey's first million-dollar player when he signs a five-year contract Aug. 26 with the Boston Bruins for $200,000 a year. "I'm very happy with the amount," Orr says. His agent, Alan Eagleson, goes one step further: "It's a safe assumption to say that Bobby's contract is the richest in NHL history." Orr proves he's worth it, winning the Hart Trophy for the third straight season–the last time a defenseman cops the honor.

3. Habs add Lafleur and Bowman

The NHL's June meetings could be described as the Montreal Canadiens' show. The Habs use the first pick overall, acquired the previous season from the California Golden Seals, to select junior star Guy Lafleur in the amateur draft. Veteran winger John Ferguson joins Beliveau in retirement, then the defending champions complete their changes, naming St. Louis Blues' coach Scotty Bowman to replace Al MacNeil.

Great Expectations

A 10-year-old, 70-pound center named Wayne Gretzky is an intermission guest on *Hockey Night In Canada* after a Toronto newspaper article chronicles how he scored 378 goals in one season for his novice team in Brantford, Ont.

HOCKEY LISTS OF THE CENTURY
Rewriting NHL Record Book

Bobby Orr sets single-season standards for goals, assists or points by a defenseman nine times during a six-year period in the late 1960s and early 1970s. All are raised incrementally by Orr himself. But, it makes for a fascinating comparison to look at the records before Orr enters the league in 1966-67. Only his goal record has been eclipsed since; Coffey ups it by two in 1985-86. Orr is the only blueliner to win a scoring title (1969-70, 1974-75).

Single-Season Standards

Goals		
Flash Hollett, Det., '44-45	20
Bobby Orr, Bos., '74-75	46
Per-cent Increase	*130%*
Paul Coffey, Edm., '85-86	48

Assists		
Pat Stapleton, Chi., '68-69	50
Bobby Orr, Bos., '70-71	102
Per-cent Increase	*101%*

Points		
Pierre Pilote, Chi., '64-65	59
Bobby Orr, Bos., '70-71	139
Per-cent Increase	*138%*

Chalk Talk

"We played them pretty even, but they had Bobby Orr and we didn't."

New York forward Vic Hadfield on what decided the Stanley Cup final between Boston and the Rangers

 **1972-73**

Scene of Crime

Boston's Carol Vadnais is arrested in Philadelphia twice–first after a fan presses assault charges, then when he is mistaken for a bank robber. In both cases, the charges are dropped. "I guess this isn't my town," Vadnais says.

HOCKEY LISTS OF THE CENTURY

International Ice: Canada & USA

Ten North American highs:

1. '72 Summit Series
Canada nips Soviets on Henderson's third winner.

2. '80 Miracle On Ice
U.S. collegians win Olympic gold.

3. '87 Canada Cup
Lemieux beats Soviets on pass from Gretzky.

4. '96 World Cup
U.S. upsets Canada for title after losing series opener.

5. '75-76 Super Series
Red Army ties Habs, walks off ice in Philly.

6. '76 Canada Cup
Sittler's OT goal wins it for Team Canada.

7. '84 Canada Cup
Coffey blocks pass, sets up Bossy in OT against Soviets.

8. '98 Olympics
U.S. upsets Canada in first battle for women's gold.

9. '97 World Juniors
Canada blanks U.S. 2-0 for record fifth straight title.

10. '90 Women's Worlds
Canada beats U.S. in first global tournament.

Chalk Talk

"We gave up a lot for this series–money, our vacations. We didn't deserve it."

Phil Esposito, reacting angrily after fans in Vancouver loudly boo Canadian players following a 5-3 loss to the Soviets

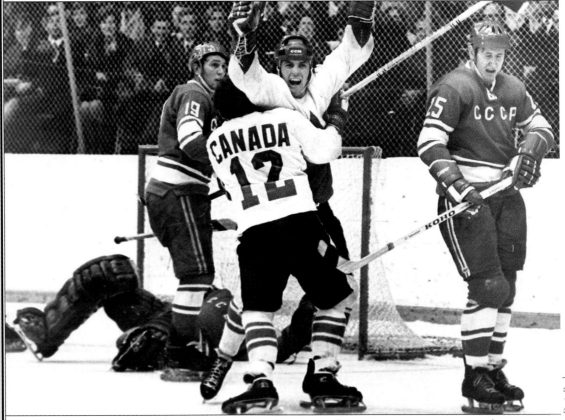

Denis Brodeur

Paul Henderson is embraced by Yvan Cournoyer after scoring the Summit Series-winning goal.

No. 1 STORY: Canada squeaks by Soviets in Summit Series clash

Most experts predict the eight-game, September series between Canada and the Soviets will be a mismatch. But Soviet goalie Vladislav Tretiak, just 20, is brilliant as his team stuns the Canadians 7-3 in Game 1 and takes a 3-1-1 lead after five games. Team Canada is in turmoil from Day 1. Stars Bobby Hull, Derek Sanderson, Gerry Cheevers and J.C. Tremblay are dropped after jumping to the rival World Hockey Association and the injured Bobby Orr can't play. All looks lost until Paul Henderson scores two winning goals to tie the series. With all Canadians glued to their TV sets, Henderson then becomes a national hero by scoring with 34 seconds left in Game 8 as Canada wins 6-5 on Moscow ice to take the series.

2. Start-up WHA steals stars from NHL

NHL moguls are not impressed by the World Hockey Association, which promises to be a major league rival. The laughing stops when Chicago Black Hawks' superstar Bobby Hull signs a $1-million deal with the Winnipeg Jets. Gerry Cheevers, Derek Sanderson, Bernie Parent and John McKenzie are other prominent NHLers to jump. The NHL's reserve clause, which ties a player to one team for life, is defeated in court by the WHA, opening the door to free agency.

3. Expansion Islanders set record for losses

As the league grows from 14 to 16 teams, the Atlanta Flames, coached by former Montreal star Bernie 'Boom Boom' Geoffrion, win 25 of 78 games and fare much better than their expansion cousins the New York Islanders, who set an NHL record with 60 losses.

▶ IMPACT PERSON

Paul Henderson

Henderson goes from local hero with Toronto to national icon in sparking Team Canada past the Soviet Union. "After I scored the winner in the seventh game, I figured I'd had the biggest moment of my hockey life," Henderson says. "But when I got the winner in the eighth game, I couldn't believe it. It was the thrill of a lifetime."

Graphic Artists/HHOF

1973-74 Stanley Cup: Philadelphia Flyers

Marty, Gordie and Mark Howe, Houston Aeros

O-Pee-Chee Collection/HHOF

▶ IMPACT PERSON

Bernie Parent

The original Flyer is booed at the start of the season because popular Doug Favell is traded to get Parent back from Toronto after the latter's return from the WHA. Catcalls change to cheers as Parent wins the Vezina Trophy. Parent adds the Conn Smythe Trophy after leading the Flyers to the Stanley Cup, the first of two straight for both.

London Life – Portnoy/HHOF

No. 1 STORY: Flyers first expansion team to win title

Philadelphia's rugged Broad Street Bullies, who set an NHL penalty minutes record in 1972-73, become the first of the 1967 expansion teams to win the Stanley Cup. Billed as the team against the superstar, the Flyers, led by captain Bobby Clarke, defeat the Boston Bruins in six games. "They had (Bobby) Orr and he can do an awful lot," says Flyers' coach Fred Shero. "But we've got 17 good hockey players and every one of them put out. It was 17 against one."

2. Howe teams with sons in WHA

One year after grabbing Bobby Hull, the WHA stages another coup, luring NHL career scoring leader Gordie Howe out of retirement. The Houston Aeros sign Howe, 45, to play on the same team with his sons Mark and Marty. The old man shows no rink rust, leading the Aeros in scoring with 100 points although he has been away from the game two years. Howe finishes third in league scoring and is named the league's MVP. With the Howes in the lineup, Houston wins the Avco Cup title.

3. Horton killed in car accident

Buffalo GM Punch Imlach lures Tim Horton out of retirement with a signing bonus of an Italian-made Ford Pantera sports car. It turns out to be a fatal decision. The 44-year-old defenseman is driving the car from Toronto to Buffalo after a game Feb. 21 when he loses control and crashes near St. Catharines, Ont. Horton is killed instantly. The night before, he had been named one of the three stars as the Sabres dropped a 4-2 decision to the Maple Leafs.

2nd Toronto Team

Toronto gets a second team when the WHA Ottawa Nationals move, becoming the Toronto Toros. With regular season games at tiny Varsity Arena, the club averages 4,291 fans. Its overall attendance of 167,432 is second-lowest in the league.

HOCKEY LISTS OF THE CENTURY
Swedish Blueliner Pioneer For Euros

Borje Salming paves the way for the European invasion. The gaunt Swedish defenseman joins Toronto in 1973-74 and quickly develops into an all-star. He is not the best European ever in the NHL–that honor belongs to Peter Stastny or Jaromir Jagr–but he's the most important. Salming withstands physical and verbal attacks ('Chicken Swede'), particularly from the Philadelphia Flyers, to establish himself as a star player and open the door for Europeans to follow. Here's a list of facts about Salming's 17-year career. On pg. 77 is a list of six other Europeans who have made a huge impact on the game.

The Salming File
Born: April 17, '51
NHL: Tor., Det., '73-74 – '89-90

GP	G	A	Pts	PIM
1,148	150	637	787	1,344

1st all-star (1), 2nd all-star (5)
Elected to Hall of Fame ('96)

Chalk Talk

"Last year there were six goaltenders making more than I. The Canadiens are not an impoverished organization."

Ken Dryden explaining why he'll sit out the season and article with a Toronto law firm for $134 a week

Marcel Dionne, Detroit Red Wings

O-Pee-Chee Collection/HHOF

1974-75

Stanley Cup: Philadelphia Flyers

No. 1 STORY: More expansion leads to realignment

Expansion franchises in Washington and Kansas City lead to the biggest changes in the NHL since 1967-68. The league moves to a four-division format, naming them after NHL icons Lester Patrick, Conn Smythe, Jim Norris and Jack Adams. Expansion teams win three of four divisions– Philadelphia (Patrick), Vancouver (Smythe) and Buffalo (Adams). The Capitals go 8-67-5 and set NHL records of 17 straight losses and the lowest winning percentage in history–.131.

2. Orr and Espo enjoy one last hurrah together

Boston teammates Bobby Orr and Phil Esposito put on another explosive scoring display. Little does anyone realize it's their swan song together. Orr pots a record 46 goals for a defenseman and wins his second Art Ross and eighth straight Norris Trophy. Esposito leads the league in goals for the sixth straight season with 61, and finishes behind Orr with 127 points. Neither would reach that output again. Esposito is traded next season while Orr, whose knees begin to go, never plays a full season again.

3. Islanders join '42 Leafs with miraculous comeback

The New York Islanders are down 3-0 to the Pittsburgh Penguins in their quarterfinal, but when coach Al Arbour replaces goalie Billy Smith with rookie Glenn Resch, the tables turn. The Isles win four straight, including 1-0 in Game 7. They join the 1942 Toronto Maple Leafs as the only teams to rally from such a deficit. In the next series, New York trails the Philadelphia Flyers 3-0, then wins three straight before losing 4-1 in Game 7.

▶ IMPACT PERSON

Bobby Clarke

For the first time since 1967-68, someone other than Phil Esposito is at center on the NHL's first all-star team. It's Clarke, the spiritual leader of the Stanley Cup-champion Philadelphia Flyers. He posts the second 100-point season of his career, and despite scoring champion Bobby Orr's record 46-goal season, Clarke earns his second of three Hart Trophies, as league MVP.

London Life – Portnoy/HHOF

Marcel's Magic

At 23, Marcel Dionne scores 47 goals for Detroit and places third in league scoring behind Bobby Orr and Phil Esposito. Dionne demands a trade and is dealt to Los Angeles, where he blossoms beginning in 1975-76.

HOCKEY LISTS OF THE CENTURY Transition Europeans

Borje Salming is the first great European in the NHL, but not the last. Of the hundreds who follow, here's a list of the six most important, including Jari Kurri, who plays for five teams (only two are listed). Asterisks (*) indicate active players.

Anders Hedberg, Win., NYR	Best Euro in WHA, which embraces Euros before NHL
Peter Stastny, Que., N.J., St.L	Special all-around talent has seven 100-point seasons
Jari Kurri, Edm., LA	Seven-time 40-goal man, highest scoring Euro ever
Igor Larionov, Van., S.J., Det.*	Courage and conviction leads to Soviet open-door policy
Teemu Selanne, Win., Ana.*	Rookie record-setter, first winner of Richard Trophy
Jaromir Jagr, Pit.*	Four-time scoring champ, game's best player

Chalk Talk

"It wasn't something I liked to do, but I was pretty good at it."

Philadelphia's Dave 'The Hammer' Schultz on fighting. The Broad Street Bully earns an NHL record 472 penalty minutes in 1974-75

Broad Street Bullies: Don 'Big Bird' Saleski, Andre 'Moose' Dupont, Bob 'Houndog' Kelly, Dave 'The Hammer' Schultz

True Hockey News

Soviets Leave Ice

Angry that referee Lloyd Gilmour calls no penalty when Philadelphia's Ed Van Impe hits its star, Valeri Kharlamov, early in a Jan. 11 game, the Central Red Army team leaves the ice. It returns but suffers a 4-1 loss.

HOCKEY LISTS OF THE CENTURY
Hockey Violence Before The Courts

There are more dramatic legal results of hockey violence–Dino Ciccarelli is jailed for a day in 1988–but 1975 and 1976 stand out as the busiest period. Here are four cases from that time.
Jan. 4, '75: Dave Forbes butt-ends Henry Boucha, fracturing his cheekbone. Charge: Aggravated assault. Verdict: Hung jury.
Nov. 5, '75: Dan Maloney hits Brian Glennie from behind, giving him a concussion. Charge: Assault Verdict: Not guilty.
April 11, '76: Rick Jodzio ambushes Marc Tardif, giving him a concussion. Charge: Assault. Verdict: Guilty plea to lesser charge.
April 15, '76: Joe Watson, Mel Bridgman, Bob Kelly and Don Saleski get in fight with fans. Charge: Assault, possession of dangerous weapon. Verdict: Watson, Kelly plead guilty to lesser charge. Charges against Bridgman, Saleski dropped.

Chalk Talk

"They were completely outclassed from start to finish, except on the scoreboard and in the nets."

Montreal coach Scotty Bowman after his club's 3-3 New Year's Eve tie with the Soviet Red Army in which the Habs outshoot the visitors 38-13 at the Forum

---

► IMPACT PERSON

Reggie Leach

Teamed with Bobby Clarke, his old junior center, Leach becomes the second player to score 60 goals (61), then really lights it up in the playoffs. He sets a Stanley Cup record with 19 goals, including five in Philadelphia's semifinal win over Boston. "I can release the puck as fast as anyone," says Leach, who wins the Conn Smythe Trophy. "Within 15-20 feet of the net, I'm deadly."

London Life – Portnoy/HHOF

No. 1 STORY: Bruins trade Esposito to Rangers

In a move that would have been unthinkable when the two teams were on top of the NHL standings, the Boston Bruins trade all-star Phil Esposito and Carol Vadnais to the New York Rangers Nov. 7 for two other all-stars, Jean Ratelle and Brad Park, as well as fringe defenseman Joe Zanussi. Esposito scores only 35 goals, 26 fewer than in 1974-75. "I think there should be a rule protecting veterans from trades after you've been with a team for five or seven years." says Esposito, a five-time NHL scoring champion.

2. Ontario Attorney General goes after NHL hooligans

Following a brawl-filled playoff game in Toronto, the Philadelphia Flyers' Mel Bridgman, Bob Kelly, Don Saleski and Joe Watson are charged with assault. It's all part of Ontario Attorney General Roy McMurtry's crackdown on hockey violence. The Detroit Red Wings' Dan Maloney also faces charges after a November incident when he pounds the head of the Toronto Maple Leafs' Brian Glennie into the ice. Watson and Kelly plead guilty to common assault and are fined $750 and $200, respectively. The other players are cleared of all charges.

3. Sittler's record night a perfect 10

In an 11-4 win over Boston Feb. 7, Toronto's Darryl Sittler scores six times and adds four assists for an NHL-record 10 points. Then in Game 6 of a quarterfinal series with Philadelphia, Sittler equals a Stanley Cup record with five goals. But he lists neither as his most memorable moment. "I figured I'd had my share of once-in-a-lifetime happenings back in 1971-72, when I had a perfect hand in cribbage."

Bobby Orr, Chicago Black Hawks

1976-77

Stanley Cup: Montreal Canadiens

No. 1 STORY: First Canada Cup stays home

For the first time, the world's top six hockey-playing nations stage a true championship. The Canada Cup tournament ends when Canada sweeps a best-of-three final from Czechoslovakia, the only country to beat the Canadians in the preliminary round. The Soviet Union keeps eight of its greatest stars at home and finishes third. Skating virtually on one leg following a series of knee operations, Canada's Bobby Orr is named MVP. "This is the greatest hockey team in the world," proclaims Canada's Darryl Sittler, whose OT winner decides Game 2 of the final.

2. Orr leaves Beantown for Windy City

First, Phil Esposito is traded. Now Bobby Orr jumps ship–signing a $3-million free agent deal with the Chicago Black Hawks June 9–leaving Boston minus its two icons. Bruins' fans turn sour when they learn Boston didn't try to keep Orr. "We were offered the same deal as Chicago was," admits Boston president Paul Mooney. "We just didn't take it." Boston considers filing suit for compensation, but elects not to pursue the matter.

3. Cup-winning Habs win most games in NHL history

Perhaps the most dominant team in league history, the Montreal Canadiens roll to an NHL-record 60 victories and 132 points, then go 12-2 in the playoffs to win the Stanley Cup for the second straight season. The Canadiens are 33-1-6 at home and win a league-record 27 road games. Steve Shutt establishes a league record for left wingers by scoring 60 goals to lead the league.

▶ IMPACT PERSON

Denis Potvin

Coming off a 98-point, Norris Trophy-winning season, Potvin stars in the first Canada Cup with nine points in eight games. He then picks up 80 points for the Islanders, helping them to the Final Four. In four NHL seasons Potvin has Calder and Norris Trophy wins, three all-star selections and 308 points. He will become the first NHL blueliner to score 1,000 points.

On The Move

For the first time since 1934-35 when Ottawa left for St. Louis, a franchise changes towns. Kansas City goes to Colorado while California moves to Cleveland. It doesn't help. Both teams still finish last in their divisions.

HOCKEY LISTS OF THE CENTURY 6th Decade All-Stars

Bobby Orr is a first all-star and Norris Trophy winner eight straight seasons during the NHL's sixth decade (1967-68 through 1976-77). Brad Park is a Norris runner-up five times.

	The Hockey News' First Team		The Hockey News' Second Team
G	**Ken Dryden**, Mon. *Four-time all-star*	G	**Bernie Parent**, Phi. *Two Smythes*
D	**Bobby Orr**, Bos. *Revolutionary force*	D	**Denis Potvin**, NYI. *Orr's offensive heir*
D	**Brad Park**, Det. *Norris bridesmaid*	D	**Borje Salming**, Tor. *First Euro star*
LW	**Bobby Hull**, Chi. *100-mph shot*	LW	**Rick Martin**, Buf. *French connector*
C	**Phil Esposito**, Bos. *1st 100-point man*	C	**Bobby Clarke**, Phi. *Heart for Hart*
RW	**Guy Lafleur**, Mon. *Flower Power*	RW	**Yvan Cournoyer**, Mon. *'Roadrunner'*

Chalk Talk

"Some of the things the Flyers have done are disgraceful."

Former Broad Street Bully Dave 'The Hammer' Schultz after being traded from Philadelphia to Los Angeles

1977-78

Stanley Cup: Montreal Canadiens

Mike Bossy, New York Islanders

No. 1 STORY: Bossy shatters rookie goal record

Passed over until the 15th pick of the NHL amateur draft, right winger Mike Bossy from Laval of the Quebec League proves to be the find of the decade for the New York Islanders. Bossy's quick release allows him to score 53 goals, breaking the NHL rookie record of 44 set in 1971-72 by the Buffalo Sabres' Rick Martin. Complacency isn't an issue for Bossy. The name over his dressing room stall remains written on masking tape with magic marker well into the season. "Maybe I'll get a nameplate like everyone else when they decide I can stay," Bossy says.

2. Linesman fights draft law and wins

Signed by the WHA's Birmingham Bulls, 19-year-old center Ken Linseman is refused permission to play by league president Harold Baldwin. The president is honoring an agreement with amateur hockey that the league will not sign or draft players under the age of 20. However, Linseman challenges the system in court and wins–opening the door to the drafting of underaged amateurs, a process which starts in the NHL in 1979.

3. Ziegler replaces Campbell as president

Clarence Campbell winds up his 31-season reign as president of the NHL, announcing his retirement prior to the season. John Ziegler, a lawyer employed as vice-president of the Detroit Red Wings, is recommended by Campbell and unanimously selected as his replacement by the 18 team owners. Ziegler is the first American to serve as NHL president.

Denis Brodeur

▶ **IMPACT PERSON**

Guy Lafleur

After struggling through his early NHL days, 'The Flower' blooms in the mid-1970s, developing into the force Montreal anticipated when drafting him No. 1 in 1971. Lafleur enjoys his best season, setting an NHL record for right wingers with 60 goals. His 132 points win him the Art Ross Trophy for the third straight season and he also gets his second consecutive Hart Trophy.

O-Pee-Chee Collection/HHOF

Defensive Gains

A new award is created and it could almost be renamed after its first winner. Montreal's Bob Gainey wins the Frank Selke Trophy as the NHL's best defensive forward. He also wins it the next three seasons.

HOCKEY LISTS OF THE CENTURY Big Screen Snapshots

Slap Shot and *Mystery, Alaska* are the best hockey movies on a list that peters out quickly.

1. *Slap Shot* (1977)
Paul Newman, Hanson Bros. rough it up
2. *Mystery, Alaska* (1999)
Small-town boys vs. New York Rangers
3. *Idol of the Crowds* (1937)
Hockey star John Wayne battles gangsters
4. *The Mighty Ducks* (1992)
Kiddie comedy spawns real NHL team

5. *Hockey Night* (1984)
Megan Follows tries out for boys team
6. *Gross Misconduct* (1992)
Atom Egoyan's Brian Spencer life story
7. *Youngblood* (1985)
Rob Lowe learns about hockey life
8. *Face-off* (1971)
Canadian classic features Jim McKenny

Chalk Talk

"He's a know-nothing shrimp."

Toronto owner Harold Ballard on NHL president John Ziegler, after being ordered to have names on the backs of jerseys

Guy Lafleur, Montreal Canadiens

London Life – Portnoy/HHOF

1978-79
Stanley Cup: Montreal Canadiens

No. 1 STORY: Gretzky stars in final WHA season

In what will be its final season, the WHA stages a major coup when Indianapolis owner Nelson Skalbania signs Wayne Gretzky to a $1.75-million personal services contract. In November, the Racers sell his contract to Edmonton, where he places third in WHA scoring with 110 points. Then in March, the NIIL votes 14-3 to adopt four WHA franchises–the Edmonton Oilers, Hartford Whalers, Quebec Nordiques and Winnipeg Jets–in 1979-80.

2. Cherry bomb helps Habs win fourth straight title

Leading Montreal 4-3 with 2:34 left in Game 7 of the semifinals, Boston blows its Stanley Cup chances with a foolish too-many-men-on-the-ice penalty. Guy Lafleur scores, then Yvon Lambert wins it in OT and Bruins' coach Don Cherry is fired as a result. It's the fourth consecutive Cup for the powerhouse Montreal Canadiens and the fifth straight 50-goal season for Lafleur. Three prominent Habs–Yvan Cournoyer, Jacques Lemaire and Ken Dryden–retire at the end of the season. All three will be inducted into the Hockey Hall of Fame within the next five years.

3. Bad knees end Orr's career

The only thing that stops Bobby Orr is his health. The Chicago superstar, who has knee surgery six times, retires Nov. 8 at the age of 30. He finishes his 12-year career with 270 goals and 915 points, both NHL records for defensemen, as well as three Hart and eight Norris Trophies. Inducted into the Hockey Hall of Fame the next year, he's the youngest person to receive the honor.

▶ **IMPACT PERSON**

Bryan Trottier

The Islanders' captain has his best season as the club wins the regular season title with 116 points. Trottier wins the Art Ross Trophy, setting club records with 87 assists and 134 points. The gritty center also wins the Hart Trophy and is named to the first all-star team for the second straight season. Toronto coach Roger Neilson calls him "the best player in the world."

Bruce Bennett/BBS

Murdoch Sits Out

Rangers' winger Don Murdoch, 21, is suspended for the 1978-79 season and fined $500 after being convicted of cocaine possession. But his suspension is lifted after 40 games and New York signs him to a new contract.

HOCKEY LISTS OF THE CENTURY All-Time WHA Team

The World Hockey Association lives only seven seasons, 1972-73 through 1978-79, but its renegade ways change the face of pro hockey. Below is the all-time WHA team. Listed are primary teams, WHA years, games, goals, assists, points and penalty minutes.

G	**Ron Grahame**	Houston	'73-'77		LW	**Bobby Hull**	Winnipeg	'72-'78
	143 games, 2.56 GAA					411 - 303 - 335 - 638 - 183		
D	**Paul Shmyr**	Cleveland	'72-'79		C	**Ulf Nilsson**	Winnipeg	'74-'78
	511 - 61 - 248 - 309 - 860					300 - 140 - 344 - 484 - 341		
D	**Lars Sjoberg**	Winnipeg	'74-'78		RW	**Anders Hedberg**	Winnipeg	'74-'78
	295 - 25 - 169 - 194 - 42					286 - 236 - 242 - 478 - 141		

Chalk Talk

"Hell, we were so close to it and so excited, I had to pull back two other guys or we would have had eight guys on the ice."
Bruin coach Don Cherry after too-many-men-on-the-ice penalty costs team semifinal series with Montreal

1979-80 Stanley Cup: New York Islanders

America's all-time favorite hockey team celebrates its historic victory over the Soviets Feb. 22 at the Lake Placid Olympics.

Canapress

▶ **IMPACT PERSON**

Herb Brooks

Brooks has operated in obscurity while guiding Minnesota to three U.S. college championships. "When this is over, I'll be known as 'Herb Who?,'" the U.S. Olympic coach says en route to the gold medal at Lake Placid. He's wrong. Brooks is named coach of the New York Rangers in 1981 and 13 U.S. Olympians go on to NHL careers.

No. 1 STORY: 'Miracle on Ice' ignites hockey interest in U.S.

Mike Eruzione's third period goal gives a spirited group of American collegians a stunning 4-3 upset victory over the Soviet Union at the 1980 Lake Placid Olympics. Unknown goalie Jim Craig is spectacular as the Americans are outshot 39-16 in the Feb. 22 game. Team USA goes on to defeat Finland 4-2 Feb. 24 to win the gold medal, igniting U.S. hockey interest as never before. It's the first time since 1960, when the Americans also won at Squaw Valley, any nation other than the Soviet Union wins gold.

2. Four WHA refugees make NHL debuts

The NHL starts 1979-80 with four new teams–the Edmonton Oilers, Hartford Whalers, Quebec Nordiques and Winnipeg Jets–as the senior league absorbs the four strongest WHA franchises. This officially brings to an end a seven-year battle between the two leagues. Launched with 12 teams in 1972-73, the WHA peaks with 14 in 1974-75 and finishes in 1978-79 with six. The other two remaining franchises–the Cincinnati Stingers and Birmingham Bulls–are dissolved. At age 51, Hartford's Gordie Howe scores 15 goals in his first NHL campaign since 1970-71. It's 'Mr. Hockey's' 26th and final NHL season.

3. Gretzky begins reign as NHL king

WHA graduate and Edmonton Oilers' sensation Wayne Gretzky begins a decade of dominance in the NHL. At 19, he becomes the youngest player to score 50 goals as well as win the Hart and Lady Byng Trophies. Although he ties Marcel Dionne with a league-high 137 points, Dionne wins the Art Ross Trophy because he has more goals (53 to 51). Gretzky is ruled ineligible for the Calder Trophy because of his WHA experience.

HOCKEY LISTS OF THE CENTURY
USA! USA! USA!
Americans Win

The U.S. wins its second Olympic gold medal, surprising the mighty Soviets 4-3 just days after losing 10-3 to them in an exhibition game. The Americans go on to win the gold medal, defeating Finland 4-2. Here's the list of countries that have won Olympic gold medals.

Country	No.
1. Soviet Union/Russia	8
2. Canada	5
3. USA	2
4. Sweden	1
Great Britain	1
Czech Republic	1

Wayne Gretzky, Edmonton Oilers

Bruce Bennett/BBS

1980-81

Stanley Cup: New York Islanders

No. 1 STORY: Gretzky breaks Esposito and Orr scoring marks

Wayne Gretzky has a record-breaking week that will become all too familiar. The Edmonton center records three assists March 30 at Pittsburgh, vaulting him past Phil Esposito's 10-year-old NHL record of 152 points. Two nights later, Gretzky collects his 103rd assist, breaking the NHL mark of 102 set by Esposito's teammate Bobby Orr in 1970-71. Gretzky finishes with 109 assists and 164 points and his 2.05 points-per-game average is the highest since Joe Malone's 2.40 in 1917-18, the NHL's first season.

2. Stastnys defect to play in Quebec

Stars of Czechoslovakia's national team the Stastny brothers, Peter and Anton, defect and sign with the Quebec Nordiques. "I want to see what the best hockey league in the world is going to be like," says Anton. Peter garners a rookie-record 109 points and wins the Calder Trophy. Their defection leads to an agreement with the Czechoslovak federation allowing other talented players to leave the country legally to play in the NHL the next season. That includes Marian Stastny, who joins his brothers in Quebec.

3. Dionne king of Triple Crown line

Los Angeles' center Marcel Dionne places second to Wayne Gretzky in the scoring race with 58 goals and 135 points. He leads the Kings' Triple Crown line, with wingers Dave Taylor and Charlie Simmer, to a banner season. The line produces 161 goals and 191 assists for 352 points. Dionne also records his 1,000th career point in only his 740th game, the fastest anyone has ever reached 1,000.

▶ IMPACT PERSON

Bruce Bennett/BBS

Mike Bossy

Needing two goals in his 50th game to join Rocket Richard as the only players to score 50 in 50 games, New York Islanders' Mike Bossy scores a pair on Quebec goalie Ron Grahame with less than five minutes remaining in the game. "I had never been so frustrated in all my hockey career," he says. Bossy finishes with a league-high 68 goals and goes on to score 50 or more in each of his first nine seasons.

Howe's Lucky Crash

The career of Hartford's Mark Howe almost ends after he crashes into the net Dec. 27. His buttock is punctured and the point inside the cage just misses his spine. The net design is later changed to a straight bar across the back.

HOCKEY LISTS OF THE CENTURY All-Time AHL Team

Johnny Bower plays a decade in the American League before a Hall-of-Fame career in the NHL. He is THN's choice as captain of the all-time AHL team. Listed are primary teams, AHL years, games, goals, assists, points and penalty minutes.

G	**Johnny Bower**	Cleveland	'47-'58	LW	**Dick Gamble**	Rochester	'54-'70
	595 games, 45 shutouts				899 - 468 - 424 - 892 - 295		
D	**Frank Mathers**	Pittsburgh	'48-'62	C	**Willie Marshall**	Hershey	'52-'72
	799 - 67 - 340 - 407 - 636				1,205 - 523 - 852 - 1,375 - 520		
D	**Al Arbour**	Rochester	'62-'67	RW	**Fred Glover**	Cleveland	'48-'68
	324 - 15 - 86 - 101 - 381				1,201 - 520 - 814 - 1,334 - 2,402		

Chalk Talk

"You should have seen the room when the players first came in. It was like they'd won the Stanley Cup."
Winnipeg coach Bill Sutherland after the Jets end an NHL-record 30-game winless streak

1981-82

Stanley Cup: New York Islanders

Wayne Gretzky beats Buffalo goalie Don Edwards for his record 77th goal of the season.

▶ IMPACT PERSON

Wayne Gretzky

Gretzky breaks Phil Esposito's record of 76 goals when he scores three times in the final 6:36 of a 6-3 win over Buffalo Feb. 24. The Oilers' superstar finishes with amazing 92-120-212 totals and signs a 21-year contract with Edmonton Jan. 30. "My father saw him play when he was 14 and told me: 'I've just watched the kid who's going to break all your records,'" Esposito says.

No. 1 STORY: Gretzky scores 92 goals and tops 200 points

Wayne Gretzky ravages the record book. He begins by scoring 50 goals in record time, hitting the magic mark in just 39 games. Gretzky puts an exclamation mark on the record by scoring five goals in game No. 39 against the Philadelphia Flyers. The 21-year-old prodigy finishes the season with 92 goals and shatters his own assists mark with 120. He becomes the first and only NHLer to top the 200-point plateau with 212, 48 more than his previous record. Gretzky helps Edmonton become the first team to score more than 400 goals in a season (417).

2. Soviets toy with Canadians in Canada Cup blowout

For the second time in three seasons, the Soviet national team embarrasses some of the NHL's best players, trouncing Canada 8-1 in the final of the Canada Cup tournament. Tourney organizer Alan Eagleson draws the champs' ire by refusing to allow them to take the trophy home. Canada defeats the Soviets 7-3 in round robin play and 3-2 in a pre-tourney test. "We beat them two out of three, but didn't win the one that counts," says Canadian defenseman Brian Engblom.

3. Playoff realignment intensifies divisional rivalries

The NHL changes its playoff format to emphasize divisional play. Instead of seeding teams one to 16, each division plays down to a champion, followed by a conference final, with the conference champs meeting for the Stanley Cup. The change creates an imbalance. Only two teams in the Campbell Conference have winning records while all four playoff teams in the Adams Division are over .500.

Royal Shocker

Los Angeles bumps off favored Edmonton in the first round of the playoffs. Down 5-0 in the last period of Game 3, L.A. ties it with five seconds left, then Darryl Evans wins it for the Kings 2:34 into OT. The comeback is dubbed the 'Miracle on Manchester.'

HOCKEY LISTS OF THE CENTURY
The Mt. Rushmore Of American Hockey

Detroit defenseman Reed Larson records the fifth of nine straight 55-plus point seasons in 1981-82. It is a mark equalled by only three other players (Phil Housley, 11 straight seasons, Ray Bourque and Paul Coffey, 15 each) and confirms his place among the best Americans ever in the NHL. Here are eight other seminal Americans in NHL history and when they played.

Player	
Frank Brimsek	'30s-'40s
One of best goalies ever	
Tommy Williams	'60s-'70s
Lone American for a time	
Rod Langway	'70s-'90s
Best defensive defenseman	
Joe Mullen	'80s-'90s
Most prolific goal-scorer	
Brian Lawton	'80s-'90s
First drafted No. 1 overall	
Pat LaFontaine	'80s-'90s
Paves way to major junior	
Phil Housley	'80s-'90s
Top offensive defenseman	
Tom Barrasso	'80s-'90s
Highly decorated goalie	

Chalk Talk

"Tretiak has been the dominant goalie in hockey for the past 10 years. We knew he wasn't going to fold if his teammates gave him a two-goal lead."
Team Canada's Denis Potvin, on the great Soviet goalie, after losing 8-1 in the Canada Cup final

Denis Potvin celebrates the Islanders' fourth consecutive Cup.

1982-83

Stanley Cup: New York Islanders

No. 1 STORY: Islander Cup dynasty hits four years

The New York Islanders make it look easy, sweeping aside the upstart Edmonton Oilers in a four-game final, and holding scoring champion Wayne Gretzky goalless, to join the Montreal Canadiens as the only NHL teams to win four straight Stanley Cups. Immediately, talk begins of the Canadiens' record of five consecutive Cups (1956-60). "Our guys are never satisfied," says Islanders' GM Bill Torrey. "Who knows how long they'll keep it up?"

2. Brain hemorrhage ends Leveille's career

In a tragic end to a brief career, Boston Bruins' forward Normand Leveille, 19, collapses Oct. 23 during the first intermission in Vancouver. He's rushed to hospital and found to have suffered a brain hemorrhage. The 1981 first round draft pick is left partially paralyzed and his career is over after just 75 games. Almost 13 years later at the Boston Garden closing ceremony, Leveille receives a standing ovation as he skates on to the ice with the help of Bruin greats Ray Bourque and Terry O'Reilly.

3. Draft day blues for St. Louis

The St. Louis Blues seem destined to relocate to the Canadian prairies when they are sold to Saskatoon, Sask., interests April 19. When NHL governors vote 15-3 to reject the sale, team owners Ralston Purina begin the process of liquidating the franchise and the Blues don't participate in the NHL entry draft. The league assumes control of the team and sells it to Harry Ornest in July for the bargain basement price of $3 million.

▶ IMPACT PERSON

Billy Smith

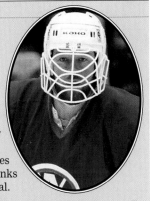

His numbers are seldom the best during the regular season, but there's no better netminder than Smith in the playoffs. 'Battlin' Billy' puts a punctuation mark on his importance to the Isles, winning the Conn Smythe Trophy with a playoff-best 2.68 GAA. He becomes the first goalie in 99 games to shut out the Oilers when he blanks them 2-0 in Game 1 of the Cup final.

Great Assistance

Wayne Gretzky not only sets a new high for assists (125), he matches Bill Cowley's 1940-41 record of earning more assists than anyone has points. Runner-up Peter Stastny's 124 points are a record 72 behind Gretzky's 196 points.

HOCKEY LISTS OF THE CENTURY High (School) Jumpers

Phil Housley jumps directly from high school hockey to the NHL, the second of three straight American schoolboys drafted in the first round to do so. Here are the details behind an amazing period in NHL draft history. Listed are draft number, first NHL year games, goals, assists, points, win-loss-tie mark and goals-against average.

Draft	No.	Player	High School Team	NHL Team	GP	G	A	P
1981	3rd	Bobby Carpenter, C	St. John's (Mass.)	Washington	80	32	35	67
1982	6th	Phil Housley, D	South St. Paul (Minn.)	Buffalo	77	19	47	66
1983	5th	Tom Barrasso, G	Acton-Boxboro (Mass.)	Buffalo	26-12-33, 2.84			

*Housley is second in rookie-of-the-year voting; Barrasso is rookie of the year

Chalk Talk

"The Oilers are so damn cocky. The thing that really bugs me is they don't give us any respect. The Flyers respect us. So do the Rangers and Bruins. Edmonton doesn't respect anyone."
Islander Bob Bourne's opinion of the Oilers

Bruce Bennett/BBS

1983-84

Stanley Cup: Edmonton Oilers

Conn Smythe-winning Mark Messier, Edmonton Oilers

Bruce Bennett/BBS

▶ IMPACT PERSON

Paul Coffey

The most productive blueliner since Bobby Orr, Coffey ranks second in NHL scoring with 40 goals and 126 points. "(Edmonton coach) Glen (Sather) tells me he doesn't mind me carrying the puck," Coffey says. Despite his extraordinary numbers, Coffey places second to Washington's Rod Langway in Norris voting.

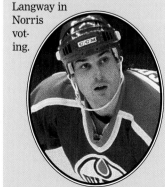

O-Pee-Chee Collection/HHOF

No. 1 STORY: 1. Edmonton strikes oil to win first Stanley Cup

The cocky Edmonton Oilers continue to rewrite the record book. Wayne Gretzky sets NHL records for goals per game (1.18), assists per game (1.59) and points per game (2.77) and runs up a record 51-game scoring streak. Regular season and playoffs combined, he scores 100 goals. Teammates Jari Kurri and Glenn Anderson join him in the 50-goal club, while Paul Coffey scores 40 as Edmonton finishes with a record 446 goals. Art Ross runner-up Coffey scores the most points (126) for a defenseman since Bobby Orr, but finishes a record 79 points behind Gretzky (205). The Mark Messier-led Oilers continue the assault in the playoffs, ending the New York Islanders' dynasty, to bring the Stanley Cup to Edmonton for the first time.

2. NHL works OT back into regular season

After a 41-year hiatus, overtime is reintroduced to NHL regular season games with a five-minute sudden-death period. Although 54 of 140 games are decided in the extra session, not everyone is a fan of the brief period. "Five minutes of overtime is like 15 seconds of sex," says New York Islanders' GM Bill Torrey. "If we're going to have overtime, then let's play to a finish."

3. Rookie Barrasso raises bar in Buffalo

Jumping from Acton-Boxboro high school in Massachusetts, Buffalo Sabres' goalie Tom Barrasso, 18, surprises with a 26-12-3 record and 2.84 goals-against average, earning first all-star status and winning both the Calder and Vezina Trophies. Barrasso, Frank Brimsek (1939) and Tony Esposito (1970) are the only three goalies to win both trophies in the same year.

Mickey Mouse Club

Wayne Gretzky accuses New Jersey of "putting a Mickey Mouse operation on the ice", after the Oilers blast the Devils 13-4 Nov. 19. To show their disgust, New Jersey fans don Mickey Mouse ears on Edmonton's next visit.

HOCKEY LISTS OF THE CENTURY
Dynasty Means At Least Three Cups

Edmonton ends one dynasty and begins another with its Stanley Cup win over the New York Islanders. The NHL has seen the rise and fall of eight dynasties.

Team	Cups
Tor. '47, '48, '49	3
Broda's Leafs lose five playoff games in three years	
Det. '50, '52, '54, '55	4
Howe powers overwhelming Red Wings	
Mon. '56, '57, '58, '59, '60	5
Rocket Richard's Canadiens are best-ever NHL team	
Tor. '62, '63, '64	3
Armstrong's veteran team saves best for playoffs	
Mon. '65, '66, '68, '69	4
Beliveau's big red machine wins four times	
Mon. '76, '77, '78, '79	4
Lafleur's Habs do it with style and grace	
NYI '80, '81, '82, '83	4
Potvin's gritty Islanders beat 'em every which way	
Edm. '84, '85, '87, '88	4
Gretzky's goal-scorers rack up four Cups	

Chalk Talk

"No question, I can see we're going to try to keep this Cup in Edmonton. It's going to be awfully tough to get it out of here."

Edmonton owner Peter Pocklington, after his Oilers win the Stanley Cup

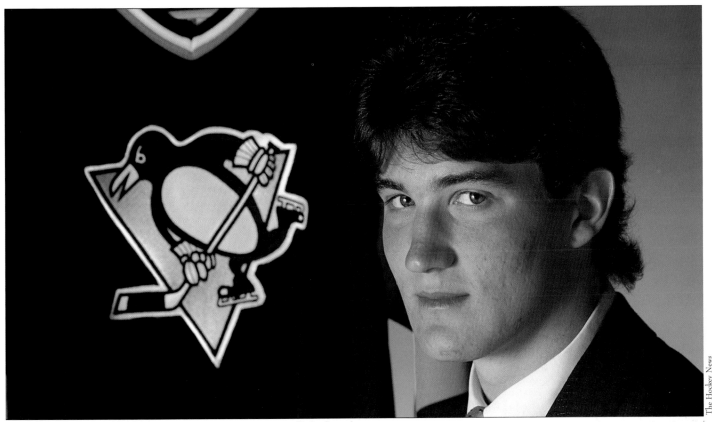

Mario Lemieux, Pittsburgh Penguins' 1984 No. 1 overall draft pick

Star Spangled Cap

Washington's Bobby Carpenter–the first American drafted in the first round and first high schooler to go directly to the NHL (1981-82)–becomes the first American to score 50 goals (53), the highest total of his career.

Chalk Talk

"We should attach a bucket of chicken to the net, or some hamburgers. If we're going to have water bottles, let's have lunch."

Edmonton coach Glen Sather, complaining about the water bottle Flyers' goalie Pelle Lindbergh keeps on his net

No. 1 STORY: Lemieux brings magic to Pittsburgh

After scoring 282 points in his last junior season at Laval, Mario Lemieux, the most heralded draft prospect since Guy Lafleur, goes to the Pittsburgh Penguins first overall in the entry draft. Viewed as the savior of a franchise that hasn't won a playoff series since 1979, Lemieux declines to go to the podium when his name is called. "I didn't want to shake the hand of (Penguins' GM) Eddie Johnston if he does not want to give me a good contract," says Lemieux, who later signs a three-year, $600,000 deal. He scores on his first NHL shift and finishes with 100 points to win the Calder Trophy.

2. Coffey saves Team Canada's bacon

Canada is on the ropes when Soviet players Vladimir Kovin and Alexander Skvortsov get a two-on-one break in overtime of the Canada Cup semifinals. But Paul Coffey makes a game-saving block on Kovin's pass. Seconds later, fans at the Calgary Saddledome go wild when Coffey's shot deflects in off Mike Bossy to give Canada a 3-2 win. Canada goes on to beat Sweden in straight games in an anti-climactic best-of-three final, reclaiming world hockey supremacy after its Canada Cup loss in 1981.

3. Superstars Lafleur, Clarke retire

Frustrated over reduced playing time under coach and former linemate Jacques Lemaire, Guy Lafleur, 33, retires Nov. 26. Captain Bob Gainey says Lafleur is still physically better than most players. Philadelphia Flyers' star Bobby Clarke, 35, becomes Flyers' GM after retiring in the summer of '84. He hires Mike Keenan as coach and, led by Vezina winner Pelle Lindbergh, the Flyers reach the Cup final.

▶ IMPACT PERSON

Jari Kurri

Playing with Wayne Gretzky is a great way to get points, if not attention, but Kurri's 71 goals sets an NHL mark for right wingers. He's the third NHLer to post a 70-goal campaign, joining Gretzky and Phil Esposito. The flying Finn also equals Reggie Leach's Stanley Cup record with 19 goals, including a playoff-record four hat tricks.

1985-86 Stanley Cup: Montreal Canadiens

Bruce Bennett/BBS

Paul Coffey, Edmonton Oilers

▶ IMPACT PERSON

Wayne Gretzky

Gretzky breaks his own points record for the third time and the assists mark for the fifth time with 52-163-215 totals to win the Art Ross and Hart Trophies. Gretzky's assist total is 22 higher than second-place finisher Mario Lemieux's point total. The NHL's only 200-point scorer ever, Gretzky has now done it four times in five seasons.

Bruce Bennett/BBS

No. 1 STORY: Smith gaffe ends Oilers' Cup streak

In a bid to slow down the high-flying Edmonton Oilers, the NHL changes its rule to allow for substitutions during offsetting penalties–effectively limiting four-on-four manpower situations. Still, the Oilers roar to their fifth straight Smythe Division title. But they lose in the division final, blowing a 2-0 third period lead in Game 7 against the Calgary Flames. Defenseman Steve Smith's clearing attempt bounces into the Edmonton net off goalie Grant Fuhr and Calgary wins 3-2, ending Edmonton's two-year Cup reign. "I don't know if I'll ever live this down, but I will have to keep on living," Smith says.

2. Coffey breaks Orr's goal record

It's a mark that looks unbeatable, but Edmonton's Paul Coffey surpasses Bobby Orr's 1974-75 defenseman record of 46 goals when he scores his 46th and 47th April 2 against the Vancouver Canucks. Coffey finishes with 48 and his 138 points are one shy of Orr's record for points (1970-71). Coffey, who wins his second straight Norris Trophy, also has an eight-point outing in a March 14 win over the Detroit Red Wings, tying Tom Bladon's 1977-78 record.

3. Lindbergh killed in car accident

After celebrating the club's 10th straight victory with a night on the town, 26-year-old Philadelphia Flyers' goalie Pelle Lindbergh dies after crashing his Porsche into a concrete wall. It's determined he was driving 60 miles per hour in a 35 mph zone. His blood-alcohol level is measured at .24, twice the legal limit. "We'd sat him down and talked to him about driving fast," says Flyers' GM Bob Clarke. "But when you're that young and that strong, you just feel invincible."

GM Gets His Man

After serving one year in prison for vehicular manslaughter, former Bruin Craig MacTavish is signed by Edmonton. "I'm not a do-gooder," says Oilers' GM Glen Sather. "I want him because he's a whale of a player."

HOCKEY LISTS OF THE CENTURY
99 Raises Bar To Best-Ever Levels

Wayne Gretzky sets single-season standards for goals, assists and points nine times during a six-year period of unprecedented statistical domination in the 1980s. Already the owner of the NHL assist and point records from 1980-81, 'The Great One' smashes all three marks in 1981-82. Gretzky's best single-season totals during his career destroy the NHL's previous goal, assist and point records before he entered the league in 1979-80 with Edmonton.

Single-Season Standards

Goals	
Phil Esposito, Bos., '70-71	76
W. Gretzky, Edm., '81-82	92
Per-cent Increase	17%

Assists	
Bobby Orr, Bos., '70-71	102
W. Gretzky, Edm., '85-86	163
Per-cent Increase	60%

Points	
Phil Esposito, Bos., '70-71	152
W. Gretzky, Edm., '85-86	215
Per-cent Increase	41%

Chalk Talk

"Who am I going to trade him for–Lee Trevino?"

Philadelphia GM Bobby Clarke on Flyers' forward Todd Bergen, who quits the team, insisting he'll pursue a career on the PGA Tour

Toronto's Borje Salming is cut by a skate for more than 200 stitches.

1986-87

Stanley Cup: Edmonton Oilers

No. 1 STORY: Junior players die in bus crash

Traveling to Regina for a Dec. 30 Western League game, the bus carrying the Swift Current Broncos careens out of control on a curve, flips over and slams to the ground on its right side. Four players–Scott Kruger, 19, Trent Kresse, 20, Chris Mantyka, 19 and Brent Ruff, 16–are killed. Among the survivors are future NHLers Joe Sakic and Sheldon Kennedy. The Broncos regroup from the tragedy, finish the season and, in 1989, win the Memorial Cup.

2. Rendez-vous '87 masterpiece on ice

For the second time, the All-Star Game takes on an NHL vs. Soviet Union format as the league's stars and Soviets' best clash in an exciting two-game series in Quebec City. "That was hockey the way it's supposed to be played," Wayne Gretzky says after the NHL and the USSR split, 4-3 for the NHL and 5-3 for the Soviets. Twenty-year-old Soviet star Valeri Kamensky sparkles in the second game, scoring two brilliant second period goals to give his team a 3-1 lead.

3. Junior tournament punch-up ends in darkness

Leading the Soviets 4-2 on the last day of the World Junior Championship in Piestany, Czechoslovakia, Canada will take the gold medal if it wins by five goals. But a vicious, bench-clearing brawl erupts in the second period. Referee Hans Ronning of Norway leaves the ice with his linesmen, and the lights are turned out. In the aftermath, both teams are disqualified and Finland is awarded its first gold medal at the event.

▶ IMPACT PERSON

Ron Hextall

A third generation NHLer, whose grandfather Bryan Hextall Sr. won the 1941-42 scoring title, this Hextall prevents goals. The Philadelphia rookie wins the Vezina Trophy and records 106 PIM, a new mark for goalies. Hextall backstops the Flyers to the Stanley Cup final. Although they lose in seven games to Edmonton, he's awarded the Conn Smythe Trophy.

New Iron Man

After playing 11-plus seasons without missing a game, Hartford's Doug Jarvis breaks Garry Unger's ironman record of 914 straight games Dec. 26. Jarvis wins the Masterton Trophy for dedication to hockey.

HOCKEY LISTS OF THE CENTURY 7th Decade All-Stars

Edmonton and the Islanders combine for seven Stanley Cups during the NHL's seventh decade (1977-78 through 1986-87) and take seven spots on THN's all-star teams.

The Hockey News' First Team		The Hockey News' Second Team	
G	**Billy Smith**, NYI *Money goalie*	G	**Grant Fuhr**, Edm. *Big save 'keeper*
D	**Ray Bourque**, Bos. *All-around all-star*	D	**Denis Potvin**, NYI *Captain of dynasty*
D	**Paul Coffey**, Edm. *Blazing speed*	D	**Larry Robinson**, Mon. *'Big Bird'*
LW	**Michel Goulet**, Que. *Accurate sniper*	LW	**Mark Messier**, Edm. *All-time leader*
C	**Wayne Gretzky**, Edm. *The Greatest*	C	**Bryan Trottier**, NYI *Two-way player*
RW	**Mike Bossy**, NYI *Lightning release*	RW	**Jari Kurri**, Edm. *The Finn-isher*

Chalk Talk

"It's not important that Team NHL did not win this series, or that the Soviet Union did not win this series. What is important is that hockey was the winner."

Soviet coach Viktor Tikhonov following Rendez-vous '87

1987-88

Stanley Cup: Edmonton Oilers

Mario Lemieux scores the '87 Canada Cup-winning goal; it's his record 11th goal of the tournament.

▶ IMPACT PERSON

Ray Bourque

Bourque earns his ninth consecutive all-star berth and second straight Norris Trophy in 1987-88. The Bruins make the Cup final for the first time in 10 years. By the end of the 1999-2000 season, new Colorado defenseman Bourque has 1,520 career points, seven shy of Paul Coffey's record for most points by a defenseman (1,527).

No. 1 STORY: Lemieux and Gretzky Canada's dynamic duo

Three exciting 6-5 games decide the Canada Cup final between Canada and the Soviets, with the teams splitting two OT verdicts. The score is tied 5-5 late in Game 3 when Canada's Wayne Gretzky, Mario Lemieux and Larry Murphy get a three-on-one break. Gretzky feeds Lemieux a perfect pass and Super Mario blasts the puck past Sergei Mylnikov at 18:34, sending fans at Hamilton's Copps Coliseum into hysteria. It's a coming-of-age party for Lemieux, who scores the deciding goal in both Canadian wins. Later in the season the Pittsburgh Penguins' center wrests the Art Ross and Hart Trophies away from Gretzky.

2. Donutgate leaves NHL in hole

Angry following a 6-1 loss to the Boston Bruins in Game 3 of the Wales Conference final, New Jersey Devils' coach Jim Schoenfeld confronts referee Don Koharski, calling him a "fat pig" and suggesting he "have another donut." Schoenfeld is suspended by the NHL, but gets a court injunction and is back for Game 4. NHL officials refuse to work the game and amateurs are used in their place as the league endures one of its most embarrassing moments ever. NHL president John Ziegler can't be found to help resolve the issue.

3. Penguins brew up Coffey deal

Edmonton GM Glen Sather makes the first move in the undoing of the Oilers' dynasty. Demanding to renegotiate his contract, two-time Norris Trophy-winning defenseman Paul Coffey holds out and is shipped Nov. 24 to Pittsburgh in a seven-player deal.

Soviet streak ends

After clinching the Olympic gold medal two days earlier in round-robin play, the Soviets fall behind 1-0 to Finland and lose their final game 2-1. It's the first time the Soviets have trailed in an Olympic match since their 4-3 upset loss to the U.S. in 1980.

HOCKEY LISTS OF THE CENTURY
He Shoots, He Scores And Still Makes Saves

Philadelphia's Ron Hextall becomes the first NHL goalie to shoot in a goal, Dec. 8 against Boston. Even before Hextall scores, he heralds the dawn of a new era of goalies handling the puck. The game has never seen a goalie who shoots as hard as some forwards. Before Hextall, Billy Smith was awarded a 1979 goal when he was the last Islander to touch the puck before Colorado scored into its own net. The first pro goalie who actually shoots the puck in the net for a goal is Michel Plasse, who makes history in a 1970-71 Central League game. Listed are NHL goalies credited with goals.

Goalie	Yr.
Billy Smith, NYI	'78-79
Ron Hextall, Phi.	'87-88
Ron Hextall, Phi.	'88-89
Chris Osgood, Det.	'95-96
Martin Brodeur, NJ	'96-97
Damian Rhodes, Ott.	'98-99
Martin Brodeur, NJ	'99-00

Chalk Talk

"This is my greatest thrill ever. I think I've answered a few questions in this tournament."

Pittsburgh's Mario Lemieux silences his critics with 11 goals in the Canada Cup

Ciccarelli Jailed

Minnesota winger Dino Ciccarelli serves a day in jail and is fined $1,000 for clobbering Toronto's Luke Richardson with his stick during a game Jan. 19. It's a rare conviction for an on-ice offense in NHL history.

HOCKEY LISTS OF THE CENTURY
The Great One Bests Other Five

Wayne Gretzky outscores all five assets Edmonton obtains in the Aug. 9 trade by 148 points over the remainder of his career. They are Jimmy Carson, Martin Gelinas, Jason Miller, Martin Rucinsky and Nick Stajduhar. Edmonton wins one post-Gretzky Cup, but Los Angeles has a better post-trade regular season record than the Oilers over the remaining 11 seasons of 99's career. Listed are games, goals, assists, points, wins, losses, ties and winning percentages.

The Great One

Gretzky	791	311	877	1,188

The Traded Ones

Carson	466	183	192	375
Gelinas	663	181	176	357
Miller	6	0	0	0
Rucinsky	462	126	182	308
Stajduhar	2	0	0	0
Totals	1,599	490	550	1,040

Post-Trade '88-89 – '98-99

Team	W	L	T	WP
L.A.	361	389	114	.484
Edmonton	351	410	103	.466

Chalk Talk

"I didn't test the market, but I heard scalpers were getting $500 or $1,000 for a good pair."

Canadiens' winger Mike McPhee on the return of Guy Lafleur to the Forum in Rangers' colors, Feb. 4

Wayne Gretzky, Los Angeles Kings

Bruce Bennett/BBS

No. 1 STORY: Gretzky says goodbye to Edmonton

It was rumored for days, but even after it happens people can't believe it–the Edmonton Oilers trade Wayne Gretzky. On Aug. 9, 1988, the seven-time scoring champ and eight-time Hart Trophy winner goes to the Los Angeles Kings with Mike Krushelnyski and Marty McSorley for Jimmy Carson and Martin Gelinas, three first round draft picks and $15 million. The media says Oilers' owner Peter Pocklington needs the cash, but 'Peter Puck' claims it was Gretzky's idea. "The people to blame, I guess, are myself, Pocklington and (Kings' owner Bruce) McNall," Gretzky says. "We're the people who created the transaction."

2. Lemieux within one of 200 points

At 23, Mario Lemieux scores 85 goals and wins his second straight scoring title. His assists (114) and points (199) are the highest in NHL history for any player other than Wayne Gretzky. His most impressive effort comes New Year's Eve against the New Jersey Devils. He scores for the cycle–five goals in five different situations–at even strength, on the power play, short-handed, on a penalty shot and into an empty net.

3. Soviets irate after Mogilny defection

Unheralded Soviet Sergei Priakhin, 25, debuts with the Calgary Flames March 31 with his federation's blessing, but when the talented Alexander Mogilny, 20, defects May 4 and signs with the Buffalo Sabres, Soviet officials cry foul. After the World Championship in Sweden, Mogilny surreptitiously leaves his hotel and flies to the U.S. with Sabres' GM Gerry Meehan and player development director Don Luce. The Soviets call him a traitor.

▶ **IMPACT PERSON**

Wayne Gretzky

Los Angeles has had only two winning seasons in the 1980s. But with Gretzky scoring 54 goals and 168 points, the Kings post a 42-31-7 record. Attendance at the Forum jumps more than 3,000 per game. Gretzky averages two points per game in the playoffs as the Kings oust Edmonton, before losing to eventual Cup-champion Calgary.

Bruce Bennett/BBS

Viacheslav Fetisov, New Jersey Devils

1989-90

Stanley Cup: Edmonton Oilers

No. 1 STORY: Soviet invasion begins in NHL

Following years of negotiations, the Soviet Ice Hockey Federation agrees to release veterans to the NHL. Center Igor Larionov, 28, and left winger Vladimir Krutov, 29, sign with the Vancouver Canucks. Defensemen Viacheslav Fetisov, 31, and Sergei Starikov, 30, join the New Jersey Devils and right winger Sergei Makarov, 31, goes to the Calgary Flames. Larionov, Fetisov and Makarov make big contributions, but Krutov is cut loose by the Canucks and Starikov lasts just 16 games with the Devils.

2. 'The Great One' passes 'Mr. Hockey'

Los Angeles Kings' megastar Wayne Gretzky treats his Oiler fans when he overtakes Gordie Howe as the NHL career scoring leader in a 5-4 victory in Edmonton Oct. 15. He records a first period assist to tie Howe's 1,850 points and, with 53 seconds left to play, sets the record by beating Oilers' goalie Bill Ranford to send the game into overtime. The crowd gives the former Oiler a five-minute standing ovation. Gretzky adds the overtime winner.

3. Eagleson on the way out as NHLPA leader

Three major events combine to change the course of events in NHL Players' Association history. First, executive director Alan Eagleson loses the players' support and agrees to step down, effective Dec. 31, 1991. Second, at the 1990 All-Star Game in Pittsburgh, the players name hard-nosed Detroit lawyer Bob Goodenow to succeed Eagleson. And third, the players agree to salary disclosure, a primary catalyst for salary escalation. Players release a salary survey for the first time in February.

▶ **IMPACT PERSON**

Igor Larionov
Writing an article critical of the Soviet system, the national team center lights the fire that leads to freedom for Soviet veterans. Larionov is temporarily dropped from the national team, as is captain Viacheslav Fetisov. But in the end, they win the battle and Larionov collects 44 points for Vancouver in his first NHL season.

Bruce Bennett/BBS

Bruce Bennett/BBS

Ruskie Rookie

Tongues wag when Calgary's Sergei Makarov, with 11 years of international experience, is named rookie of the year at 31. The NHL rules that, in future, no player who starts the season at 26 or older will be eligible.

HOCKEY LISTS OF THE CENTURY Pink Power Prevails

Women's hockey takes a leap forward at the first Women's World Championship in 1990. Canada wears pink and defeats the U.S. in a thriller before a capacity crowd in Ottawa. Listed are five key players from the most important decade in women's hockey.

Player	Mark in the Game
1. **Manon Rheaume**, G, Canada	Raises level of consciousness with brief pro stint
2. **Cammi Granato**, C, USA	Highest-scoring and best-known American ever
3. **Geraldine Heaney**, D, Canada	Recognized as best player much of decade
4. **France St-Louis**, C, Canada	Tremendous athlete cornerstone of program
5. **Karyn Bye**, RW, USA	Hard shooter consistently among world's elite

Chalk Talk

"Sometimes in the dearness of his heart he just had trouble making the right decisions."

Former Toronto star Darryl Sittler, after the death of controversial owner Harold Ballard

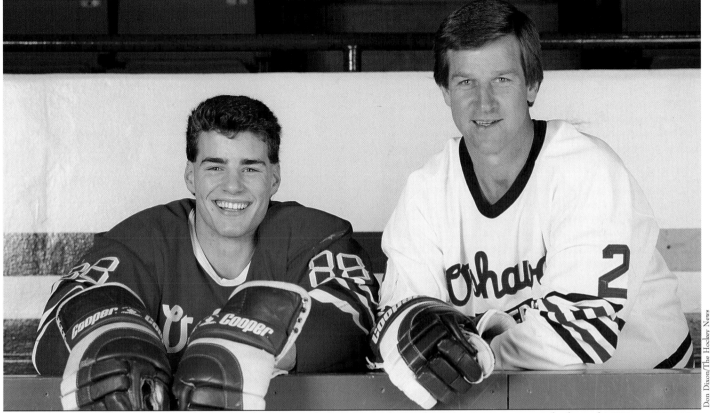

Eric Lindros and Bobby Orr, the best players in Oshawa Generals' history: Lindros is the Ontario League scoring leader and MVP in 1990-91.

Don Dixon/The Hockey News

Sergei Wings It

Slipping away from the Soviet national team at the Goodwill Games in Seattle, star center Sergei Fedorov, 20, signs with Detroit July 24, 1990. In 1993-94, Fedorov will become the first Russian to win the Hart Trophy.

Chalk Talk

"It was sick. I was nearly crying that people would use this as some kind of humor."

Blues' defenseman Paul Cavallini, who loses the tip of a finger in a game, then learns it is being auctioned off by a St. Louis radio station

No. 1 STORY: Lemieux backs Pens to first Stanley Cup

Pittsburgh Penguins' captain Mario Lemieux misses the first 50 games with a back injury, but the club keeps battling under new coach Bob Johnson to win the Patrick Division, a franchise first. Aided by new arrivals Ron Francis and Ulf Samuelsson, Pittsburgh wins its first Stanley Cup, ousting the Minnesota North Stars in six games in the final. Lemieux wins the Conn Smythe Trophy with 44 points in 23 games, the second-most points in NHL playoff history.

2. North Stars find way to San Jose

The first franchise split in NHL history is arranged: it's revealed that the North Stars will be divided into two teams after 1990-91, with the Gund brothers selling the team in exchange for a new franchise in San Jose. The roster will be split to stock the teams and an expansion draft held for both clubs. Bobby Clarke, fired as the Philadelphia Flyers' GM, takes over in Minnesota and hires Bob Gainey as coach. Meanwhile, the league grants new franchises to Ottawa (Senators) and Tampa Bay (Lightning) for the 1992-93 season.

3. Stevens' signing causes outrage

Sparks fly when the St. Louis Blues sign restricted free agent defenseman Scott Stevens to a four-year, $5.145-million contract, surrendering five first round draft picks as compensation. "It scares the hell out of me," says Vancouver Canucks' GM Pat Quinn, of how the deal might affect the NHL salary structure. Stevens' stay in St. Louis doesn't last long. One season later, he's awarded as compensation to New Jersey after St. Louis signs another free agent–Brendan Shanahan.

▶ **IMPACT PERSON**

Brett Hull

After scoring an NHL-leading 86 goals, a record for right wingers, Brett joins dad Bobby as the only father-son combo to win Hart Trophies. Hull joins another exclusive group, the 50-goals-in-50-games club, scoring his 50th in game No. 49: "This is the most exciting thing that has happened to me," he says after the goal. "I was in dreamland."

Bruce Bennett/BBS

1991-92

Stanley Cup: Pittsburgh Penguins

NHL president John Ziegler, left, and NHLPA executive director Bob Goodenow announce peace plans.

Scott Levy/BBS

▶ IMPACT PERSON

Eric Lindros

Picked first overall by Quebec in the 1991 entry draft, the 18-year-old center refuses to join the Nordiques, who after the season trade him twice in the same day–to Philadelphia and the Rangers. It's ruled June 30 Lindros is the property of the Flyers. Lindros costs Philadelphia six players, two first round picks and $15 million.

Doug MacLellan/HHOF

No. 1 STORY: Stanley Cup threatened by 10-day walkout

It's no April Fool's joke when players walk off the job for the first time April 1. With the playoffs in jeopardy, the league and NHL Players' Association reach an agreement April 10, saving the NHL's 75th season. The NHL makes concessions in card-licensing monies and free agency, grants a 15 per-cent raise in the minimum salary and a guarantee no salary cap will be installed. "I believe we got the best deal under the circumstances," says Toronto's Ken Baumgartner, a member of the NHLPA bargaining committee.

2. Penguins rally after Badger Bob's death

On the eve of the 1991 Canada Cup, U.S. coach 'Badger' Bob Johnson of Stanley Cup-champion Pittsburgh Penguins is diagnosed with a brain tumor, an illness which claims his life Nov. 26. The American team tries desperately to win the tourney for him, but falls short losing to Canada in the final. "His will was contagious and I think his spirit will be contagious for a long time," says Penguins' center Bryan Trottier. Player development director Scotty Bowman, the NHL's winningest coach, takes over and, after a rough start, leads Pittsburgh to a second straight Cup.

3. Record deal brings Gilmour to Toronto

Doug Gilmour is the big prize in a 10-player trade, the largest in NHL history. The Calgary Flames send Gilmour, Jamie Macoun, Rick Wamsley, Ric Nattress and Kent Manderville to Toronto Jan 2. for Gary Leeman, Alexander Godynyuk, Jeff Reese, Michel Petit and Craig Berube. Gilmour brings respectability back to the Maple Leafs, leading Toronto to the semi-finals the next two seasons.

94

Passing Potvin

Paul Coffey breaks Denis Potvin's career assists and points records for a defenseman on the same night. Coffey's two assists in Pittsburgh's 8-5 win over the Islanders Oct. 17 puts him over Potvin's totals of 742 assists and 1,052 points.

HOCKEY LISTS OF THE CENTURY
Canada Dominates Cup History

Will it be remembered as the Canada Cup or Canada's Cup. The founding nation beats the U.S. in 1991, claiming its fourth title in five events. The Soviets win just once, demolishing Canada 8-1 in the 1981 final. It's the U.S., however, that wins the newly named World Cup in 1996. Here's what you need to know about the tournament recognized as the unofficial world championship...by North Americans anyway.

Tournament Records
Most goals
Mario Lemieux, 11, '87
Most assists
Wayne Gretzky, 18, '87
Most points
Wayne Gretzky, 21, '87
Best goals-against average
Vladislav Tretiak, 1.33, '81
Most Valuable Players
Bobby Orr, '76, Vladislav Tretiak, '81, John Tonelli, '84 (MVPs only named three times)

Chalk Talk

"I thought I was going to be able to tell everybody I had a fight at Caesar's Palace, but Marty McSorley and Jay Miller didn't dress."

Rangers' Tie Domi, after a pre-season game with L.A. on an outdoor rink at the Las Vegas casino

First For Females

Goalie Manon Rheaume is the first woman to play in a game involving two NHL teams, seeing a period of action with Tampa Bay in a Sept. 23 exhibition against St. Louis. She faces nine shots and surrenders two goals.

HOCKEY LISTS OF THE CENTURY

NHL's Ultimate Roll: Stanley Cup Winners

From the Montreal Shamrocks, who win the first Stanley Cup of the century in 1900, to the New Jersey Devils, who win the last in 2000, here are the leaders in Cup victories. Included are pre-NHL champions (1899-1900 through 1916-17) as appropriate and all Original Six teams. Any team that has captured two Cups or more is included.

Team	No.
Montreal Canadiens	24
Toronto Maple Leafs	13
Detroit Red Wings	9
Boston Bruins	5
Edmonton Oilers	5
New York Islanders	4
New York Rangers	4
Ottawa Silver Seven	4
Montreal Wanderers	4
Chicago Blackhawks	3
Philadelphia Flyers	2
Pittsburgh Penguins	2
Quebec Bulldogs	2
Montreal A.A.A.	2
Winnipeg Victorias	2
Ottawa Senators	2
New Jersey Devils	2

Chalk Talk

"He's the whole package, Mario (Lemieux) and Wayne (Gretzky), they don't play a physical game."

Philadelphia winger Mark Recchi, assessing rookie teammate Eric Lindros

Manon Rheaume, pioneer goalie

No. 1 STORY: Lemieux makes incredible recovery from cancer

A superhuman player faces a very human ordeal as Pittsburgh Penguins' superstar Mario Lemieux is diagnosed Jan. 11 with Hodgkin's disease–cancer of the lymph nodes. "It's scary when you hear that word, cancer," Lemieux says. He makes an amazing recovery following surgery and radiation treatments, returning March 2 against the Philadelphia Flyers. He scores a goal and an assist after having a radiation treatment in the morning. He leads the Penguins to the longest winning streak in NHL history–17 games from March 9-April 10. Lemieux scores 56 points in his final 20 games to overtake the Buffalo Sabres' Pat Lafontaine for the Art Ross Trophy. He is also awarded the Hart and Masterton at season's end.

2. Bettman named NHL commissioner

Gary Bettman, vice-president of the National Basketball Association, switches from roundballs to round pucks when he's named the NHL's first commissioner Dec. 11. He starts his job Feb. 1, taking over from Gil Stein, who has served as interim president since John Ziegler resigned in June. "I believe the opportunities that face this league are virtually limitless," Bettman says.

3. NHL homes get warmer and warmer

Two new teams, the Ottawa Senators and Tampa Bay Lightning, begin play, while two other cities–Miami (Florida Panthers) and Anaheim (the Mighty Ducks) are awarded franchises Dec. 10, to begin play in 1993-94. Another team heads south at the end of the season, when the Minnesota North Stars announce they are relocating to Dallas.

▶ **IMPACT PERSON**

Teemu Selanne

The Winnipeg Jets' right winger becomes the most prolific rookie scorer in NHL history. Selanne shatters Mike Bossy's goal-scoring record of 53 with a hat trick March 2 against Quebec and finishes with 76 goals and 132 points, another record. Selanne sets or ties 16 Jets' marks and wins the Calder Trophy.

1993-94

Stanley Cup: New York Rangers

Goal No. 802: Wayne Gretzky takes over lead in all major career and single-season offensive categories.

▶ IMPACT PERSON

Mark Messier

It's not as dramatic as Babe Ruth's called shot home run in 1932, but Mark Messier's guarantee of a win in Game 6 of the conference final against New Jersey is a treasured moment in New York sports lore. Messier backs up his vow with three goals in a 4-2 victory. The Rangers win the series and edge Vancouver in the Cup final.

No. 1 STORY: Rangers end 54-year Stanley Cup jinx

The endless chants of "1940" stop at Madison Square Garden, as the New York Rangers score a seven-game Stanley Cup final win over Vancouver, their first title since 1939-40. Mike Keenan coaches his first Cup winner, but the party's barely over when he signs as coach-GM of the St. Louis Blues. The Rangers charge Keenan with breach of contract. The NHL fines the Blues and Detroit Red Wings–who also negotiate with him–for tampering. Keenan is suspended 60 days and the Blues' Petr Nedved is awarded to the Rangers in exchange for Esa Tikkanen and Doug Lidster as part of a compensation package.

2. Gretzky shoots past Howe's goal mark

In his last truly great season, Los Angeles Kings' center Wayne Gretzky becomes the greatest goal-scorer in NHL history. His goal against Vancouver Canucks' goalie Kirk McLean March 23 is No. 802, surpassing Gordie Howe's NHL career mark. Gretzky had previously overtaken Howe on the all-time lists of leaders in assists and points. The Great One wins his 10th and last Art Ross Trophy with 130 points, but he misses the playoffs for the first time in his career.

3. Sweden's Olympic win gets stamp of approval

Peter Forsberg becomes a folk hero in Sweden, scoring a spectacular goal in a shootout of the final game to give his country its first Olympic gold medal. Forsberg's incredible one-handed, backhand goal on Canada's Corey Hirsch is commemorated on a Swedish stamp, but Hirsch refuses permission to have his image on it.

HOCKEY LISTS OF THE CENTURY
International Ice: 10 Euro Memories

Two handfuls of highlights.
 1. **'98 Olympics** Hasek carries Czech Republic to Olympic gold in Nagano.
 2. **'94 Olympics** Forsberg's shootout goal gives Swedes first gold.
 3. **'81 Canada Cup** Soviets humiliate Team Canada 8-1 in final game.
 4. **'74 WHA Series** Soviets beat new league's best Canadians 4-1-3.
 5. **'79 Challenge Cup** Soviets embarrass NHL all-stars 6-0 in final.
 6. **'92 Olympics** Soviet Union breaks up, but Unified Team wins gold.
 7. **'87 Rendez-vous** Soviets and NHL all-stars split masterpiece on ice.
 8. **'89 World Juniors** Fedorov-Bure-Mogilny line sparkles in Soviet victory.
 9. **'77 Worlds** Soviets outscore Canadian NHLers 19-2 in two games.
 10. **'95 Worlds** Finland wins first gold ever on arch-rival Sweden's ice.

Chalk Talk

"We knew Dominik was an NHL goaltender, but I don't think we thought he'd be letting in fewer than two goals a game."

Buffalo coach John Muckler on Dominik Hasek's 1.94 GAA, the lowest in 20 seasons

1994-95

Glow Puck Fizzles

The FOX network pays $155 million for the rights to air a limited number of NHL games over the next five years. FOX experiments with a glowing puck on the screen, starting with the 1996 All-Star Game in Boston, but abandons it before the 1998-99 season.

HOCKEY LISTS OF THE CENTURY
Goalies Pull Plug On Red Light

One year after Dominik Hasek is the first goalie in 20 years to record a goals-against average under 2.00, he leads the NHL again with a 2.11 mark in 1994-95. Listed are the best GAA's by decade. To list by the Early and Modern Eras would see all the best marks concentrated in the low-scoring 1920s and 1950s. Goalies must have played half their team's games to qualify.

Goalie	GAA
George Hainsworth	0.92
Mon., '28-29 ('20s)	
Wilf Cude	1.47
Det., Mon., '33-34 ('30s)	
Turk Broda	2.00
Tor., '40-41 ('40s)	
Al Rollins	1.77
Tor., '50-51 ('50s)	
Gump Worsley	1.98
Mon., '67-68 ('60s)	
Tony Esposito	1.77
Chi., '71-72 ('70s)	
Pete Peeters	2.36
Bos., '82-83 ('80s)	
Ron Tugnutt	1.79
Ott., '98-99 ('90s)	

Chalk Talk

"If I was Gary Bettman, I'd be worried about my family. Some crazed fan or player might figure if they get him out of the way, this might get settled."

Chicago's Chris Chelios utters bizarre remark during the lockout, for which he later apologizes

Doug MacLellan/HHOF

The battle between owners and players descends to murky depths when Chris Chelios, right, speaks his mind.

No. 1 STORY: Lockout knocks out season until new year

Hockey fans are left in the dark when NHL owners lock out the players Sept. 30 because there is no collective bargaining agreement in place. As Christmas approaches there's still no hockey and the owners give Bettman approval Dec. 12 to shut down the season. It looks like that will happen when both sides reject each other's "final offers" Jan. 7. But four days later, the NHLPA negotiating committee switches gears and endorses the owner's offer. An agreement is reached six days later, ending a 103-day lockout. A 48-game season begins Jan. 20—the shortest schedule since the 1941-42 season.

2. Former players win pension suit

Former NHLers, led by a group including Carl Brewer and Brad Park, win their lawsuit that contends the NHL skimmed surplus money from the pension fund, when the Supreme Court of Canada dismisses the league's appeal July 28, 1994. In 1992, an Ontario court ruled the NHL contravened bylaws established in 1949. The league is estimated to owe as much as $40 million to retired players.

3. Super Mario sits out season

Ill health forces Mario Lemieux to put his career on hold. The four-time scoring champion, limited to 22 games in 1993-94, announces he'll sit out the 1994-95 season. "There's a strong possibility I will be able to come back," says Lemieux, who acknowledges after the season he will return for the 1995-96 campaign. The Pittsburgh Penguins still finish third overall, thanks mainly to Jaromir Jagr, who wins his first Art Ross Trophy with 70 points.

▶ **IMPACT PERSON**

Bob Goodenow

A Detroit lawyer, who grew up playing minor hockey alongside Gordie Howe's sons Mark and Marty, Goodenow establishes the cozy days of the NHL's working with Alan Eagleson are over. The NHLPA leader oversees the first players' strike in 1992, and keeps his union solid during a 103-day lockout.

Bruce Bennett/BBS

1995-96

Stanley Cup: Colorado Avalanche

No. 1 STORY: Old Nordiques make smashing debut as Avalanche

Quebec Nordiques' fans miss their just rewards when, after years of last-place finishes, the club is bought May 25 by COMSAT and moved to Denver where it shines as the Colorado Avalanche. The Avs sweep the Florida Panthers in the 1996 final to become the only NHL team to win the Stanley Cup in its first season in a new city. Uwe Krupp scores the Cup-clinching goal in triple overtime. Quebec isn't the only Canadian city to receive bad news. On Jan. 19, the NHL approves the sale and transfer of the Winnipeg Jets to Phoenix, where they begin play as the Coyotes in 1996-97.

2. Wings soar to record heights

It's a winning season for captain Steve Yzerman's Detroit Red Wings. They finish with an NHL-record 62-13-7 slate, bettering Montreal's 60-win campaign of 1976-77. The Red Wings also equal the 1974-75 Philadelphia Flyers' record for home wins (36). It's a personal triumph for coach Scotty Bowman, who also guided the 1976-77 Habs. He moves past Al Arbour (1,606) into first spot on the all-time list of games coached, finishing with 1,654. All is not perfect though; the Wings lose to Colorado in the conference final.

3. NHL stars to play in Olympics

At an Oct. 2 meeting involving the NHL, NHLPA and International Ice Hockey Federation, the Canada Cup is renamed the World Cup. More importantly, plans are unveiled to make the 1998 Olympic tournament in Nagano, Japan a 'dream team' event featuring NHL stars. The league will take a 17-day break in the middle of the season to let the players participate.

► **IMPACT PERSON**

Patrick Roy

Embarrassed when he's left in for nine goals in an 11-1 loss to Detroit Dec. 2, Roy approaches team president Ron Corey during the game to tell him he has played his last game for Montreal. Four days later he's dealt to Colorado. Roy earns his third Stanley Cup ring with the Avs, posting three playoff shutouts, including a dramatic 1-0 triple OT win in the Cup clincher against Florida.

Doug MacLellan/HHOF

Bruce Bennett/BBS

Miami's Rat Trick

Florida's Scott Mellanby kills a rodent in the dressing room before a game with Calgary, then scores twice in a 4-3 win. It's dubbed a 'rat trick' and fans start throwing plastic rats on the ice when the Panthers score.

HOCKEY LISTS OF THE CENTURY Buffalo's Save-ior

Buffalo's Dominik Hasek is the only goalie to record a .930-or-better save percentage since the NHL began recording the stat in 1982-83. Hasek kicks off a string of six straight SP titles in 1993-94, and 1995-96 is the only season he doesn't hit .930. He sets the SP standard of .937 in 1998-99. Here's how the five-time Vezina Trophy winner's feats compare to those of other greats. The Vezina is awarded to the NHL's best goalie.

Hasek ('93-94 – '98-99)	Comparable
Five-time first all-star	Bill Durnan first all-star six times in seven years ('44-'50)
Six-time SP leader	Patrick Roy leads in SP four times in five years ('88-'92)
Five-time Vezina winner	Patrick Roy wins Vezina three times in four years ('89-'92)

Chalk Talk

"I'm excited by this challenge. I feel like a young kid again."
Wayne Gretzky on the Feb. 27 trade that sends him from L.A. to St. Louis...for a brief time, as 99 signs with the Rangers in July as an unrestricted free agent

Ruling The World

Superb goaltending by Mike Richter sparks the U.S. to a 5-2 upset win over Canada in the deciding game of the first World Cup final. The Americans drop the first game of the best-of-three series in Philadelphia, then win twice in Montreal.

HOCKEY LISTS OF THE CENTURY

8th Decade All-Stars

Mario Lemieux wins the scoring race six times during the NHL's eighth decade (1987-88 through 1996-97, plus 1997-98 through 1999-00).

THN's First Team

G **Patrick Roy**, Mon.
Cocky and confident

D **Ray Bourque**, Bos.
Four Norris Trophies

D **Chris Chelios**, Chi.
Tough and talented

LW **Luc Robitaille**, L.A.
Seven 40-goal seasons

C **Mario Lemieux**, Pit.
Magnificent moves

RW **Jaromir Jagr**, Pit.
Mario Jr.

THN's Second Team

G **Dominik Hasek**, Buf.
Dominator unbeatable

D **Al MacInnis**, Cgy.
Bullet slapshot

D **Brian Leetch**, NYR
Big-time passer

LW **John LeClair**, Phi.
Power, scoring combo

C **Wayne Gretzky**, L.A.
All-time ambassador

RW **Brett Hull**, St.L
As Golden as Bobby

Chalk Talk

"I thought we outplayed Canada and I don't ever remember when a U.S. coach has been able to say that."

Coach Jeff Jackson's lament after his team's 2-0 loss to Canada, which wins a record fifth consecutive world junior gold medal

Mario Lemieux scores the second last goal of his career, against Philadelphia's Garth Snow April 23.

No. 1 STORY: Junior coach James guilty of sexual assault

The hockey world is shocked when Graham James, coach of the Western League's Swift Current Broncos, is convicted on charges of sexually assaulting two players. Boston right winger Sheldon Kennedy and another player, who chooses not to give his name, provide police with details. "I felt I had to come forward and deal with this issue," Kennedy says. James is sentenced to 3-1/2 years in federal prison; a statement of facts says James committed about 350 offenses against the two players.

2. Triumph and tragedy in Hockeytown

Detroit sweeps Philadelphia to win the Stanley Cup for the first time since 1954-55. There's joy in Hockeytown USA, but it's shortlived. Six days after the final game, a limousine transporting Red Wings' defensemen Vladimir Konstantinov and Viacheslav Fetisov, with team masseur Sergei Mnatsakanov, veers out of control and hits a tree in a Detroit suburb. Mnatsakanov, 43, and Konstantinov, 30, a second-team all-star in 1995-96, suffer debilitating brain injuries, ending their careers. Fetisov, 39, has minor injuries, but will play one more season and win another Cup.

3. Lemieux retires with 11 records

Mario Lemieux can boast that he went out on top. The Pittsburgh Penguins' center scores 50 goals and wins his sixth Art Ross Trophy with 122 points, then retires after 12 seasons. Hampered during his magnificent career by Hodgkin's disease and serious back problems, Lemieux, 31, leaves with 11 league marks and an NHL-record career goals-per-game average of .823.

Sheldon Kennedy

Kennedy's public acknowledgement of being sexually abused by Graham James leads to imprisonment for James and upheaval in hockey. It also helps explain Kennedy's problems with substance abuse and the Bruin begins the process of reclaiming his life. "I still have trouble with loving and trusting others," he says.

1997-98

Stanley Cup: Detroit Red Wings

No. 1 STORY: Hasek leads Czechs to Olympic gold

In a battle of NHL 'dream teams', the Czech Republic blanks Russia 1-0 to win the Olympic gold medal in Japan, behind the spectacular goaltending of Dominik Hasek. The Czechs reach the final after shocking Canada in the semifinal. Tied 1-1 after a score-less 10-minute overtime, the Czechs win in a shootout when Hasek stones all five Canadians and Robert Reichel beats Patrick Roy. Finland upsets Canada 3-2 for the bronze, while the U.S. goes home in shame, trashing rooms in the Olympic Village after losing in the quarterfinals. In the first women's Olympic event, Shelley Looney scores the winner as the U.S. beats Canada 3-1 in the gold game.

2. Eagleson sent to sin bin

Facing more than 30 charges of racketeering, fraud, obstruction of justice, embezzlement and accepting kickbacks, hockey czar Alan Eagleson pleads guilty to three counts of fraud Jan. 6 in a Boston court. He does the same the next day in a Toronto court-room and is sentenced to 18 months in a minimum security cor-rectional center and fined $1 million.

3. NHL shooters caught in trap

Pittsburgh Penguins' star Jaromir Jagr is the NHL's only 100-point scorer. His 102 points are the lowest Art Ross-winning total in a full season since 1967-68 as teams employ the neutral zone trap and scoring drops to a 40-year low of 5.28 goals per game. Player crease violations become a major issue; a total of 304 reviews conducted by video goal judges result in 110 goals being disallowed.

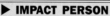

▶ **IMPACT PERSON**

Dominik Hasek

'The Dominator' accomplishes an NHL first; he wins back-to-back Hart Trophies. He carries the Czech Republic to the Olympic gold medal and takes Buffalo to the Stanley Cup final four, posting 13 regular season shutouts. He wins his fourth Vezina Trophy in five sea-sons and leads the league in save per-centage for the fifth straight season.

Expanding Horizons

The NHL announces it will add four teams over three seasons–Nashville (1998-99), Atlanta (1999-2000), Columbus (2000-01) and Minnesota (2000-01). Meanwhile, the Hartford Whalers relocate to Carolina.

HOCKEY LISTS OF THE CENTURY Top NHLers of All-Time

THN names the Top 50 NHL Players of All-Time to mark our 50th anniversary. Players are listed here on all-star teams according to overall ranking (in parentheses).

Pos.	First Team	Second Team	Third Team
G	Terry Sawchuk, Det. (8)	Jacques Plante, Mon. (13)	Glenn Hall, Chi. (16)
D	Bobby Orr, Bos. (2)	Eddie Shore, Bos. (10)	Denis Potvin, NYI (19)
D	Doug Harvey, Mon. (6)	Ray Bourque, Bos. (14)	Red Kelly, Det. (22)
LW	Bobby Hull, Chi. (8)	Ted Lindsay, Det. (21)	Frank Mahovlich, Tor. (26)
C	W. Gretzky, Edm. (1)	Mario Lemieux, Pit. (4)	Jean Beliveau, Mon. (7)
RW	Gordie Howe, Det. (3)	Maurice Richard, Mon. (5)	Guy Lafleur, Mon. (11)

Chalk Talk

"This isn't like most injuries. It's a very confus-ing state because you're definitely not yourself." *Rangers' center Pat LaFontaine is forced to retire. He's one of a grow-ing number of victims of post-concussion syndrome.*

The Great One bids adieu April 18, 1999.

Bruce Bennett/BBS

1998-99

Stanley Cup: Dallas Stars

No. 1 STORY: The Great One says good-bye

Following weeks of speculation, Wayne Gretzky acknowledges April 16 he's retiring. Two days later, he plays his final game for the Rangers in New York. Before the puck is dropped, NHL commissioner Gary Bettman declares that No. 99 will be retired across the league. Gretzky picks up one final point–an assist on Brian Leetch's goal in a 2-1 OT loss to Pittsburgh. New York Rangers' coach John Muckler calls timeout in the final minute of regulation and the crowd has one last chance to salute The Great One. "That's when it really hit me that I'm done," says Gretzky, who finishes his amazing career with 894 goals and 1,963 assists for 2,857 points, just three of the 61 NHL records he holds or shares.

2. Stars Hull home Cup amidst video dispute

The Stanley Cup finds itself deep in the heart of Texas for the first time, as the Dallas Stars defeat the Buffalo Sabres. Controversy erupts when cameras show Brett Hull's skate is in the crease on his Cup-winning goal in triple OT. The NHL says the goal was reviewed and Hull had control of the puck, making it legal. Two days later the league returns jurisdiction over crease violation calls, which had rested with the video replay judge, to on-ice officials.

3. Chiasson killed in car crash

Losing control of his truck following a season-ending party, Carolina Hurricanes' defenseman Steve Chiasson is killed May 3. Chiasson, 32, has a blood-alcohol count three times the legal limit, isn't wearing a seatbelt and is speeding at the time of the accident.

▶ IMPACT PERSON

Jaromir Jagr

It's fitting that Jagr scores the winning goal in Wayne Gretzky's final game. "Everyone always talks about passing torches," Gretzky says. "He caught it." Jagr wins his first Hart Trophy and third Art Ross with 127 points. He figures in 52.5 per cent of Pittsburgh's 242 goals, a percentage Gretzky never matched in his career.

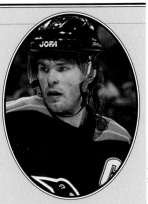

Dave Sandford/HHOF

4-on-4 To Work OT

The NHL unveils plans to use 4-on-4 play for 1999-2000 regular season overtime. It results in 44 per cent of OT games being settled, compared to 27 in '98-99. But the number of games ending in ties drops only from 162 to 146.

HOCKEY LISTS OF THE CENTURY Superstars' last games

Ted Williams homered in his last at-bat and Michael Jordan won a National Basketball Association title with his final shot. Here's what the top six players in NHL history did. Listed are their last teams, ages at retirement, dates of final game and game results.

1. **Wayne Gretzky**, NYR   38   Apr. 18, '99   One assist. 2-1 loss in OT to Pittsburgh
2. **Bobby Orr**, Chi.   30   Nov. 1, '78   No points. 1-0 loss to Vancouver
3. **Gordie Howe**, Hfd.   52   Apr. 11, '80   No points. 4-3 loss in OT to Montreal
4. **Mario Lemieux**, Pit.   31   Apr. 27, '97   One goal, one assist. 6-3 loss to Philadelphia
5. **Rocket Richard**, Mtl.   38   Apr. 14, '60   No points. 4-0 win over Toronto to win Cup
6. **Doug Harvey**, St. L   44   Mar. 29, '69   No points. 3-1 win over Los Angeles

Chalk Talk

"I'm very excited about the opportunity to come back. It's a dream come true."

Mario Lemieux, on becoming the first ex-NHLer to buy his old team, when he assembles a group to purchase the bankrupt Pittsburgh Penguins

1999-00

Stanley Cup: New Jersey Devils

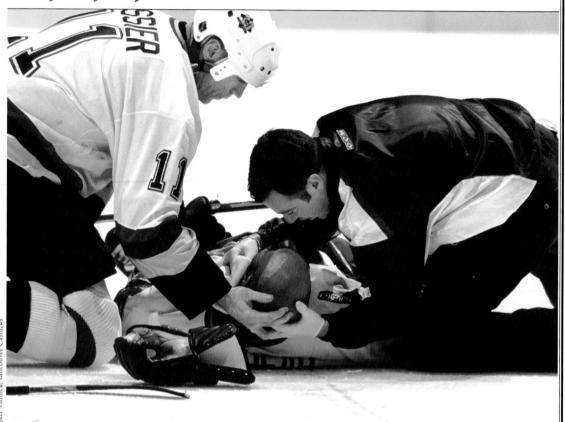

Vancouver trainer Mike Burnstein and captain Mark Messier tend to Donald Brashear after a vicious high-sticking.

▶ IMPACT PERSON

Larry Robinson

Replacing Robbie Ftorek as coach with eight games left in the regular season, Robinson guides New Jersey to the Stanley Cup. His dressing room tirade after the Devils trail 3-1 to Philadelphia in the Eastern Conference final is seen as the turning point. Asked if the club could have won with Ftorek, center Bobby Holik says, "No way."

No. 1 STORY: NHL endures season from hell

Controversy and brutality mark the NHL campaign. Montreal's Trent McCleary chokes and nearly dies Jan. 29 when his larynx is broken by a shot from Philadelphia's Chris Therien. Toronto's Bryan Berard almost loses his right eye March 11 after he is clipped by the stick of Ottawa's Marian Hossa. Boston's Marty McSorley faces assault charges after rendering Vancouver's Donald Brashear unconscious with a baseball-swing slash to the head Feb. 21. Meanwhile, Philadelphia coach Roger Neilson battles cancer and Ottawa star Alexei Yashin sits out the entire season rather than live up to the terms of his contract.

2. Headaches for Lindros, Flyers

Eric Lindros is stripped of the captaincy after ripping Philadelphia's training staff in the wake of his being allowed to play four games with what is later diagnosed as a concussion. While recuperating, Lindros suffers another concussion after colliding with minor leaguer Francis Lessard in practice. Lindros returns for Game 6 of the Eastern Conference final and scores in a 2-1 Flyers' loss, but absorbs a devastating hit from New Jersey's Scott Stevens in Game 7, suffering his fourth concussion in five months.

3. Cancer claims the Rocket

A legend passes away when Maurice (Rocket) Richard, 78, succumbs to abdominal cancer May 27. The Montreal right winger was the NHL's first 500-goal scorer and the first to post a 50-goal season. Among those paying their final respects at Richard's funeral are Canadian Prime Minister Jean Chretien and Hall of Famers Gordie Howe and Jean Beliveau.

Bye-bye Beantown

After 21 seasons and 1,518 games with the Boston Bruins, Ray Bourque is traded to Colorado March 6. Only Detroit's Gordie Howe (1,687) and Alex Delvecchio (1,549) have played more games in one team's uniform than Bourque.

HOCKEY LISTS OF THE CENTURY
The NHL From '17-18 to '99-00

The NHL grows from a league that spans a triangle measuring no more than 350 miles at its farthest—an axis formed by Toronto, Montreal and Ottawa—to a league that spans most of North America and embraces much of Europe during its 83-season history in the 20th century. Players grow from an average age of 5-foot-8 and 172 pounds to 6-foot-1 and 199 pounds. Average salary grows even more–rocketing from $1,000 (Cdn.) to $1,400,000 (U.S.).

'17-18	NHL	'99-00
3	Teams	28
45	Players	661
5-8	Avg. Ht.	6-1
172	Avg. Wt.	199
43	Canadians	372
(96%)		(56%)
2	Americans	106
(4%)		(16%)
0	Europeans	183
(0%)		(28%)
$1,000	Avg. Salary	$1.4m
(Cdn.)		(U.S.)

Chalk Talk

"I pity him. I feel sorry for him. What's it like to be 27 years old and have your mom and dad running your life?"

Philadelphia GM Bob Clarke's assessment of Flyer center Eric Lindros' relationship with his parents

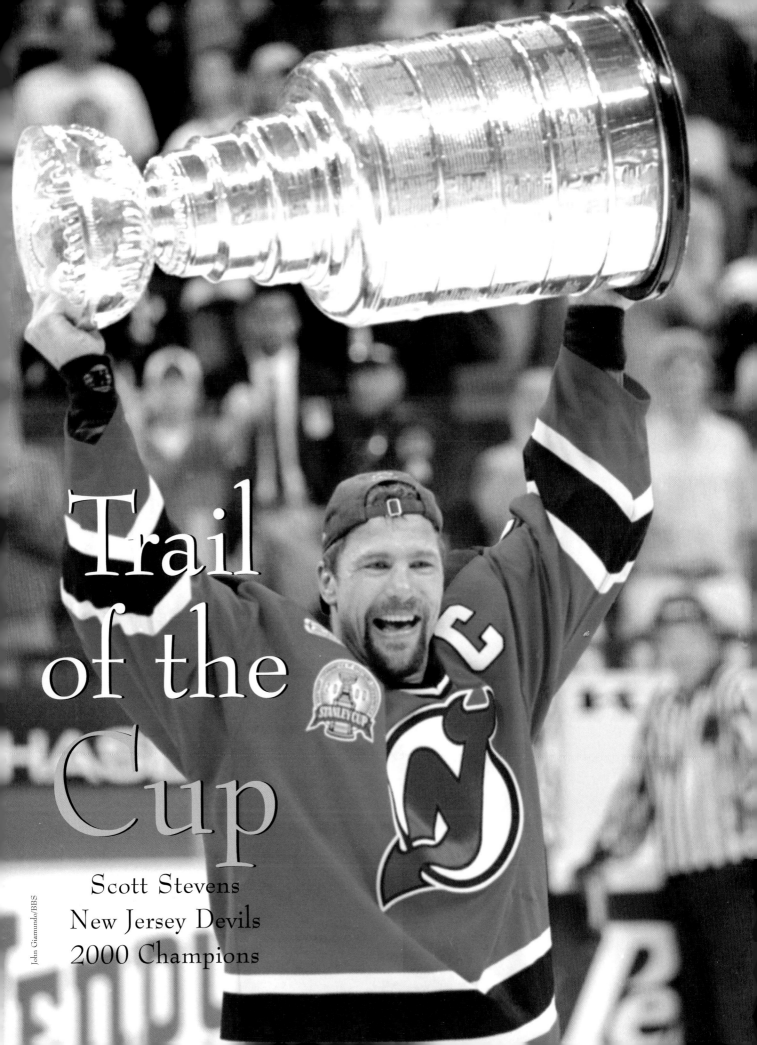

Trail
of the
Cup

Scott Stevens
New Jersey Devils
2000 Champions

1917-18 The Toronto Arenas are the first NHL team to win the Cup, edging the Vancouver Millionaires of the Pacific Coast Association 3-2 in games. Vancouver's Fred 'Cyclone' Taylor is the individual star with nine goals.

1918-19 With the Montreal Canadiens and PCHA's Seattle Metropolitans tied 2-2 in games, the series is cancelled when several Montreal players, suffering from the Spanish flu, can't play. The Habs' Joe Hall dies days later.

1919-20 Warm weather forces two games to be moved from Ottawa to Toronto. Jack Darragh nets all game-winners as the Senators beat the PCHA's Seattle three games to two.

1920-21 A total of 51,000 fans, including the largest crowd (11,000) to see a hockey game in Game 1 at Vancouver, take in the final as Ottawa defeats the PCHA's Millionaires 3-2.

1921-22 Vancouver of the PCHA allows the Toronto St. Pats to use Ottawa's Eddie Gerard for one game when Harry Cameron and Ken Randall are injured. Toronto wins 3-2, giving Gerard his third of four straight Cups.

1922-23 Ottawa sweeps the best-of-three final from the Edmonton Eskimos of the Western Canada League, playing on neutral ice in Vancouver. Edmonton won't have a team in the final again until the Oilers make it in 1983.

1923-24 Rookie Howie Morenz scores seven goals in six games as the Montreal Canadiens go unbeaten in the playoffs, ousting the WCHL's Calgary Tigers in two straight to win their first Cup in the NHL.

1924-25 The WCHL's Victoria Cougars defeat the Canadiens 3-1 in games to win the Cup. Victoria is the last team from outside the NHL to capture Lord Stanley's mug.

1925-26 Dunc Munro, who has captained teams to Memorial and Allan Cups and Canada to Olympic gold already, wears the 'C' for the Montreal Maroons in their 3-1 Cup series conquest of Victoria.

1926-27 Ottawa wins its fourth Cup in eight years, defeating the Boston Bruins in the first all-NHL Stanley Cup final. The Senators win twice and there are two ties–the last in Cup final history.

1927-28 Coach Lester Patrick, 44, backstops the New York Rangers to victory in Game 2, then farmhand Joe Miller wins twice as the Blueshirts cop their first Cup, 3-2 in games over the Maroons.

1928-29 Boston defeats the Rangers in two straight games to win its first Cup. The final series features 13 future Hall-of-Famers, including coaches Cy Denneny of the Bruins and Lester Patrick of New York.

1929-30 The Canadiens sweep Boston in two straight games in one of the biggest upsets in NHL history. The Bruins had not lost back-to-back games all season and finished 26 points ahead of Montreal.

1930-31 Boston coach Art Ross makes history in the semi-finals against the Canadiens, pulling goalie Tiny Thompson in an unfruitful bid to score. The Habs oust the Bruins, then top the Chicago Black Hawks 3-2 in the final.

1931-32 The Toronto Maple Leafs sweep the 'tennis series' final 6-4, 6-2, 6-4 from the Rangers, in three different cities–Toronto, New York and Boston. The circus takes over Madison Square Garden, forcing the move to Beantown.

1932-33 Bill Cook scores the first overtime Cup-winning goal, as the Rangers defeat the Maple Leafs 3-1 to become the first third-place club to win a championship. It's the first Cup final rematch in NHL history.

1933-34 'Mush' March, who scored the first goals at Maple Leaf Gardens and Chicago Stadium, connects in overtime as the Black Hawks win their first Cup, 3-1 over the Detroit Red Wings.

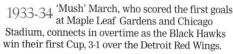

The original Stanley Cup, 1893

1934-35 Tommy Gorman becomes the only coach in NHL history to win successive Cups with two teams, as the Maroons sweep Toronto in three games. He guided Chicago to victory in 1934.

1935-36 'Mud' Bruneteau ends the longest game in NHL history after 176:30 of playing time as Detroit blanks the Maroons 1-0 in a semi-final match. The Wings win the series, then outplay Toronto 3-1 in the final.

1936-37 Earl Robertson fills in for injured goaltender Normie Smith and posts two shutouts in the final as Detroit becomes the first U.S.-based team to win back-to-back Cups, defeating the Rangers 3-2 in the final.

1937-38 Chicago owner Major Frederic McLaughlin realizes a dream when American Bill Stewart coaches the Black Hawks to a 3-1 Cup win over Toronto with eight U.S.-born players in the lineup.

1938-39 Mel 'Sudden Death' Hill scores three overtime goals, including the series clincher, for Boston in its seven-game, semifinal win over the Rangers. The Bruins top Toronto 4-1 in the Cup final.

1939-40 The Rangers win the Cup final 4-2 over Toronto on Bryan Hextall's overtime goal, despite having to play the last four games at Maple Leaf Gardens. A circus is playing in New York.

1940-41 Boston's four-game sweep of Detroit in the Cup final is anti-climactic after the Bruins squeak past Toronto in a thrilling seven-game semi-final series, winning three of the last four games 2-1.

The Cup, 1894-1927

1941-42 Toronto rallies from a 3-0 deficit to win four straight games over Detroit in the greatest comeback in Cup final history. A 9-3 Maple Leafs' romp in Game 5 at Toronto turns the series around.

1942-43 Detroit rebounds from its heartbreaking 1942 loss to Toronto by sweeping Boston. It's the final hurrah for goalie Johnny Mowers, who enlists in the Canadian Army and plays only seven more NHL games.

1943-44 Montreal's Rocket Richard scores five goals in a 5-1 semifinal win at Toronto and is awarded all three stars. The line of Richard, Toe Blake and Elmer Lach scores 10 goals in the final as the Habs sweep Chicago.

1944-45 Toronto wins the first three games of the final, then Detroit takes three straight before the Leafs prevail 2-1 in Game 7. As in 1942, the Wings win three straight games, but don't win the Cup, the only team ever to do this.

1945-46 The Canadiens oust Boston in a five-game final in which three games are decided in overtime. In Game 1, Montreal's Rocket Richard nets the first of a record six career playoff overtime goals.

1946-47 Toronto tops the favored Canadiens 4-2 in the first all-Canadian final since 1935, rallying from a 6-0 loss in Game 1, and answering Habs' goalie Bill Durnan's question about how they got into the playoffs in the first place.

1947-48 Toronto sweeps Detroit to retain the Cup, in a career cross-over for two stars. Leafs' captain Syl Apps retires after hoisting the Cup, while Gordie Howe of the vanquished Red Wings plays in his first final.

1948-49 The first NHL team to win three straight Stanley Cups, Toronto is also the first to sweep back-to-back finals. Once again Detroit is the victim.

1949-50 Pete Babando's OT goal gives Detroit the Cup over the Rangers, who have to play all games on the road–two in Toronto, five in Detroit–because the circus is at Madison Square Garden.

1950-51 Toronto's Bill Barilko scores in overtime as the Leafs eliminate the Canadiens 4-1, in a nailbiting series in which all games are decided in overtime. Barilko dies in a plane crash that summer.

1951-52 Detroit wins the Cup in the minimum eight games, sweeping Toronto and Montreal, and giving up only five goals. Terry Sawchuk matches an NHL record with four shutouts.

1952-53 Trailing 3-2 in their semifinal series with Chicago, the Canadiens turn to rookie goalie Jacques Plante, who posts a 3-0 shutout. The Habs win the series and beat Boston 4-1 in the Cup final.

1953-54 Tony Leswick's shot banks in off Canadiens' defenseman Doug Harvey in OT, as Detroit wins a tough, seven-game final. Montreal had rallied from a 3-1 deficit in games to tie the series.

1954-55 Gordie Howe picks up a playoff-record 20 points, leading Detroit to a semifinal sweep of Toronto and a difficult 4-3 conquest of favored Montreal in the final.

1955-56 Jean Beliveau scores 12 playoff goals, seven against defending-champion Detroit in the five-game final, leading the Habs to the first of five straight Cups and stamping himself as a big-time player.

1956-57 Jacques Plante holds Boston to six goals in a five-game final series and Rocket Richard scores four times in a 5-1 Game 1 victory as the Canadiens win back-to-back titles for the first time since 1929-30 and 1930-31.

1957-58 After missing 28 games recovering from a ruptured bowel, Bernie Geoffrion scores six goals in 10 games as Montreal beats Detroit, then Boston. Rocket Richard's Game 5 OT goal propels Montreal to a six-game triumph.

1958-59 The Canadiens score 14 of 39 goals on the power play, becoming the first NHL team to win four straight Cups. Toronto loses to the Habs in five games in its first Cup final appearance since 1951.

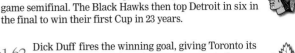 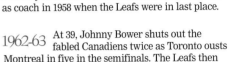 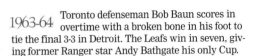 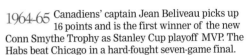  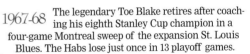 

The Cup, 1928-1947

1959-60 Montreal sweeps Chicago and Toronto to win a record fifth straight Cup, as Jacques Plante posts three shutouts and allows just two goals in four road games. He limits the Leafs to five goals in the four-game final.

1960-61 Chicago uses muscle to curtail Montreal's bid for a sixth consecutive Cup, sidelining the Habs in a six-game semifinal. The Black Hawks then top Detroit in six in the final to win their first Cup in 23 years.

1961-62 Dick Duff fires the winning goal, giving Toronto its first title since 1951 in a six-game conquest of Chicago. Victory is sweet for Punch Imlach, who took over as coach in 1958 when the Leafs were in last place.

1962-63 At 39, Johnny Bower shuts out the fabled Canadiens twice as Toronto ousts Montreal in five in the semifinals. The Leafs then beat Detroit in five to win their second straight Cup.

1963-64 Toronto defenseman Bob Baun scores in overtime with a broken bone in his foot to tie the final 3-3 in Detroit. The Leafs win in seven, giving former Ranger star Andy Bathgate his only Cup.

1964-65 Canadiens' captain Jean Beliveau picks up 16 points and is the first winner of the new Conn Smythe Trophy as Stanley Cup playoff MVP. The Habs beat Chicago in a hard-fought seven-game final.

1965-66 Montreal rallies from 2-0 down to beat Detroit in the Cup final. Wings' goalie Roger Crozier is the first player from the losing side to win the Conn Smythe Trophy.

1966-67 A superb two-way effort by Conn Smythe Trophy winner Dave Keon leads Toronto past Montreal in a six-game final. The Leafs are the oldest team (average age 31.4) ever to win the Cup.

1967-68 The legendary Toe Blake retires after coaching his eighth Stanley Cup champion in a four-game Montreal sweep of the expansion St. Louis Blues. The Habs lose just once in 13 playoff games.

1968-69 Rookie coach Claude Ruel, 29, follows Blake's lead, guiding the Habs to a four-game sweep of St. Louis. Serge Savard is the first defenseman to win the Conn Smythe Trophy.

1969-70 Bobby Orr scores in overtime, as Boston wins its first title since 1940-41, sweeping St. Louis. Montreal and Toronto miss the playoffs, making this the Stanley Cup's first all-American post-season.

1970-71 Rookie goalie Ken Dryden comes to the rescue for Montreal, while Henri Richard scores the tying and winning goals as the Canadiens rally from a 2-0 deficit for a 3-2 win over Chicago in Game 7 of the Cup final at Chicago.

1971-72 Phil Esposito and Bobby Orr score 24 playoff points apiece, as Boston beats the Rangers in a six-game final after easily eliminating Toronto and St. Louis in earlier rounds. Orr wins his second Conn Smythe Trophy.

1972-73 Captain Henri Richard, 37, wins a record 11th Stanley Cup, as Montreal beats Chicago in a six-game final. Conn Smythe Trophy winner Yvan Cournoyer leads all playoff scorers with 15 goals and 25 points.

1973-74 Philadelphia's brawling Flyers become the first expansion team to win the Cup, upsetting Boston 4-2 in the final series. Bernie Parent shuts the Bruins out 1-0 in the clincher at Philly and wins the Conn Smythe Trophy.

1974-75 Game 4 of the final in Buffalo is halted to clear fog from the ice. Coach Freddie 'The Fog' Shero guides Philadelphia to its second straight Cup, this time in six games over the Sabres, who are finalists for the first time.

 1975-76 The speedy and skillful Canadiens sweep the physical Flyers in the Cup final. But Philadelphia winger Reggie Leach sets an NHL record by scoring 19 goals in 16 games to win the Conn Smythe Trophy.

 1976-77 Jacques Lemaire nets three game winners, including the Cup-clincher, as Montreal sweeps Boston in the final. The Habs' Guy Lafleur wins the Conn Smythe Trophy with a playoff-high 26 points.

 1977-78 Conn Smythe Trophy winner Larry Robinson is a tower of strength on defense, as the Canadiens beat Boston in a six-game final. Robinson also collects 21 points in 15 games.

 1978-79 A penalty for too many men on the ice costs Boston a chance to end Montreal's three-year reign as Cup champion in the semifinals. The Habs win, then beat the Rangers in a five-game final.

1979-80 The New York Islanders win their first Cup, in six games over Philadelphia, on Bob Nystrom's OT goal. Defenseman Ken Morrow wins a Cup and Olympic gold medal in the same season.

1980-81 Mike Bossy sets a playoff record with 35 points in 18 games, leading the Islanders to their second straight Cup victory. The Isles defeat the Minnesota North Stars in a five-game final.

1981-82 The Vancouver Canucks (30-33-17) stage an improbable run to the final before being swept by the Islanders, who join Toronto and Montreal as the only NHL teams to win three straight Cups.

1982-83 The Edmonton Oilers outscore opponents 74-33 in the first three playoff rounds. But they are swept in the final by the Islanders, who outscore them 17-6. Islanders' goalie Billy Smith wins the Conn Smythe Trophy.

 1983-84 Edmonton's tenacious Mark Messier earns the Conn Smythe Trophy with 26 points, as Edmonton wins its first Stanley Cup, ousting the four-time champion Islanders in a five-game final.

1984-85 Wayne Gretzky equals a Cup final record with seven goals and sets playoff marks with 30 assists and 47 points, as Edmonton repeats as Cup champion in a five-game victory over Philadelphia in the final.

1985-86 Ten rookies help Montreal win the Cup in five games over the Calgary Flames, appearing in their first final. Habs' goalie Patrick Roy, just 20, earns the Conn Smythe Trophy with a sparkling 1.92 GAA in 20 games.

1986-87 Edmonton edges Philadelphia in a seven-game final, but it's an Islanders' first round win over Washington which has everybody talking. Pat LaFontaine ends the fifth-longest game in Cup history after 68:47 of OT.

1987-88 A second period power outage causes the suspension of Game 4 of the final at Boston Garden with the score tied 3-3. The series moves back to Edmonton, where the Oilers complete a four-game sweep to win the Cup.

1988-89 The final is a fond farewell for Calgary star Lanny McDonald, who scores his last goal in the Cup-clinching win over Montreal. The Flames are the only visiting team ever to beat the Habs for the Cup at the Forum.

1989-90 Former Bruin Bill Ranford wins the Conn Smythe Trophy, backstopping Edmonton to a five-game final win over Boston. Petr Klima's goal at 55:13 of OT in Game 1 ends the longest game in Cup final history.

1990-91 Minnesota is the first No. 16 seed to reach the final, after upsetting No. 1 Chicago and No. 2 St. Louis earlier. But the Pittsburgh Penguins win their first Cup in six games with an 8-0 win in Game 6.

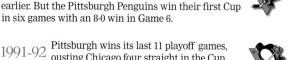

1991-92 Pittsburgh wins its last 11 playoff games, ousting Chicago four straight in the Cup final. Mario Lemieux becomes just the second player in history to win two straight Conn Smythe Trophies.

1992-93 Montreal wins 10 straight overtime games, including three in its five-game final win over Los Angeles, to win a 24th Cup. It's the Kings' first Cup final and the last for Wayne Gretzky.

1993-94 Vancouver phenom Pavel Bure scores 16 playoff goals, but the Rangers edge the Canucks in a seven-game final, ending a 54-year Cup drought at Madison Square Garden.

1994-95 The New Jersey Devils use the neutral zone trap to win their first Cup, with rumors circulating the club will move to Nashville. The Devils sweep Detroit in the final.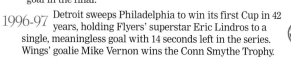

1995-96 The first-year Colorado Avalanche upsets heavily favored Detroit, which lost just 13 of 82 regular season games, in a six-game semifinal, then sweeps the upstart Florida Panthers on Uwe Krupp's OT goal in the final.

1996-97 Detroit sweeps Philadelphia to win its first Cup in 42 years, holding Flyers' superstar Eric Lindros to a single, meaningless goal with 14 seconds left in the series. Wings' goalie Mike Vernon wins the Conn Smythe Trophy.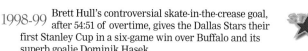

1997-98 Scotty Bowman wins his eighth Cup as a coach, tying the record of the Canadiens' Toe Blake, as Detroit sweeps the Washington Capitals. Red Wings' captain Steve Yzerman takes home the Conn Smythe Trophy.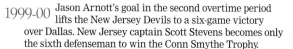

1998-99 Brett Hull's controversial skate-in-the-crease goal, after 54:51 of overtime, gives the Dallas Stars their first Stanley Cup in a six-game win over Buffalo and its superb goalie Dominik Hasek.

1999-00 Jason Arnott's goal in the second overtime period lifts the New Jersey Devils to a six-game victory over Dallas. New Jersey captain Scott Stevens becomes only the sixth defenseman to win the Conn Smythe Trophy.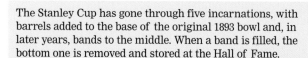

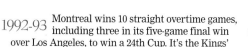

The Cup,
1948-

The Stanley Cup has gone through five incarnations, with barrels added to the base of the original 1893 bowl and, in later years, bands to the middle. When a band is filled, the bottom one is removed and stored at the Hall of Fame.

NHL Stanley Cup Honor Roll

Season	Champion (Cup number) Runner-Up	Coach	General Manager	Captain	Cup-Winning Goal
1917-18	**TORONTO ARENAS** (1*)	**Dick Carroll**	**Charlie Querrie**	**Harry Mummery**	**Corb Denneny**
	Vancouver Millionaires	*Frank Patrick*	*Frank Patrick*	*Lloyd Cook*	
1918-19	**NO DECISION**	The final between the Seattle Metropolitans and Montreal Canadiens is cancelled because of an influenza epidemic. The Habs' Joe Hall dies of the illness.			
1919-20	**OTTAWA SENATORS** (1)	**Pete Greene**	**Tommy Gorman**	**Eddie Gerard**	**Jack Darragh**
	Seattle Metropolitans	*C.P. Muldoon*	*C.P. Muldoon*	*Jack Walker*	
1920-21	**OTTAWA SENATORS** (2)	**Pete Greene**	**Tommy Gorman**	**Eddie Gerard**	**Jack Darragh**
	Vancouver Millionaires	*Frank Patrick*	*Frank Patrick*	*Lloyd Cook*	
1921-22	**TORONTO ST. PATS** (2*)	**George O'Donoghue**	**Charlie Querrie**	**Reg Noble**	**Babe Dye**
	Vancouver Millionaires	*Frank Patrick*	*Frank Patrick*	*Lloyd Cook*	
1922-23	**OTTAWA SENATORS** (3)	**Pete Greene**	**Tommy Gorman**	**Eddie Gerard**	**Punch Broadbent**
	Edmonton Eskimos	*Kenny McKenzie*	*Kenny McKenzie*	*Duke Keats*	
1923-24	**MONTREAL CANADIENS** (1)	**Leo Dandurand**	**Leo Dandurand**	**Sprague Cleghorn**	**Howie Morenz**
	Calgary Tigers	*Herb Gardiner*	*Herb Gardiner*	*Eddie Oatman*	
1924-25	**VICTORIA COUGARS** (1)	**Lester Patrick**	**Lester Patrick**	**Clem Loughlin**	**Gizzy Hart**
	Montreal Canadiens	*Leo Dandurand*	*Leo Dandurand*	*Sprague Cleghorn*	
1925-26	**MONTREAL MAROONS** (1)	**Eddie Gerard**	**Eddie Gerard**	**Dunc Munro**	**Nels Stewart**
	Victoria Cougars	*Lester Patrick*	*Lester Patrick*	*Clem Loughlin*	
1926-27	**OTTAWA SENATORS** (4)	**Dave Gill**	**Dave Gill**	**George Boucher**	**Cy Denneny**
	Boston Bruins	*Art Ross*	*Art Ross*	*No Captain*	
1927-28	**NEW YORK RANGERS** (1)	**Lester Patrick**	**Lester Patrick**	**Bill Cook**	**Frank Boucher**
	Montreal Maroons	*Eddie Gerard*	*Eddie Gerard*	*Dunc Munro*	
1928-29	**BOSTON BRUINS** (1)	**Cy Denneny**	**Art Ross**	**Lionel Hitchman**	**Bill Carson**
	New York Rangers	*Lester Patrick*	*Lester Patrick*	*Bill Cook*	
1929-30	**MONTREAL CANADIENS** (2)	**Cecil Hart**	**Cecil Hart**	**Sylvio Mantha**	**Howie Morenz**
	Boston Bruins	*Art Ross*	*Art Ross*	*Lionel Hitchman*	
1930-31	**MONTREAL CANADIENS** (3)	**Cecil Hart**	**Cecil Hart**	**Sylvio Mantha**	**Johnny Gagnon**
	Chicago Black Hawks	*Dick Irvin*	*Fred McLaughlin*	*Ty Arbour*	
1931-32	**TORONTO MAPLE LEAFS** (3)	**Dick Irvin**	**Conn Smythe**	**Hap Day**	**Ace Bailey**
	New York Rangers	*Lester Patrick*	*Lester Patrick*	*Bill Cook*	
1932-33	**NEW YORK RANGERS** (2)	**Lester Patrick**	**Lester Patrick**	**Bill Cook**	**Bill Cook**
	Toronto Maple Leafs	*Dick Irvin*	*Conn Smythe*	*Hap Day*	
1933-34	**CHICAGO BLACK HAWKS** (1)	**Tommy Gorman**	**Tommy Gorman**	**Chuck Gardiner**	**Mush March**
	Detroit Red Wings	*Jack Adams*	*Jack Adams*	*Herbie Lewis*	
1934-35	**MONTREAL MAROONS** (2)	**Tommy Gorman**	**Tommy Gorman**	**R.J. Smith**	**Baldy Northcott**
	Toronto Maple Leafs	*Dick Irvin*	*Conn Smythe*	*Hap Day*	
1935-36	**DETROIT RED WINGS** (1)	**Jack Adams**	**Jack Adams**	**Doug Young**	**Pete Kelly**
	Toronto Maple Leafs	*Dick Irvin*	*Conn Smythe*	*Hap Day*	
1936-37	**DETROIT RED WINGS** (2)	**Jack Adams**	**Jack Adams**	**Doug Young**	**Marty Barry**
	New York Rangers	*Lester Patrick*	*Lester Patrick*	*Bill Cook*	
1937-38	**CHICAGO BLACK HAWKS** (2)	**Bill Stewart**	**Bill Stewart**	**Johnny Gottselig**	**Carl Voss**
	Toronto Maple Leafs	*Dick Irvin*	*Conn Smythe*	*Charlie Conacher*	
1938-39	**BOSTON BRUINS** (2)	**Art Ross**	**Art Ross**	**Cooney Weiland**	**Roy Conacher**
	Toronto Maple Leafs	*Dick Irvin*	*Conn Smythe*	*Red Horner*	
1939-40	**NEW YORK RANGERS** (3)	**Frank Boucher**	**Lester Patrick**	**Art Coulter**	**Bryan Hextall Sr.**
	Toronto Maple Leafs	*Dick Irvin*	*Conn Smythe*	*Red Horner*	
1940-41	**BOSTON BRUINS** (3)	**Cooney Weiland**	**Art Ross**	**Dit Clapper**	**Bobby Bauer**
	Detroit Red Wings	*Jack Adams*	*Jack Adams*	*Ebbie Goodfellow*	
1941-42	**TORONTO MAPLE LEAFS** (4)	**Hap Day**	**Conn Smythe**	**Syl Apps**	**Pete Langelle**
	Detroit Red Wings	*Jack Adams*	*Jack Adams*	*Ebbie Goodfellow*	
1942-43	**DETROIT RED WINGS** (3)	**Jack Adams**	**Jack Adams**	**Sid Abel**	**Joe Carveth**
	Boston Bruins	*Art Ross*	*Art Ross*	*Dit Clapper*	
1943-44	**MONTREAL CANADIENS** (4)	**Dick Irvin**	**Tommy Gorman**	**Toe Blake**	**Toe Blake**
	Chicago Black Hawks	*Paul Thompson*	*Bill Tobin*	*Doug Bentley*	

*The Toronto Arenas became the St. Pats and then the Maple Leafs. The Maple Leafs' Stanley Cup total includes two won as the Arenas and St. Pats.

NHL Stanley Cup Honor Roll

Season	Champion (Cup number) Runner-Up	Coach	General Manager	Captain	Cup-Winning Goal
1944-45	**TORONTO MAPLE LEAFS (5)**	**Hap Day**	**Conn Smythe**	**Bob Davidson**	**Babe Pratt**
	Detroit Red Wings	*Jack Adams*	*Jack Adams*	*Flash Hollett*	
1945-46	**MONTREAL CANADIENS (5)**	**Dick Irvin**	**Tommy Gorman**	**Toe Blake**	**Toe Blake**
	Boston Bruins	*Dit Clapper*	*Art Ross*	*Dit Clapper*	
1946-47	**TORONTO MAPLE LEAFS (6)**	**Hap Day**	**Conn Smythe**	**Syl Apps**	**Ted Kennedy**
	Montreal Canadiens	*Dick Irvin*	*Frank Selke*	*Toe Blake*	
1947-48	**TORONTO MAPLE LEAFS (7)**	**Hap Day**	**Conn Smythe**	**Syl Apps**	**Harry Watson**
	Detroit Red Wings	*Tommy Ivan*	*Jack Adams*	*Sid Abel*	
1948-49	**TORONTO MAPLE LEAFS (8)**	**Hap Day**	**Conn Smythe**	**Ted Kennedy**	**Cal Gardner**
	Detroit Red Wings	*Tommy Ivan*	*Jack Adams*	*Sid Abel*	
1949-50	**DETROIT RED WINGS (4)**	**Tommy Ivan**	**Jack Adams**	**Sid Abel**	**Pete Babando**
	New York Rangers	*Lynn Patrick*	*Frank Boucher*	*Buddy O'Connor*	
1950-51	**TORONTO MAPLE LEAFS (9)**	**Joe Primeau**	**Conn Smythe**	**Ted Kennedy**	**Bill Barilko**
	Montreal Canadiens	*Dick Irvin*	*Frank Selke*	*Butch Bouchard*	
1951-52	**DETROIT RED WINGS (5)**	**Tommy Ivan**	**Jack Adams**	**Sid Abel**	**Metro Prystai**
	Montreal Canadiens	*Dick Irvin*	*Frank Selke*	*Butch Bouchard*	
1952-53	**MONTREAL CANADIENS (6)**	**Dick Irvin**	**Frank Selke**	**Butch Bouchard**	**Elmer Lach**
	Boston Bruins	*Lynn Patrick*	*Art Ross*	*Milt Schmidt*	
1953-54	**DETROIT RED WINGS (6)**	**Tommy Ivan**	**Jack Adams**	**Ted Lindsay**	**Tony Leswick**
	Montreal Canadiens	*Dick Irvin*	*Frank Selke*	*Butch Bouchard*	
1954-55	**DETROIT RED WINGS (7)**	**Jimmy Skinner**	**Jack Adams**	**Ted Lindsay**	**Gordie Howe**
	Montreal Canadiens	*Dick Irvin*	*Frank Selke*	*Butch Bouchard*	
1955-56	**MONTREAL CANADIENS (7)**	**Toe Blake**	**Frank Selke**	**Butch Bouchard**	**Maurice Richard**
	Detroit Red Wings	*Jimmy Skinner*	*Jack Adams*	*Ted Lindsay*	
1956-57	**MONTREAL CANADIENS (8)**	**Toe Blake**	**Frank Selke**	**Maurice Richard**	**Dickie Moore**
	Boston Bruins	*Milt Schmidt*	*Lynn Patrick*	*Fern Flaman*	
1957-58	**MONTREAL CANADIENS (9)**	**Toe Blake**	**Frank Selke**	**Maurice Richard**	**Bernie Geoffrion**
	Boston Bruins	*Milt Schmidt*	*Lynn Patrick*	*Fern Flaman*	
1958-59	**MONTREAL CANADIENS (10)**	**Toe Blake**	**Frank Selke**	**Maurice Richard**	**Marcel Bonin**
	Toronto Maple Leafs	*Punch Imlach*	*Punch Imlach*	*George Armstrong*	
1959-60	**MONTREAL CANADIENS (11)**	**Toe Blake**	**Frank Selke**	**Maurice Richard**	**Jean Beliveau**
	Toronto Maple Leafs	*Punch Imlach*	*Punch Imlach*	*George Armstrong*	
1960-61	**CHICAGO BLACK HAWKS (3)**	**Rudy Pilous**	**Tommy Ivan**	**Eddie Litzenberger**	**Ab McDonald**
	Detroit Red Wings	*Sid Abel*	*Jack Adams*	*Gordie Howe*	
1961-62	**TORONTO MAPLE LEAFS (10)**	**Punch Imlach**	**Punch Imlach**	**George Armstrong**	**Dick Duff**
	Chicago Black Hawks	*Rudy Pilous*	*Tommy Ivan*	*Pierre Pilote*	
1962-63	**TORONTO MAPLE LEAFS (11)**	**Punch Imlach**	**Punch Imlach**	**George Armstrong**	**Eddie Shack**
	Detroit Red Wings	*Sid Abel*	*Jack Adams*	*Alex Delvecchio*	
1963-64	**TORONTO MAPLE LEAFS (12)**	**Punch Imlach**	**Punch Imlach**	**George Armstrong**	**Andy Bathgate**
	Detroit Red Wings	*Sid Abel*	*Sid Abel*	*Alex Delvecchio*	
1964-65	**MONTREAL CANADIENS (12)**	**Toe Blake**	**Sam Pollock**	**Jean Beliveau**	**Jean Beliveau**
	Chicago Black Hawks	*Billy Reay*	*Tommy Ivan*	*Pierre Pilote*	
1965-66	**MONTREAL CANADIENS (13)**	**Toe Blake**	**Sam Pollock**	**Jean Beliveau**	**Henri Richard**
	Detroit Red Wings	*Sid Abel*	*Sid Abel*	*Alex Delvecchio*	
1966-67	**TORONTO MAPLE LEAFS (13)**	**Punch Imlach**	**Punch Imlach**	**George Armstrong**	**Jim Pappin**
	Montreal Canadiens	*Toe Blake*	*Sam Pollock*	*Jean Beliveau*	
1967-68	**MONTREAL CANADIENS (14)**	**Toe Blake**	**Sam Pollock**	**Jean Beliveau**	**J.C. Tremblay**
	St. Louis Blues	*Scotty Bowman*	*Lynn Patrick*	*Al Arbour*	
1968-69	**MONTREAL CANADIENS (15)**	**Claude Ruel**	**Sam Pollock**	**Jean Beliveau**	**John Ferguson**
	St. Louis Blues	*Scotty Bowman*	*Lynn Patrick*	*Al Arbour*	
1969-70	**BOSTON BRUINS (4)**	**Harry Sinden**	**Milt Schmidt**	**No Captain**	**Bobby Orr**
	St. Louis Blues	*Scotty Bowman*	*Scotty Bowman*	*Al Arbour*	
1970-71	**MONTREAL CANADIENS (16)**	**Al MacNeil**	**Sam Pollock**	**Jean Beliveau**	**Henri Richard**
	Chicago Black Hawks	*Billy Reay*	*Tommy Ivan*	*No Captain*	
1971-72	**BOSTON BRUINS (5)**	**Tom Johnson**	**Milt Schmidt**	**No Captain**	**Bobby Orr**
	New York Rangers	*Emile Francis*	*Emile Francis*	*Vic Hadfield*	

NHL Stanley Cup Honor Roll

Season	Champion (Cup Number) Runner-Up	Coach	General Manager	Captain	Cup-Winning Goal
1972-73	**MONTREAL CANADIENS** (17)	**Scotty Bowman**	**Sam Pollock**	**Henri Richard**	**Yvan Cournoyer**
	Chicago Black Hawks	*Bill Reay*	*Tommy Ivan*	*No Captain*	
1973-74	**PHILADELPHIA FLYERS** (1)	**Fred Shero**	**Keith Allen**	**Bobby Clarke**	**Rick MacLeish**
	Boston Bruins	*Bep Guidolin*	*Harry Sinden*	*Johnny Bucyk*	
1974-75	**PHILADELPHIA FLYERS** (2)	**Fred Shero**	**Keith Allen**	**Bobby Clarke**	**Bob Kelly**
	Buffalo Sabres	*Floyd Smith*	*Punch Imlach*	*Gerry Meehan*	
1975-76	**MONTREAL CANADIENS** (18)	**Scotty Bowman**	**Sam Pollock**	**Yvan Cournoyer**	**Guy Lafleur**
	Philadelphia Flyers	*Fred Shero*	*Keith Allen*	*Bobby Clarke*	
1976-77	**MONTREAL CANADIENS** (19)	**Scotty Bowman**	**Sam Pollock**	**Yvan Cournoyer**	**Jacques Lemaire**
	Boston Bruins	*Don Cherry*	*Harry Sinden*	*Johnny Bucyk*	
1977-78	**MONTREAL CANADIENS** (20)	**Scotty Bowman**	**Sam Pollock**	**Yvan Cournoyer**	**Mario Tremblay**
	Boston Bruins	*Don Cherry*	*Harry Sinden*	*Wayne Cashman*	
1978-79	**MONTREAL CANADIENS** (21)	**Scotty Bowman**	**Irving Grundman**	**Yvan Cournoyer**	**Jacques Lemaire**
	New York Rangers	*Fred Shero*	*Fred Shero*	*Dave Maloney*	
1979-80	**NEW YORK ISLANDERS** (1)	**Al Arbour**	**Bill Torrey**	**Denis Potvin**	**Bob Nystrom**
	Philadelphia Flyers	*Pat Quinn*	*Keith Allen*	*Mel Bridgman*	
1980-81	**NEW YORK ISLANDERS** (2)	**Al Arbour**	**Bill Torrey**	**Denis Potvin**	**Wayne Merrick**
	Minnesota North Stars	*Glen Sonmor*	*Lou Nanne*	*Paul Shmyr*	
1981-82	**NEW YORK ISLANDERS** (3)	**Al Arbour**	**Bill Torrey**	**Denis Potvin**	**Mike Bossy**
	Vancouver Canucks	*Roger Neilson*	*Jake Milford*	*Kevin McCarthy*	
1982-83	**NEW YORK ISLANDERS** (4)	**Al Arbour**	**Bill Torrey**	**Denis Potvin**	**Mike Bossy**
	Edmonton Oilers	*Glen Sather*	*Glen Sather*	*Lee Fogolin*	
1983-84	**EDMONTON OILERS** (1)	**Glen Sather**	**Glen Sather**	**Wayne Gretzky**	**Ken Linesman**
	New York Islanders	*Al Arbour*	*Bill Torrey*	*Denis Potvin*	
1984-85	**EDMONTON OILERS** (2)	**Glen Sather**	**Glen Sather**	**Wayne Gretzky**	**Paul Coffey**
	Philadelphia Flyers	*Mike Keenan*	*Bobby Clarke*	*Dave Poulin*	
1985-86	**MONTREAL CANADIENS** (22)	**Jean Perron**	**Serge Savard**	**Bob Gainey**	**Bobby Smith**
	Calgary Flames	*Bob Johnson*	*Cliff Fletcher*	*Lanny McDonald*	
1986-87	**EDMONTON OILERS** (3)	**Glen Sather**	**Glen Sather**	**Wayne Gretzky**	**Jari Kurri**
	Philadelphia Flyers	*Mike Keenan*	*Bobby Clarke*	*Dave Poulin*	
1987-88	**EDMONTON OILERS** (4)	**Glen Sather**	**Glen Sather**	**Wayne Gretzky**	**Wayne Gretzky**
	Boston Bruins	*Terry O'Reilly*	*Harry Sinden*	*Rick Middleton*	
1988-89	**CALGARY FLAMES** (1)	**Terry Crisp**	**Cliff Fletcher**	**Lanny McDonald**	**Doug Gilmour**
	Montreal Canadiens	*Pat Burns*	*Serge Savard*	*Bob Gainey*	
1989-90	**EDMONTON OILERS** (5)	**John Muckler**	**Glen Sather**	**Mark Messier**	**Craig Simpson**
	Boston Bruins	*Mike Milbury*	*Harry Sinden*	*Ray Bourque*	
1990-91	**PITTSBURGH PENGUINS** (1)	**Bob Johnson**	**Craig Patrick**	**Mario Lemieux**	**Ulf Samuelsson**
	Minnesota North Stars	*Bob Gainey*	*Bobby Clarke*	*Curt Giles*	
1991-92	**PITTSBURGH PENGUINS** (2)	**Scotty Bowman**	**Craig Patrick**	**Mario Lemieux**	**Ron Francis**
	Chicago Blackhawks	*Mike Keenan*	*Mike Keenan*	*Dirk Graham*	
1992-93	**MONTREAL CANADIENS** (23)	**Jacques Demers**	**Serge Savard**	**Guy Carbonneau**	**Kirk Muller**
	Los Angeles Kings	*Barry Melrose*	*Nick Beverley*	*Wayne Gretzky*	
1993-94	**NEW YORK RANGERS** (4)	**Mike Keenan**	**Neil Smith**	**Mark Messier**	**Mark Messier**
	Vancouver Canucks	*Pat Quinn*	*Pat Quinn*	*Trevor Linden*	
1994-95	**NEW JERSEY DEVILS** (1)	**Jacques Lemaire**	**Lou Lamoriello**	**Scott Stevens**	**Neal Broten**
	Detroit Red Wings	*Scotty Bowman*	*Scotty Bowman*	*Steve Yzerman*	
1995-96	**COLORADO AVALANCHE** (1)	**Marc Crawford**	**Pierre Lacroix**	**Joe Sakic**	**Uwe Krupp**
	Florida Panthers	*Doug MacLean*	*Bryan Murray*	*Brian Skrudland*	
1996-97	**DETROIT RED WINGS** (8)	**Scotty Bowman**	**Scotty Bowman**	**Steve Yzerman**	**Darren McCarty**
	Philadelphia Flyers	*Terry Murray*	*Bobby Clarke*	*Eric Lindros*	
1997-98	**DETROIT RED WINGS** (9)	**Scotty Bowman**	**Ken Holland**	**Steve Yzerman**	**Martin Lapointe**
	Washington Capitals	*Ron Wilson*	*George McPhee*	*Dale Hunter*	
1998-99	**DALLAS STARS** (1)	**Ken Hitchcock**	**Bob Gainey**	**Derian Hatcher**	**Brett Hull**
	Buffalo Sabres	*Lindy Ruff*	*Darcy Regier*	*Michael Peca*	
1999-00	**NEW JERSEY DEVILS** (2)	**Larry Robinson**	**Lou Lamoriello**	**Scott Stevens**	**Jason Arnott**
	Dallas Stars	*Ken Hitchcock*	*Bob Gainey*	*Derian Hatcher*	

The
Top
40

Orr Soars

Landmark Scoring Title NHL's Most Important Season

By Steve Dryden

Bobby Orr and Wayne Gretzky have never played against one another, but they have faced off in two of the most heated battles of the century. When last the two hockey legends met, in a 1997 poll conducted by The Hockey News, Wayne Gretzky was the narrow choice of voters over Bobby Orr as the No. 1 player in NHL history.

This time, Bobby Orr prevailed.

Orr's Art Ross Trophy-winning performance in 1969-70, the first-ever scoring championship by a defenseman, has been voted the most significant full season performance in NHL history by a panel of 20 experts assembled by The Hockey News.

That season was ranked marginally ahead of Wayne Gretzky's seminal 92-goal, 212-point performance in 1981-82. Orr received 864 voting points compared to 857 for Gretzky, a difference of less than .8 per cent. The difference between them in voting for No. 1 NHLer of all-time was .5 per cent.

The two players share space on hockey's highest pedestal. Five of Orr's nine full seasons with the Boston Bruins are among the Top 40 single-season performances in NHL history. Eight of Gretzky's nine full seasons with the Edmonton Oilers are on the list. *(See pg. 120 for the full Top 40.)*

So, what separates the two greatest seasons? The glib answer, judging from the results of our poll, is *next to nothing*.

They were the two clear choices of voters, although Gretzky's 215-point 1985-86 season was in the mix at No. 3 with 785 points and may well have split the vote more than Orr's second Art Ross season (1974-75) that finished No. 5 behind Rocket Richard's historic 50 goals in 50 games (1944-45).

Just the same, the question begs asking: What *does* make Orr's season so special? The answer: Two things. Or, perhaps, two parts of one thing.

First, Orr changed the way the game was played. He wasn't the first defenseman to be an offensive threat; the wonderfully named Flash Hollett led NHL defensemen in goals five times and set the pre-Orr record of 20 goals in 1944-45. Others such as all-time greats Doug Harvey and Red Kelly were also significant contributors. But none of them

Single-Season Magnificence

The Hockey News asked 20 experts to select a special Top 40 list on the eve of a new century in hockey. The panel of ex-players, NHL executives and media *(see pg. 120 for listing)* was asked to "conceive the definitive ranking of individual performances that resonate greatness and will be remembered as the century's most important full regular season contributions to NHL history." The criteria? "Judge the achievements on the basis of any or all of historical significance, dramatic impact, revolutionary or defining nature, dominance over peers and statistical enormity." Playoff performances were not included because of the difficulty in comparing 50- to 84-game full season accomplishments versus playoff achievements of eight to 28 games.

accomplished what Orr did. That is, expand the job description of all defensemen who followed. No longer was it *accepted* on a limited basis for defensemen to join the offense, it was *expected* of them if teams were to have success. Longtime NHL executive Mike Smith said it best: Orr was a transition player in the game's history.

Second, Orr changed the game's landscape. While Gretzky would raise the bar to unimaginable levels within a decade, Orr replaced the bar with another. When he collected 120 points on 33 goals and 87 assists in 1969-70, it represented an 88-per-cent improvement on his own previous NHL record and, perhaps more dramatically, an increase of more than 100 per cent over any other defenseman's point total before him. Orr did for hockey what Babe Ruth did for baseball exactly 50 years before. Ruth revolutionized baseball in 1920 when he raised his own Major League Baseball record from 29 homers to 54, an 86 per-cent improvement.

Statistically, what Gretzky did in 1981-82 approximated (actually bettered) what Mark McGwire did to Roger Maris' homer record in 1998. Gretzky raised the single-season goal standard 21 per cent from Phil Esposito's 76-goal mark. McGwire, meanwhile, improved Maris' standard by 15 per cent, raising it from 61 to 70. None of this diminishes Gretzky's feats. Fact is, the boundaries of offensive achievement had been pushed significantly further by forwards by the time Gretzky arrived than by defensemen when Orr arrived.

Nonetheless, this much is true about Orr.

"In many ways, Orr was actually too good for the rest of us in the NHL," said Bobby Clarke, captain of the Philadelphia Flyers during the 1970s. "He was one of those guys you were terrified to play against. When he got the puck in his end, we wouldn't bother to send wingers in to check him because he'd blow right past them."

Orr was forced to retire at age 30, betrayed by surgery-ravaged knees. He played his last game Nov. 1, 1978, as a member of the Chicago Black Hawks.

"Losing Bobby was the biggest blow the NHL has ever suffered," Gordie Howe said.

Bobby Orr 1969-70

Rushin' Revolution

1 It was and remains the most consequential season ever recorded by a hockey player, and by the time Bobby Orr's magical winter of 1969-70 melted into its triumphant spring, he had changed forever the way hockey is played.

"He opened the game up and that's the way it's been played ever since," says Orr's former Boston Bruins' teammate John Bucyk.

By the time that season ended on May 10, 1970, with Boston's validating Stanley Cup win and Orr's joyful bellyflop frozen for eternity in the famous Ray Lussier photograph, Orr had broken scoring records by such huge margins and played with such creativity and abandon as to alter a half-century of tactical hockey orthodoxy about the proper role of a defenseman. He didn't merely redefine what a defenseman should do, he changed our concept of what was humanly possible and, in doing so, recorded a Grand Slam never before seen and of which repetition is all but impossible.

In his fourth NHL season, the 22-year-old Orr won four major individual trophies: The Hart as league MVP; the Ross as leading scorer (33 goals, 87 assists, 120 points–all records for a defenseman); the Norris as best defenseman; and the Conn Smythe as playoff MVP. "And he should have won the Vezina," says then-Bruins' goaltender Gerry Cheevers, "because he blocked more shots than half the goalies in the league."

But ask him which games, goals or points he remembers from his most important season and Orr, now a flat-bellied 51 and a player agent and partner in Boston's Bob Woolf & Associates agency, is as elusive in conversation as he was on the ice.

By Jack Falla

Brian Babineau/SA

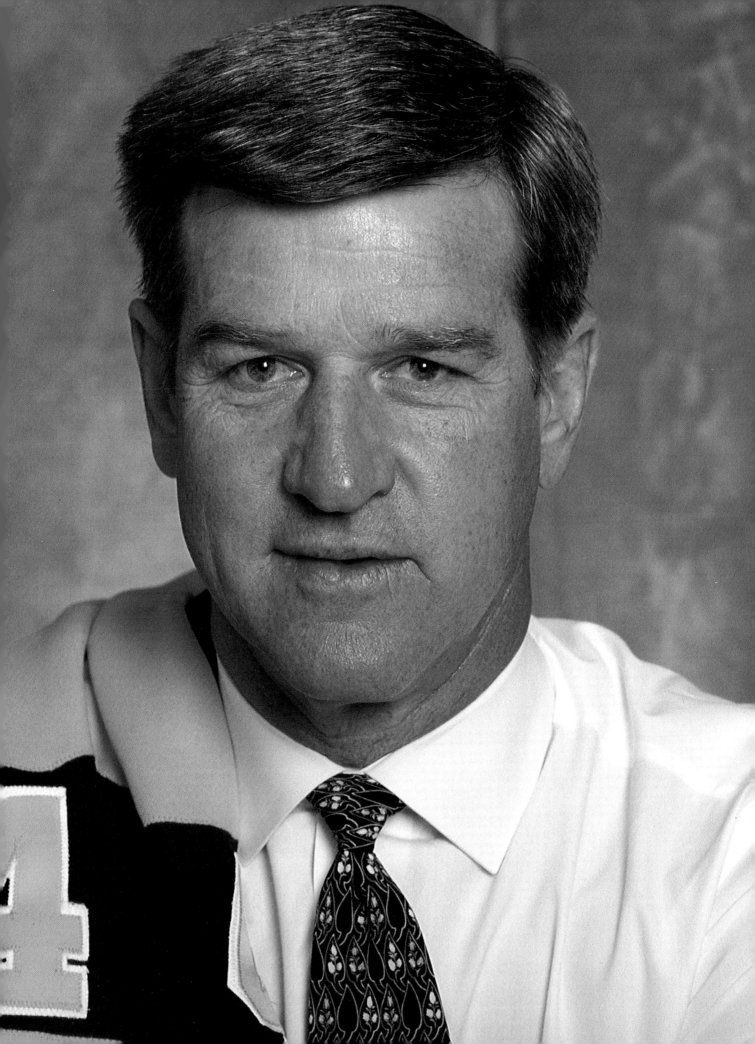

"I was never a stats guy," he says five times in a 42-minute interview in his spacious corner office on the top floor of a Back Bay office tower. "I just remember the guys and the good times." Press him and Orr seems to vaguely recall one milestone–one of the most significant in NHL history–reached on the night he became the first defenseman to record 100 points, a feat theretofore so unimaginable for a defenseman that we can only compare it to a National League pitcher leading that league in batting. "Oh, yeah...the 100th point...ah... lemme see...ah...wasn't that in Detroit? You better check... And, it might've been shorthanded...Yeah. I think it was.... But you'd better check that, too. I'm not a stats guy."

We checked. It was a shorthanded goal scored in Detroit (Orr pronounces it "De-troy-IT") after Orr weaved right to left through neutral ice and ripped a low slapshot from just inside the blueline. We are stats guys, Bobby, and we checked out some of the other statistical frontiers you rolled back in a season that challenged our imagination more than our arithmetic.

There is no intent here to in any way diminish the stature

He didn't merely redefine what a defenseman should do, he changed our concept of what was humanly possible.

and accomplishments of Wayne Gretzky as hockey's affirmed and anointed greatest player. But it is astonishing to look at the percentages by which each player bested existing records. In 1981-82–statistically his best season–Gretzky scored 92 goals to break Phil Esposito's record by 16, a 21-per-cent increase. In 1969-70, Orr broke his own record for goals by a defenseman by 12, a 57-per-cent increase over his own mark (21) and 13 more than Flash Hollett's 1944-45 record of 20 goals by a defenseman, which had stood for 24 years. In 1981-82, Gretzky broke his own assists record by 11, a 10 per-cent increase, and the points record by 48, a 29 per-cent increase; Orr broke Pat Stapleton's previous record for assists by a defenseman by 37, a whopping 74 percent jump, and broke his own record for points by 56, almost doubling his previous mark of 64 points, a barely comprehensible leap of 88 per cent. To compare Orr with players in the Mere Mortals Division, Orr bested the NHL's second-highest scoring defensemen, the Oakland Seals' Carol Vadnais and Toronto Maple Leafs' Jim McKenny (44) by 76 points.

But the numbers are less important than the changes they portended. Orr saw the ice with pan-optic vision and played the puck with a jeweler's touch; his rink-length rushes, look-off passes, speed, mobility and stubborn will to attack, attack, attack did for hockey what cavalry once did for warfare–made the infantry simultaneously more secure and dangerous.

"I guess I influenced young players and drove coaches crazy," says Orr, whose style and success begat an ongoing line of offensive defensemen from Denis Potvin to Doug Wilson to Paul Coffey to Tom Poti (the latter an Orr client whom Orr predicts will someday win the Norris Trophy). "But it drives

Bruins' goalie Gerry Cheevers guards the net while superstar teammate Bobby Orr heads for the puck in the corner.

me crazy when coaches won't let the kids play," he says. "Some coaches try to turn the kids into robots....Hey, let 'em play. Let 'em go. What if the Bruins had asked me to play a (conventional) style? I don't think I could have done it."

Nor should he have.

Yet Orr says he never, in that season, had a sense that he was changing the game. His clearest recollection from 1969-70? "Watching the guys covering the point for me trying to skate backwards when they had to play defense...Geez, some of them didn't skate backwards very well," he says and laughs at the memory. When Orr laughs–which is frequently and unrestrainedly–he squints so hard his eyes almost disappear and his face lights up. But that hawkish nose, which seems to have grown broader and more prominent over the years, takes no part in the merriment and–for the fleeting moment when the laughter stops–gives Orr's face a look of determined raptorial menace.

Orr apologizes–many times–for his inability to recall

Graphic Artists/HHOF

specifics of a season so many of us remember better than he does. Orr apparently views life solely in terms of people. "I remember like it was yesterday seeing Ted Green, who was injured then (Green lost more than one season when he was high-sticked in a fight with Wayne Maki) standing on the bench in street clothes after we won the Stanley Cup. He wasn't going to come onto the ice so (Bruins' coach) Harry (Sinden) and I went over and dragged him out. And that's what that season was all about for me. Teddy, Derek, Cash, Espie, Cheesy, Acer...Geez, we had some characters...I don't remember goals and assists. Sorry, I'm just not a stats guy."

Orr leads you out of his office past a framed copy of his

first NHL contract (calling for a base salary of $15,000 and a $5,000 bonus for playing more than half the team's games) to a bank of elevators in the lobby. But seconds after he disappears behind his office door, and before the elevator arrives, the office door swings open and there is Orr brandishing a small replica of the Stanley Cup. "Look at this prop," he says, "it's got all our names on it."

And then Robert Gordon Orr, dressed in a white shirt, dark tie, business suit and tricked-up black loafers and framed by the glass doorway to his office, lifts the replica over his head and the only thing you can read–because it is the largest writing graven in the metal–is the number at the top: "1969-1970."

Dawn Of New Era For Game

Essential Stats	Year	GP	G	A	P	Scoring champion	P	Gap
Babe Pratt, Tor.	1943-44	50	17	40	57	Herb Cain, Bos.	*82	25
Doug Harvey, Mon.	1954-55	70	6	43	49	Bernie Geoffrion, Mon.	*75	26
Bobby Orr, Bos.	1969-70	76	33	*87	*120	Bobby Orr, Bos.	*120	–
Phil Esposito, Bos.	1969-70	76	43	56	99	Bobby Orr, Bos.	*120	21

Before Bobby Orr wins the first of two scoring titles, the only defenseman in NHL history to do so, no Modern Era blueliner had challenged for the Art Ross Trophy. The closest any had come was 1943-44 (Babe Pratt, 25 points) and 1954-55 (Doug Harvey, 26). Orr demolishes that barrier in 1969-70, outscoring runner-up Phil Esposito by 21 points, then the second-highest margin of victory recorded by a scoring champion.

Legend for abbreviations appears on pg. 19

1969-70: Landmark Season

#	Date	Opponent	G	A	Pts.	G	A	Pts.
1.	Oct. 12	New York	0	2	2	0	2	2
2.	Oct. 15	Oakland	0	3	3	0	5	5
3.	Oct. 18	Pittsburgh	0	1	1	0	6	6
4.	Oct. 19	Pittsburgh	1	0	1	1	6	7
5.	Oct. 22	Minnesota	1	1	2	2	7	9
6.	Oct. 24	Oakland	0	3	3	2	10	12
7.	Oct. 25	Los Angeles	0	2	2	2	12	14
8.	Oct. 29	Toronto	0	0	0	2	12	14
9.	Nov. 1	Montreal	0	1	1	2	13	15
10.	Nov. 2	Toronto	0	3	3	2	16	18
11.	Nov. 5	St. Louis	0	0	0	2	16	18
12.	Nov. 8	Detroit	0	1	1	2	17	19
13.	Nov. 10	Oakland	0	3	3	2	20	22
14.	Nov. 13	Detroit	0	1	1	2	21	23
15.	Nov. 15	New York	2	0	2	4	21	25
16.	Nov. 16	Los Angeles	0	4	4	4	25	29
17.	Nov. 21	Chicago	0	1	1	4	26	30
18.	Nov. 23	Montreal	0	0	0	4	26	30
19.	Nov. 26	New York	0	0	0	4	26	30
20.	Nov. 27	Philadelphia	2	1	3	6	27	33
21.	Nov. 29	Montreal	0	0	0	6	27	33
22.	Nov. 30	Toronto	1	1	2	7	28	35
23.	Dec. 4	Detroit	0	2	2	7	30	37
24.	Dec. 6	Chicago	0	1	1	7	31	38
25.	Dec. 7	Minnesota	0	0	0	7	31	38
26.	Dec. 10	New York	1	1	2	8	32	40
27.	Dec. 11	New York	0	0	0	8	32	40
28.	Dec. 13	Philadelphia	0	1	1	8	33	41
29.	Dec. 14	Pittsburgh	0	0	0	8	33	41
30.	Dec. 18	St. Louis	0	1	1	8	34	42
31.	Dec. 20	Pittsburgh	0	5	5	8	39	47
32.	Dec. 21	Montreal	1	0	1	9	39	48
33.	Dec. 25	Los Angeles	1	1	2	10	40	50
34.	Dec. 28	Philadelphia	1	3	4	11	43	54
35.	Dec. 31	Detroit	0	0	0	11	43	54
36.	Jan. 3	Los Angeles	0	2	2	11	45	56
37.	Jan. 7	Oakland	0	2	2	11	47	58
38.	Jan. 10	Toronto	1	2	3	12	49	61
39.	Jan. 11	Oakland	0	0	0	12	49	61
40.	Jan. 15	Los Angeles	0	2	2	12	51	63
41.	Jan. 17	Chicago	0	0	0	12	51	63
42.	Jan. 18	Montreal	1	1	2	13	52	65
43.	Jan. 22	Philadelphia	0	1	1	13	53	66
44.	Jan. 24	New York	0	1	1	13	54	67
45.	Jan. 25	Pittsburgh	1	0	1	14	54	68
46.	Jan. 29	Minnesota	1	3	4	15	57	72
47.	Jan. 31	Montreal	1	1	2	16	58	74
48.	Feb. 1	Toronto	1	2	3	17	60	77
49.	Feb. 4	Chicago	0	0	0	17	60	77
50.	Feb. 5	Philadelphia	2	1	3	19	61	80
51.	Feb. 7	Detroit	1	0	1	20	61	81
52.	Feb. 8	St. Louis	0	1	1	20	62	82
53.	Feb. 11	St. Louis	0	2	2	20	64	84
54.	Feb. 14	Pittsburgh	1	0	1	21	64	85
55.	Feb. 17	Oakland	0	1	1	21	65	86
56.	Feb. 18	Los Angeles	1	1	2	22	66	88
57.	Feb. 21	Minnesota	2	1	3	24	67	91
58.	Feb. 22	Chicago	0	2	2	24	69	93
59.	Feb. 26	New York	0	0	0	24	69	93
60.	Feb. 28	Chicago	0	0	0	24	69	93
61.	Mar. 1	St. Louis	1	0	1	25	69	94
62.	Mar. 4	St. Louis	0	0	0	25	69	94
63.	Mar. 7	Philadelphia	0	1	1	25	70	95
64.	Mar. 8	Montreal	0	2	2	25	72	97
65.	Mar. 11	Chicago	0	0	0	25	72	97
66.	Mar. 14	Toronto	0	0	0	25	72	97
67.	Mar. 15	Detroit	2	2	4	27	74	101
68.	Mar. 19	Chicago	0	0	0	27	74	101
69.	Mar. 21	Minnesota	1	2	3	28	76	104
70.	Mar. 22	Minnesota	2	2	4	30	78	108
71.	Mar. 25	New York	0	1	1	30	79	109
72.	Mar. 28	Detroit	1	2	3	31	81	112
73.	Mar. 29	Detroit	0	2	2	31	83	114
74.	April 1	Montreal	1	2	3	32	85	117
75.	April 4	Toronto	1	1	2	33	86	119
76.	April 5	Toronto	0	1	1	33	87	120

	GP	G	A	Pts.	+/–	PIM	PP	SH	GW
1969-70	76	33	87	120	+54	125	11	4	3

Bobby Orr's Season Milestones

GP, games; **G**, goals; **A**, assists; **Pts.**, points; **+/–**, plus-minus; **PIM**, penalty minutes; **PP**, power play goals; **SH**, shorthanded goals; **GW**, game-winning goals

1. Jan. 15 Records two assists against Los Angeles to break single-season record of 50 assists for a defenseman, set in 1968-69 by Pat Stapleton of Chicago.

2. Jan. 18 Collects one goal and one assist against Montreal to break his own single-season record of 64 points by a defenseman, set in 1968-69.

3. Feb. 18 Scores 22nd goal against Los Angeles to break his own record of 21 for defensemen, set in 1968-69.

4. March 15 Collects two goals and two assists against Detroit to become first defenseman to record 100 points.

5. March 22 Scores two goals and adds two assists against Minnesota to break teammate Phil Esposito's single-season record of 77 assists, set in 1968-69.

6. April 5 Becomes first defenseman in history to earn Art Ross Trophy by winning league scoring championship.

7. April 16 Scores sixth and seventh playoff goals against New York to break defenseman record of five, set by Earl Seibert of Chicago in 1937-38.

8. May 5 Earns two assists against St. Louis to surpass defenseman record of 16 playoff points, set by Toronto's Tim Horton in 1961-62.

9. May 10 Wins Conn Smythe Trophy (playoff MVP) after scoring Cup-winning goal against St. Louis in overtime.

10. June Becomes only player in history to win four major trophies in one season: the Hart (regular season MVP), Norris (best defenseman), Art Ross and Conn Smythe.

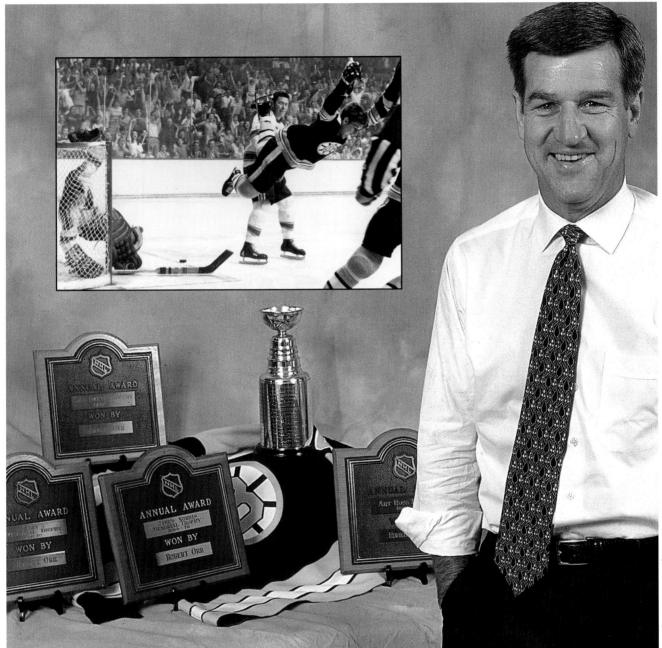

Bobby Orr is flanked by momentoes of his record-setting 1969-70 season—plaques representing four individual trophies and a miniature Stanley Cup. INSET, The most famous picture in hockey: Orr flying through the air after scoring the 1970 Cup-winning goal in overtime.

Brian Babineau/SA Inset–Fred Kennan/HHOF

Playoffs

	Date	Opponent	G	A	Pts.	G	A	Pts.
1.	Apr. 8	New York	2	1	3	2	1	3
2.	Apr. 9	New York	0	1	1	2	2	4
3.	Apr. 11	New York	1	0	1	3	2	5
4.	Apr. 12	New York	1	0	1	4	2	6
5.	Apr. 14	New York	1	1	2	5	3	8
6.	Apr. 16	New York	2	0	2	7	3	10
7.	Apr. 19	Chicago	0	2	2	7	5	12
8.	Apr. 21	Chicago	1	0	1	8	5	13

	Date	Opponent	G	A	Pts.	G	A	Pts.
9.	Apr. 23	Chicago	0	1	1	8	6	14
10.	Apr. 26	Chicago	0	1	1	8	7	15
11.	May 3	St. Louis	0	1	1	8	8	16
12.	May 5	St. Louis	0	2	2	8	10	18
13.	May 7	St. Louis	0	1	1	8	11	19
14.	May 10	St. Louis	1	0	1	9	11	20

	GP	G	A	Pts.	PIM	PP	SH	GW
1969-70	14	9	11	20	14	3	2	1

Wayne Gretzky 1981-82

Gretzky Worth Weight In Goal

By Jim Matheson

2 After Wayne Gretzky scores 50 goals in his first 39 games in 1981-82, Glen Sather dangles a carrot in front of No. 99.

"I hope Wayne passes my NHL career in one year," says the Edmonton Oilers' coach-GM, who had 80 goals in 10 NHL seasons. Gretzky listens to Sather and rolls past his career numbers with five weeks to go, finishing with the highest goal total in history–92.

How great is Gretzky in this prolific season? Gretzky has 42 goals in the final 41 Oiler games and people say he is in a slump. Gretzky doesn't score a goal in 25 of 80 Oiler games, but still has 92.

He has a run of six games in early to mid-March in which he doesn't beat any goalies, the only real drought of the year. But he has seven hat tricks, two four-goal nights and the five-goal highlight reel against the Philadelphia Flyers Dec. 30.

Gretzky has 11 shots on the night, including one into an empty net with Pete Peeters pulled for an extra attacker. That goal, No. 50 in just 39 games, establishes the most amazing of all Gretzky standards–50 goals before the new year and in 11 fewer games than anyone else has ever done it.

Gretzky has a staggering 15 goals in a five-game stretch against the Minnesota North Stars, Calgary Flames, Vancouver Canucks and Los Angeles Kings, culminating with five against the Flyers. The 15 goals come on just 32 shots. Does it get any better than that?

"I think I'm more delighted with this than anything else, at least individually," Gretzky says.

"This is absolutely crazy," says Flyers' captain Bobby Clarke.

"I saw an opportunity to go for 200 points and I went after it. Who's to say the game won't tighten up in the next few years."
–Wayne Gretzky

"At least with Bobby Orr you would see him wind up in his own end and you could try to set up some kind of defense to stop him. Gretzky just comes out of nowhere…it's scary."

Defenseman Paul Coffey says, "I know things like this aren't supposed to happen. He had nine goals in two straight games, four the game before against the Kings. But when Wayne sets a goal for himself…he gets it. He wanted to do it before his 40th game. You could have bet $1 million against him doing it, but we all knew he could."

Just like beating Phil Esposito's single-season standard of 76 goals.

Gretzky does it in the Oilers' 64th game, in Buffalo against the Sabres. It takes him 54 minutes, but he squeezes three past Don Edwards before the clock runs down. "I was anxious for Phil," Gretzky says of Esposito, who follows Gretzky during the record hunt. "I wanted to get it so he could go back to work."

Esposito, who took 78 games to score his 76 in 1970-71, has a pretty good idea Gretzky would be taking his spot in the record book.

"I got a phone call from my dad one day and he said, 'Phil, there's a boy who's going to break all your records. He's 16 years old and playing in the Soo. His name is Gretzky. Wayne Gretzky.' "

Gretzky has 16 games left to get 21 goals and reach 100, but falls eight short. It is fatigue as much as a steady diet of shadows in every rink, not to mention a penchant for missing breakaways.

"That's about the only thing he wasn't great at," says Oilers' assistant coach John Muckler.

Essential Stats	Year	GP	G	A	P	Record: Goals
Wayne Gretzky, Edm.	1981-82	80	*92	*120	*212	Raises Esposito record by 16
Wayne Gretzky, Edm.	1983-84	74	*87	*118	*205	Pro-rates to 94 over full season
Brett Hull, St.L	1990-91	78	*86	45	131	1 more than Lemieux's best

NHL Single-Season Honor Roll

1.	**BOBBY ORR**, Bos., 1969-70	*Becomes first defenseman to win scoring championship*
2.	**WAYNE GRETZKY**, Edm., 1981-82	*Scores record 92 goals, including 50 in 39 games, and 212 points*
3.	**WAYNE GRETZKY**, Edm., 1985-86	*Scores record 215 points and has more assists (163) than anyone else has points*
4.	**ROCKET RICHARD**, Mon., 1944-45	*Scores record 50 goals in 50 games, the standard by which goal-scoring is measured*
5.	**BOBBY ORR**, Bos., 1974-75	*Scores record 46 goals for defensemen and leads league with 135 points*
6.	**WAYNE GRETZKY**, Edm., 1983-84	*Earns points in record 51 games and wins Art Ross by largest margin ever*
7.	**MARIO LEMIEUX**, Pit., 1988-89	*Leads league in scoring with 199 points, the highest non-Gretzky total ever*
8.	**PHIL ESPOSITO**, Bos., 1970-71	*Sets NHL records with 76 goals, 152 points and 550 shots*
9.	**MARIO LEMIEUX**, Pit., 1992-93	*Roars back from Hodgkin's Disease to win scoring championship*
10.	**PAUL COFFEY**, Edm., 1985-86	*Beats the unbeatable foe–Bobby Orr–by scoring defenseman record 48 goals*
11.	**BOBBY ORR**, Bos., 1970-71	*First player to record 100 assists and scores defenseman record 139 points*
12.	**GEORGE HAINSWORTH**, Mon., 1928-29	*Earns 22 shutouts and 0.92 goals-against average, two records that stand today*
13.	**BOBBY ORR**, Bos., 1971-72	*Last defenseman to win Hart Trophy*
14.	**WAYNE GRETZKY**, Edm., 1979-80	*19-year-old becomes youngest player to score 50 goals and win Hart*
15.	**JOE MALONE**, Mon., 1917-18	*Scores 44 goals in 20 games for the highest goals-per-game average (2.2) in history*
16.	**MIKE BOSSY**, NYI, 1980-81	*First player to score 50 goals in 50 games since Rocket Richard (1944-45)*
17.	**STAN MIKITA**, Chi., 1966-67	*First player to win Hart, Art Ross and Lady Byng Trophies in same season*
18.	**WAYNE GRETZKY**, Edm., 1984-85	*Records second-highest point total (208) in league history at the time*
19.	**GORDIE HOWE**, Det., 1952-53	*Scores 49 goals and collects record 95 points*
20.	**PHIL ESPOSITO**, Bos., 1968-69	*First player to score 100 points*
21.	**TERRY SAWCHUK**, Det., 1950-51	*Calder winner sets NHL record with 44 wins and earns 1.99 GAA*
22.	**BOBBY HULL**, Chi., 1965-66	*Sets records for goals (54) and points (97) to win Hart*
23.	**TONY ESPOSITO**, Chi., 1969-70	*Wins Calder and Vezina with Modern Day and rookie-record 15 shutouts*
24.	**DOMINIK HASEK**, Buf., 1997-98	*Only goalie to win back-to-back Hart Trophies*
25.	**BERNIE PARENT**, Phi., 1973-74	*Sets goalie mark of 47 wins and posts last sub-2.00 GAA for 20 seasons*
26.	**BRETT HULL**, St. L, 1990-91	*Scores 86 goals, third highest total of all-time*
27.	**GORDIE HOWE**, Det., 1968-69	*Forty-one-year-old icon is oldest 100-point player ever*
28.	**TEEMU SELANNE**, Win., 1992-93	*Sets rookie records with 76 goals and 132 points*
29.	**GORDIE HOWE**, Det., 1950-51	*Sets point record (86) after suffering fractured skull previous season*
30.	**RAY BOURQUE**, Bos., 1979-80	*Nineteen-year-old scores rookie-record 65 points and earns berth on first all-star team*
31.	**MIKE BOSSY**, NYI, 1977-78	*First player to score 50 goals in rookie season*
32.	**WAYNE GRETZKY**, Edm., 1982-83	*First player in 42 seasons to earn more assists (125) than anyone else has points*
33.	**EDDIE SHORE**, Bos., 1932-33	*First defenseman to win Hart Trophy with career-high 35 points*
34.	**MARIO LEMIEUX**, Pit., 1987-88	*Breaks Wayne Gretzky's string of seven straight scoring championships*
35.	**WAYNE GRETZKY**, Edm., 1986-87	*Records most decisive Art Ross title ever, in terms of percentage (69%)*
36.	**BOBBY ORR**, Bos., 1973-74	*Leads NHL in assists with 90 and finishes second in scoring with 122 points*
37.	**WAYNE GRETZKY**, Edm., 1980-81	*Sets records for assists (109) and points (164) to win Art Ross*
38.	**BILL COWLEY**, Bos., 1943-44	*Records best non-Gretzky, non-Lemieux points-per-game average of all time (1.97)*
39.	**DOMINIK HASEK**, Buf., 1993-94	*First goalie to record sub-2.00 GAA in 20 years*
40.	**TOM BARRASSO**, Buf., 1983-84	*Only goalie to go from high school to NHL, wins Vezina and Calder at 19*

Our Expert Panel: The Hockey News Selection Committee

Wayne Gretzky 1985-86

Point King Does It In 77 Of 80 Games

3 Wayne Gretzky is always chasing his own shadow. Trying to beat his own records.

But getting 215 points in 1985-86, after breaking 200 four years earlier is remarkable, even by his own elevated standards.

He has only three games in which he doesn't earn a point–in his 10th game of the season against the Buffalo Sabres, in No. 50 against the Chicago Black Hawks and in No. 69 against Buffalo. In 40 of the 80 games, he has at least three points. In 21, he has four or more. He has more assists, an all-time high 163, than anyone else has points. Mario Lemieux is a distant second in the scoring race with 141 points.

Gretzky collects seven assists against the Black Hawks Dec. 11 in the highest-scoring game in NHL history, a 12-9 Oilers' victory.

"The main thing is, I wanted to beat 212. 215's okay, but I didn't want to get too high. There's always next year."
–Wayne Gretzky

It ties Billy Taylor's record for assists in a road game. "I actually thought I had eight assists when I fed Jari (Kurri, with 36 seconds left), but I lost count, I guess," Gretzky says. "It was one of those freaky nights."

Gretzky rolls another seven on Valentine's Day, against the Quebec Nordiques. "Seven assists? That's my lucky number," Gretzky says. "That's three times now. Maybe I should change sweaters with Paul Coffey."

Before he gets to 215, Gretzky reaches 200 for the fourth time in five years. "It's something I look at with a great deal of pride," he says. "Maybe somebody will get there once, but I've done it four times. I think Mario is a great possibility." (Lemieux will fall one point shy in 1988-89.)

Gretzky breaks his own record of 212 points with three assists in Calgary in the second-last game of the year. It comes a day after he has root canal surgery. Nothing can stop Gretzky in 1985-86.

Essential Stats	Year	GP	G	A	P	Record: Points
Wayne Gretzky, Edm.	1980-81	80	55	*109	*164	Raises Esposito record by 12
Wayne Gretzky, Edm.	1981-82	80	*92	*120	*212	Raises own record by 48
Wayne Gretzky, Edm.	1985-86	80	52	*163	*215	Raises own record by 3

Rocket Richard makes history in 1944-45; he is the first NHLer to score 50 goals.

HHOF

4

Rocket Richard 1944-45

Pure Magic: 50 Goals In 50 Games

With the help of linemates Elmer Lach and Toe Blake, the Rocket scores a record 50 goals in 50 games, 18 more than runner-up Herb Cain of the Boston Bruins. In the process, Richard smashes the previous mark of 44, set by Joe Malone in the NHL's first season, 1917-18. The Rocket adds 23 assists to finish second to Lach in league scoring with 73 points. After breaking Malone's record in game No. 42, the fiery 23-year-old climbs to 49 goals entering the final game of the season. Richard hits the magical mark at 17:54 of the third period when he takes a pass from Lach and fires it into the Boston net. Richard scores eight points Dec. 28 against Detroit, a total surpassed only by Darryl Sittler's 10-point outing in 1975-76. "He looks like (Howie) Morenz from the blueline in," says Toronto manager Conn Smythe. Richard's record of 50 goals in a season is not broken until the 1965-66 campaign when Bobby Hull scores 54 in 65 games and it takes 36 years before Mike Bossy matches Richard's 50 goals in 50 games in 1980-81.

"I find if I have a plan to fool the goaler, he usually beats me. But if I don't know what I'm going to do, how can he?"
–Rocket Richard

Essential Stats	Year	GP	G	Record: Goals
Joe Malone, Mon.	1917-18	20	*44	2.2 goals per game will stand for all-time
Cooney Weiland, Bos.	1929-30	44	*43	One of four 40-goal men before Rocket
Rocket Richard, Mon.	1944-45	50	*50	Magic mark still resonates 55 years later

Photo: Imperial Oil - Turofsky/HHOF

5

Bobby Orr 1974-75

One Last Sensational Season

It's the only season Orr plays every game and it turns out to be the last of any length for the superstar. In his last hurrah in Boston, the Bruins' defenseman leads the NHL with 89 assists and 135 points–the last blueliner to do so in either category. The Art Ross Trophy winner breaks his own defenseman record with 46 goals, to win his last (and eighth straight) Norris Trophy. The goal record before Orr enters the NHL was 20, set by Flash Hollett in 1944-45. The second-highest defenseman goal total in 1974-75 is 28, scored by the Montreal Canadiens' Guy Lapointe. In defenseman points, Orr finishes a whopping 59 ahead of runner-up Denis Potvin of the New York Islanders. "The only thing saving the National Hockey League is Bobby Orr," says Winnipeg's Bobby Hull of the rival World Hockey Association. "If Orr comes with us, they're done." Orr stays in the NHL, but he only plays 36 games over the next four seasons because of chronic knee problems. Orr sets four single-season defenseman goal-scoring records during his career and is eventually surpassed by Paul Coffey.

"He is the only one in the world who can play his style as a defenseman and get away with it. He can rush and get back in time to play defense."
–Boston GM Harry Sinden

Essential Stats	Year	GP	G	Essential Stats	Year	GP	G
Flash Hollett, Det.	1944-45	50	20	Bobby Orr, Bos.	1970-71	78	37
Bobby Orr, Bos.	1968-69	67	21	Bobby Orr, Bos.	1974-75	80	46
Bobby Orr, Bos.	1969-70	76	33	Paul Coffey, Edm.	1985-86	79	48

Photo: London Life - Portnoy/HHOF

Wayne Gretzky 1983-84

'The Great One' Streaks To Record

They aren't the highest totals of his career, but if Gretzky doesn't miss six games with a shoulder injury, it might rate as the best NHL season of all-time. He records the best goal- and point-scoring averages in NHL Modern-Era history (1.18 goals and 2.77 points per game); over a full 80-game schedule, his numbers pro-rate to a record 94 goals and 222 points. He finishes with 87 goals and 205 points. Art Ross Trophy-runner-up and Edmonton Oilers' teammmate Paul Coffey (126 points) finishes an NHL-record 79 points behind Gretzky, who also captures the Hart. 'The Great One' strings together an NHL-record 51-game points streak, racking up 61 goals and 153 points, including his 100th point of the season in a record 34 games. "I admire a guy like Joe DiMaggio for what he must have gone through (during the baseball great's 56-game hitting streak in 1941)," Gretzky says. No. 99 averages an astonishing three points per game during the streak, three-quarters of a point more than Mario Lemieux averaged during the second-longest streak ever. Gretzky leads the first-place Oilers to the NHL's highest goal total (446) of all-time in his first season as Edmonton's captain.

Essential Stats	Year	Streak	G	A	P	GPG	APG	PPG
Wayne Gretzky, Edm.	1983-84	51 games	61	92	153	1.20	1.80	3.00
Mario Lemieux, Pit.	1989-90	46 games	39	64	103	.848	1.39	2.24
Wayne Gretzky, Edm.	1985-86	39 games	33	75	108	.846	1.92	2.77

Photo: O-Pee-Chee Collection/HHOF

> *"I'm not like a Perreault or a Lafleur, where I'll skate through a whole team. The secret to our success is moving the puck and going to the holes."*
> *—Wayne Gretzky*

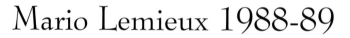

Mario Lemieux 1988-89

No. 66 Comes Within Whisker Of 200

Another player enters the Wayne Gretzky stratosphere. Lemieux misses joining 'The Great One' in the 200-point club by one in the most productive season by a player not wearing No. 99. The Pittsburgh Penguin center's 85 goals are fourth-most in NHL history and only Gretzky's four 200-point seasons surpass Lemieux's total of 199. Lemieux wins the Art Ross Trophy and joins Gretzky and Bobby Orr as the only players to record more than 100 assists in one season with 114. In addition, the 23-year-old pulls off an unusual first that not even Gretzky accomplishes. Lemieux scores for the cycle in a New Year's Eve game against New Jersey–he scores a goal at even strength, on a power play, while shorthanded, on a penalty shot and into an empty net. Forty-four of his goals come on the special teams–31 on the power play and an NHL-record 13 while shorthanded. Lemieux averages more than two points per game for a second successive season; he also averages more points per game than Gretzky for the first time (2.62` vs. 2.15). No. 66 will lead the league in points per game the remaining five full seasons of his career.

Essential Stats	Year	GP	P	PPG	PPG Noteworthy
Mario Lemieux, Pit.	1988-89	76	*199	2.62	5th highest all-time
Wayne Gretzky, LA	1988-89	78	168	2.15	12th highest all-time

Photo: Bruce Bennett/BBS

> *"Steve Yzerman is having an extraordinary season and Gretzky will always be 'The Great One.' But once again this season, the translation of Lemieux's surname ('The Best') says it all."*
> *—The Hockey News*

8

Phil Esposito 1970-71

Shooting Star Demolishes Hull Record

"Bobby's been my buddy since I centered for him in Chicago. I don't consider myself as good as him. Heck, what's he got in his career, 540 goals? I'll never score that many."
–Phil Esposito, who will outscore Hull 717-610

Never has any player blitzed NHL goalies as much as Esposito does this season. The Boston Bruins' center scores 76 goals, 18 more than Bobby Hull's previous NHL record, the highest-ever step up in the goal record and still fifth-highest total in NHL history. He adds 76 assists and wins the Art Ross Trophy with 152 points, breaking his old mark (126) set two seasons before. Neither record will be topped until Wayne Gretzky enters the NHL a decade later. One mark Gretzky never comes close to touching is Esposito's 550 shots on net, most of them coming from the slot, his second home. His total is 136 more than Hull had during his 58-goal season in 1968-69. (In 1998-99, the Mighty Ducks of Anaheim's Paul Kariya will come the closest with 429 shots.) "I see him taking all these shots and I wonder why his arms don't fall off," says Montreal Canadiens' goalie Ken Dryden. Although not a smooth skater, Esposito uses his ability to control the pace of the game to set nine different individual records during the year and help the Bruins to a then-record 121-point, 399-goal season.

Essential Stats	Year	GP	G	A	P	Record: Goals
Bobby Hull, Chi.	1968-69	74	*58	49	107	Raises own record by four
Phil Esposito, Bos.	1970-71	78	*76	*76	*152	Raises Hull record 31%
Wayne Gretzky, Edm.	1981-82	80	*92	*120	*212	Raises Esposito record 21%

Photo: London Life - Portnoy/HHOF

9

Mario Lemieux 1992-93

A Comeback For The Ages

"If he wins the Hart, it will be because of his heart. Look what he has overcome. Let's face it, if he hadn't missed those 23 games, he'd probably be going for 193 (points)."
–Buffalo center Pat Lafontaine

En route to challenging Wayne Gretzky's record of 215 points, Lemieux is confronted with the biggest battle of his life. The Pittsburgh Penguins' superstar learns Jan. 11 he has Hodgkin's disease after doctors find cancer in one lymph node in his neck. "After they gave me the news, I could hardly drive between the tears," he says. But the 27-year-old makes a tremendous recovery over the next two months. After undergoing radiation treatment, Lemieux flies to Philadelphia March 2 for a game that night and scores a goal and an assist. Before the game, Lemieux sits 12 points behind Buffalo's Pat Lafontaine in the scoring race. By season's end, he's 12 points ahead of the Sabres' center, scoring 56 points in his last 20 games. Lemieux finishes with 69 goals and 160 points in only 60 games to win the Art Ross and Hart Trophies. His 1.15 goals-per-game average is the second-best in the Modern Era and 2.67 points-per-game average is third-best. Nobody has won a scoring title playing a smaller percentage of games (60 of 84 games, 71 per cent); the three lowest marks have been recorded by Lemieux.

Essential Stats	Year	Games	Pct.	P	Noteworthy
Mario Lemieux, Pit.	1991-92	64/80	80%	*131	Wins Art Ross by 8 points
Mario Lemieux, Pit.	1992-93	60/84	71%	*160	Wins Art Ross by 12 points
Mario Lemieux, Pit.	1995-96	70/82	85%	*120	Wins Art Ross by 12 points

Photo: Bruce Bennett/BBS

10

Paul Coffey 1985-86

Oiler Surpasses Legend's Goal Total

"When I got that goal, I had a good feeling before the end of the night I'd get the 47th. I felt I had 1,000 pounds removed from my back. You knew I'd be sniffing in there as much as I could."
–Paul Coffey

It's hard to believe, but Bobby Orr's record of 46 goals in one season by a defenseman lasts only 11 years. Coffey scores on a coast-to-coast effort April 2 against Vancouver to equal the 1974-75 mark, then breaks it later in the night with his second goal of the game. The Edmonton Oiler also takes aim at Orr's 1970-71 points record (139). Needing one point in the last game of the season and two goals to reach the magical 50-goal plateau, Coffey is held pointless to finish the season with 48 goals and 138 points. Helping Coffey along the way is a 28-game point streak, smashing the old defenseman record of 17 set by Ray Bourque in 1984-85. Coffey scores an incredible 55 points over that span. The Norris Trophy winner also ties Tom Bladon's 1977-78 blueliner record of eight points in one game. "(Coach) Glen Sather was the guy who taught me to be the fourth man on rushes," Coffey says. "I didn't do that in juniors. Who knows, if I was picked by Washington with the pick ahead of Edmonton (in 1980), maybe I would have never played this way."

Essential Stats	Year	GP	G	A	P	Defenseman Notes
Bobby Orr, Bos.	1970-71	78	37	*102	*139	Current record for points
Bobby Orr, Bos.	1974-75	80	46	*89	*135	Goal record lasts 11 years
Paul Coffey, Edm.	1985-86	79	48	90	138	Current record for goals

Photos: Bruce Bennett/BBS

Paul Coffey scores an NHL-record 48 goals and a career-high 138 points during a sensational 1985-86 season.

11

Bobby Orr 1970-71

Defenseman First To 100 Assists

"Howe could do everything, but not at top speed. Hull went at top speed, but couldn't do everything. Orr can do everything, and do it at top speed."
–Boston GM Harry Sinden

Orr pulls off what looks impossible when the Boston Bruins' defenseman becomes the first player to record 100 assists. Only Wayne Gretzky (10 times) and Mario Lemieux (once) will ever surpass Orr's total of 102. The Hart and Norris Trophy winner finishes a whopping 76 points ahead of the next highest defenseman's total (139 to 63, 121 per cent more points) and winds up a record plus-124.

Essential Stats	Year	P	No. 2 Defenseman	P	Gap	Noteworthy
Bobby Orr, Bos.	1969-70	120	Carol Vadnais, Oak.	44	76	173% more points
Bobby Orr, Bos.	1970-71	*139	J.C. Tremblay, Mon.	63	76	121% more points
Bobby Orr, Bos.	1974-75	*135	Denis Potvin, NYI	76	59	78% more points

Photo: London Life - Portnoy/HHOF

12

George Hainsworth 1928-29

Untouchable Marks In Year Of The Shutout

"He was much like the man the Vezina Trophy commemorates–cool in the nets and almost mechanical in his perfection."
–Hockey Hall of Fame

Hainsworth establishes the two most amazing single-season goalie records in NHL history. The Montreal Canadien's 0.92 goals-against average and 22 shutouts (in 44 games) earn him the Vezina Trophy in the year of the shutout. Rule changes are made the following season allowing forward passing in all three zones, and guaranteeing the marks will never be equalled.

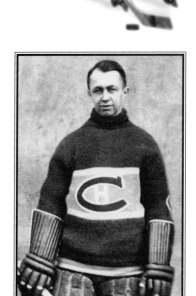

Essential Stats	Year	W	L	T	SO	GAA	Noteworthy
George Hainsworth, Mon.	1928-29	22	7	15	*22	*0.92	5-foot-6, 150 pounds
Tiny Thompson, Bos.	1928-29	*26	13	5	*12	1.15	5-foot-10, 160 pounds
Roy Worters, NYA	1928-29	16	12	10	13	1.15	5-foot-3, 135 pounds

Photo: HHOF

13

Bobby Orr 1971-72

Last Blueliner To Win Hart

"There really wasn't much to choose between the two teams, but the difference probably was Orr. He just seems to control everything."
–Rangers' left winger Vic Hadfield

Orr becomes the last defenseman to win the Hart Trophy with another Norris-winning season. The Boston Bruins' legend finishes second in scoring with 117 points–behind teammate Phil Esposito (133). Orr leads the league in assists with 80. His 37 goals tie for the second-most of his career. Doug Harvey and Denis Potvin are the defensemen who come closest to winning the Hart before and after Orr's arrival.

Essential Stats	Year	GP	G	A	P	Noteworthy
Doug Harvey, NYR	1961-62	69	6	24	30	Runner-up to Jacques Plante
Bobby Orr, Bos.	1971-72	76	37	*80	117	Ken Dryden runner-up to Orr
Denis Potvin, NYI	1975-76	78	31	67	98	Runner-up to Bobby Clarke

Photo: London Life - Portnoy/HHOF

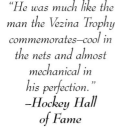

Wayne Gretzky 1979-80

'Rookie' Begins Record Book Assault

After one season in the World Hockey Association (making him ineligible for rookie of the year), the Edmonton Oiler becomes the NHL's youngest 50-goal-scorer, Hart and Lady Byng Trophy winner. His 137 points tie Marcel Dionne for the scoring title, but he misses out on the Art Ross Trophy because of goal differential (53 to 51).

Essential Stats	Year	GP	G	A	P	First Year Scoring Standards
Peter Stastny, Que.	1980-81	77	39	70	109	Age: 24 Assist record lofty target**
Wayne Gretzky, Edm.	1979-80	79	51	*86	*137	Age: 19 Real assist, point standards
Teemu Selanne, Win.	1992-93	84	*76	56	132	Age: 22 Goals never to be equalled?
**Joe Juneau, 25, also earns 70 assists, in 1992-93 with Boston						

Photo: Bruce Bennett/BBS

14

"Is he something or what? He's 19 going on 35."
—Edmonton goalie Ron Low

Joe Malone 1917-18

NHL's First Star Sets First Goals Standard

Malone's 44 goals during the NHL's inaugural season remains the league's greatest scoring burst. The Montreal Canadien's 2.20 goals-per-game average (in 20 games) remain a league record some 81 seasons later and his goal total isn't broken until Rocket Richard pots 50 in 1944-45. The top three GPG marks in history are recorded in the NHL's first season.

Essential Stats	Year	GP	G	A	P	GPG	Early Era
Joe Malone, Mon.	1917-18	20	*44	4	*48	*2.20	His next best is 1.63
Cy Denneny, Ott.	1917-18	20	36	*10	46	1.80	His next best is 1.42
Newsy Lalonde, Mon.	1917-18	14	23	7	30	1.64	His next best is 1.61

Photo: HHOF

15

"Quite often, I played 50 or 55 minutes a game. They didn't bother too much about changing lines. Only individuals."
—Joe Malone

Mike Bossy 1980-81

50-Goals-In-50-Games Club Doubles

Bossy equals hockey's most magical record–Rocket Richard's 50 goals in 50 games. The New York Islander scores Nos. 49 and 50 in the dying minutes of his 50th game. "If I didn't get the record, it would have been embarrassing because I had made it such a big thing," says Bossy, who finishes with 68 goals. The first three players to hit 50-in-50 are Richard, Bossy and Wayne Gretzky, who does it in 39 games.

Essential Stats	Year	G	GP	Background	Total
Rocket Richard, Mon.	1944-45	*50	50	1 goal vs. Boston in Game 50	*50
Mike Bossy, NYI	1980-81	50	50	2 goals vs. Quebec in Game 50	*68
Wayne Gretzky, Edm.	1981-82	50	39	5 goals vs. Philadelphia in Game 39	*92

Photo: Bruce Bennett/BBS

16

"The pressure never bothered me. I like the attention."
—Mike Bossy after scoring 50 in 50

Superstar Mike Bossy becomes only the second NHL player to score 50 goals in 50 games, in 1980-81.

Stan Mikita 1966-67

17

Gentleman First Three-Trophy Winner

The Chicago Black Hawks' center wins an unprecedented three major awards–Art Ross (scoring), Hart (MVP) and Lady Byng (sportsmanship). His 97 points ties teammate Bobby Hull's 1965-66 NHL record and Mikita breaks his own assists record (59) with 62. The native of Czechoslovakia, who has four seasons of more than 100 penalty minutes under his belt, finishes with a career-low 12 PIMS.

"I thought I'd try to beat the other guy with my skills instead of knocking his head off."
–Stan Mikita

Essential Stats	Year	GP	G	A	P	Record: Assists
Stan Mikita, Chi.	1964-65	70	28	*59	*87	Raises shared record by 1
Stan Mikita, Chi.	1966-67	70	35	*62	*97	First to break 60-assist barrier
Phil Esposito, Bos.	1968-69	74	49	*77	*126	Raises record by 15

Photo: Harold Barkley Archives

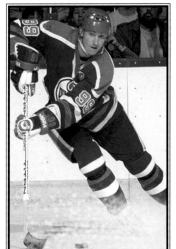

Wayne Gretzky 1984-85

18

Another Record Haul of Helpers

Gretzky breaks his own assist record (125) with 135, matching the total points of Art Ross Trophy runner-up and Edmonton Oiler teammate Jari Kurri. Gretzky also wins the Hart Trophy and records the third-highest points total (208) in NHL history. (As a point of reference, Mario Lemieux has the highest non-Gretzky assist total ever–114.) Gretzky hits the career 1,000-point mark in the fewest games ever, 424.

"Every time I come off the ice it marks one less time I will play for the Oilers. Not that I would want to play anywhere else."
–Wayne Gretzky, pondering his future after scoring point No. 1,000

Essential Stats	Year	GP	G	A	P	Record: Assists
Wayne Gretzky, Edm.	1982-83	80	*71	*125	*196	11 better than best non-99 mark
Wayne Gretzky, Edm.	1984-85	80	*73	*135	*208	21 better than best non-99 mark
Wayne Gretzky, Edm.	1985-86	80	52	*163	*215	49 better than best non-99 mark

Photo: Bruce Bennett/BBS

Gordie Howe 1952-53

19

Failed 50-Goal Hunt in Art Ross Runaway

Howe increases his two-year-old scoring record by nine points to 95. The Art Ross and Hart Trophy winner just misses joining Rocket Richard in the 50-goal club. Howe needs one goal in the last game of the season, as the Detroit Red Wings face the Montreal Canadiens, but the Habs shut him out. He finishes 24 points ahead of runner-up Ted Lindsay–a gap that won't be bettered until Phil Esposito in 1972-73.

"They call him 'Power', and that's exactly what he is to a team–power which no other man can match."
–Detroit GM Jack Adams

Essential Stats	Year	P	Runner-up	P	Gap	Noteworthy
Gordie Howe, Det.	1950-51	*86	Rocket Richard, Mon.	66	20	Previous high
Gordie Howe, Det.	1952-53	*95	Ted Lindsay, Det.	71	24	Sets standard
Phil Esposito, Bos.	1972-73	*130	Bobby Clarke, Phi.	104	26	Surpasses Howe

Photo: Imperial Oil - Turofsky/HHOF

20

Phil Esposito 1968-69

NHL's First 100-Point Player

"All I want to do is contribute to the team's success. Anything else that comes is just so much gravy."
–Phil Esposito

Esposito enters territory never approached before…and goes beyond when he becomes the first player to score 100 points. He finishes with 126 points, 29 more than the old record held by Bobby Hull and Stan Mikita, to win his first Art Ross and Hart Trophies. The Boston Bruins' center also breaks Mikita's assists mark (62) with 77, but Esposito falls one goal short of his first 50-goal season.

Essential Stats	Year	GP	G	A	P	Record: Points
Stan Mikita, Chi.	1965-66	70	35	*62	*97	Shares with Bobby Hull
Phil Esposito, Bos.	1968-69	74	49	*77	*126	Raises Mikita-Hull record 30%
Phil Esposito, Bos.	1970-71	78	*76	*76	*152	Makes another leap forward

Photo: London Life - Portnoy/HHOF

21

Terry Sawchuk 1950-51

Wings Use Rookie For Record Season

"Ever since Sawchuk turned pro, he has been the rookie of the year in each league. He doesn't intend to have the string broken now."
–The Hockey News

Detroit GM Jack Adams trades away Harry Lumley, feeling the 20-year-old Sawchuk is ready. Sawchuk responds by leading the 44-13-13 Red Wings to the NHL's first 100-point season, a record toppled by the 1968-69 Montreal Canadiens. The Calder Trophy winner records a season-high 11 shutouts, five more than any other goalie; Sawchuk's 44 wins are surpassed only once in history, by Bernie Parent in 1973-74.

Essential Stats	Year	W	L	T	SO	GAA	Noteworthy
Terry Sawchuk, Det.	1950-51	*44	13	13	*11	1.99	1st in wins, 1st in SO's
Al Rollins, Tor.	1950-51	27	5	8	5	*1.77	1st in GAA
Gerry McNeil, Mon.	1950-51	25	30	15	6	2.63	2nd in SO's, 3rd in GAA

Photo: Imperial Oil - Turofsky/HHOF

22

Bobby Hull 1965-66

Hawk First To Top 50 Goals

"You have to see it coming to really believe it. When it hits you, it feels like a piece of lead."
–Montreal goalie Jacques Plante on Bobby Hull's shot

'The Golden Jet' becomes the first player to surpass the 50-goal mark. Hull, who finishes with 54, had been tied with Rocket Richard and Bernie Geoffrion at 50. Nobody is close to Hull this season. The Chicago Black Hawk scores 23 more goals than runners-up Norm Ullman and Alex Delvecchio. Hull also breaks Dickie Moore's 1958-59 points record by one with 97 to win the Art Ross and Hart Trophies.

Essential Stats	Year	GP	G	A	P	Record: Goals
Rocket Richard	1944-45	50	*50	23	73	Original 50-goal scorer
Bobby Hull, Chi.	1965-66	65	*54	43	*97	First 50-plus goal-scorer
Bobby Hull, Chi.	1968-69	74	*58	49	107	Last of 7 goal-scoring titles

Photo: London Life - Portnoy/HHOF

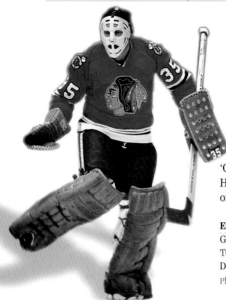

Tony Esposito 1969-70

Rookie Sets Modern Era Shutout Mark

Esposito emerges from the shadow of older brother Phil in his first full NHL season. The Chicago Black Hawks' rookie goalie racks up the second-most shutouts in history and becomes known as Tony 'O.' His 15 whitewashes are a Modern Era record and trail only George Hainsworth's 22 in 1928-29. He leads the NHL with 38 wins and is one of only four goalies to win the Calder and Vezina Tropies in the same year.

Essential Stats	Year	W	L	T	SO	GAA	Record: Shutouts
George Hainsworth, Mon.	1928-29	22	7	15	*22	*0.92	All-time SO record
Tony Esposito, Chi.	1969-70	*38	17	8	*15	*2.17	Modern record
Dominik Hasek, Buf.	1997-98	33	23	13	*13	2.09	Best since Esposito

Photo: Bruce Bennett/BBS

23

"He hates to have anyone score on him, even in practice. Many goalers today take practices too lightly, but not Tony."
—Chicago coach Billy Reay

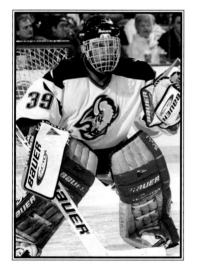

Dominik Hasek 1997-98

'The Dominator' Is All Hart…Again

As good as Hasek is in 1996-97, the Buffalo Sabre is even better this season to become the first goalie to win back-to-back Hart Trophies. His 13 shutouts are the most since Tony Esposito had 15 in 1969-70 and the league MVP also wins the Vezina Trophy. Hasek raises the bar on his own save percentage record (.930 to .932) on a team of pluggers and grinders.

Essential Stats	Year	W	L	T	SO	GAA	SP	Noteworthy
Patrick Roy, Mon.	1991-92	36	22	8	*5	*2.36	*.914	Pre-Hasek record
Dominik Hasek, Buf.	1997-98	33	23	13	*13	2.09	*.932	6-time SP leader
Dominik Hasek, Buf.	1998-99	30	18	14	9	1.87	*.937	Record SP

Photo: Dave Sandford/HHOF

24

"I don't want to say it, but this was probably the best season of my life… (but) I believe I can play better."
—Dominik Hasek

Bernie Parent 1973-74

Biggest Winner of All-Time

Parent makes a knockout return in his first season back with the Philadelphia Flyers after a year in the World Hockey Association. His 47 wins break Terry Sawchuk's NHL record of 44, and 1.89 goals-against average and 12 shutouts won't be bettered for more than two decades. Parent leads the Broad Street Bullies to a 50-16-12 record to win the Vezina Trophy.

Essential Stats	Year	W	L	T	SO	GAA	Record: Goalie Wins
Terry Sawchuk, Det.	1951-52	*44	14	12	*12	*1.90	Previous record
Bernie Parent, Phi.	1973-74	*47	13	12	*12	*1.89	Eclipses 32-year mark
Bernie Parent, Phi.	1974-75	*44	14	10	*12	*2.03	Most wins since record

Photo: Mel DiGiacomo/BBS

25

"You can't say enough about Bernie. I think he's easily the best player in hockey this year."
—Philadelphia center Bobby Clarke

26

Brett Hull 1990-91

Goal Leader By Largest Margin Ever

Hull shoots by the rest of the NHL like never before. The St. Louis Blues' sniper scores 86 goals, the third-highest total in history behind Wayne Gretzky's 92- and 87-goal seasons in 1981-82 and 1983-84, respectively. The Hart Trophy winner scores 50 goals in 49 games, but even more impressively, he finishes 35 goals ahead of any other scorer–the greatest margin of victory for a goal leader in NHL history.

Essential Stats	Year	G	Runner-up	G	Gap	Noteworthy
Wayne Gretzky, Edm.	1983-84	*87	Michel Goulet, Que.	56	31	Previous high
Brett Hull, St.L	1990-91	*86	Three others	51	35	Biggest ever
Brett Hull, St.L	1991-92	*70	Kevin Stevens, Pit.	54	16	Biggest since

Photo: Bruce Bennett/BBS

27

Gordie Howe 1968-69

Oldest Player To Hit 100 Points

Howe, the Detroit Red Wings' 23-year veteran, cracks the 100-point mark with 103 points at age 41, joining Phil Esposito (126) and Bobby Hull (107) as the first members of the exclusive group. Howe is by far the oldest player to hit triple digits. Johnny Bucyk, 35, is next oldest to score 100 points.

Stat Spotlight	Year	GP	G	A	P	Age	100-Point Seasons
Phil Esposito, Bos.	1968-69	74	49	*77	*126	27	6 (NHL)
Bobby Hull, Chi.	1968-69	74	*58	49	107	30	1 (NHL), 4 (WHA)
Gordie Howe, Det.	1968-69	76	44	59	103	41	1 (NHL), 2 (WHA)
Johnny Bucyk, Bos.	1970-71	78	51	65	116	35	1 (NHL)

Photo: Graphics Artists/HHOF

28

Teemu Selanne 1992-93

Jet Flashes By Rookie Records

Selanne demolishes two rookie records with 76 goals and 132 points. The 22-year-old Winnipeg Jet blows by Mike Bossy's 53-goal season in 1977-78 and Peter Stastny's 109 points in 1980-81; only non-rookie Wayne Gretzky does better in his first year with 137 points. Selanne wins the Calder Trophy and is named a first all-star. No player, rookie or otherwise, has scored more goals since 1992-93.

Essential Stats	Year	GP	G	A	P	Record: Rookie Points
Peter Stastny, Que.	1980-81	77	39	70	109	Betters Dale Hawerchuk by 6
Teemu Selanne, Win.	1992-93	84	*76	56	132	Raises Stastny record 21%
Mikael Renberg, Phi.	1993-94	83	38	44	82	Most rookie points since Selanne

Photo: Doug MacLellan/HHOF

Gordie Howe 1950-51

'Mr. Hockey' Becomes 'Mr. Comeback'

29

Howe sets an NHL scoring record after recovering from a fractured skull. The Detroit Red Wing faces a series of brain operations after hitting his head into the boards during the 1949-50 playoffs, but comes back and plays all 70 games in 1950-51. Howe, wearing a helmet for the season, scores an NHL-record 86 points and finishes 20 points ahead of runner-up Rocket Richard.

"Any doubts that Gordie Howe is one of the greatest players ever to lace on a pair of skates can now be cast aside."
–The Hockey News, after Howe eclipsed Herb Cain's record

Essential Stats	Year	GP	G	A	P	Record: Points
Herb Cain, Bos.	1943-44	48	36	46	*82	First season of Modern Era
Gordie Howe, Det.	1950-51	70	*43	*43	*86	Raises Cain mark by 4
Gordie Howe, Det.	1952-53	70	*49	*46	*95	Record lasts 6 seasons

Photo: Imperial Oil - Turofsky/HHOF

Ray Bourque 1979-80

Bruins' Newest Blueline Great Debuts

30

The Quebec League star is selected eighth overall by Boston in the 1979 entry draft and the 19-year-old is fantastic, scoring a defenseman rookie record 65 points, earning a berth on the first all-star team and winning the Calder Trophy. "He's the finest rookie defenseman I've ever seen come into the league," says Bruins' teammate Brad Park.

"He is way ahead of me at 19. I'm not comparing him to Bobby Orr, but he's going to be a good one."
–Montreal defenseman Guy Lapointe

Essential Stats	Year	GP	G	A	P	Record: Rookie 'D' Points
Barry Beck, Col.	1977-78	75	22	38	60	Earns share of new point mark*
Ray Bourque, Bos.	1979-80	80	17	48	65	Improves Larson-Beck standard
Larry Murphy, LA	1980-81	80	16	60	76	Shatters Bourque's record

*Detroit's Reed Larson also collects 60 points in 1977-78, including 19 goals

Photo: Bruce Bennett/BBS

Mike Bossy 1977-78

First Rookie To Score 50 Goals

31

Bossy begins his attack on NHL netminders in record fashion, becoming the first rookie to record a 50-goal season. Entering the 1977 NHL amateur draft, many teams fear he's one-dimensional and he's not selected until the New York Islanders grab him No. 15 overall. The sniper jumps right into the lineup and breaks Rick Martin's 1971-72 record of 44 goals with 53, to win the Calder Trophy.

"That kid sure knows where the net is. There aren't too many youngsters around who can set up and shoot like that."
–Chicago goalie Tony Esposito

Essential Stats	Year	GP	G	A	P	Record: Rookie Goals
Rick Martin, Buf.	1971-72	73	44	30	74	Raises Gil Perreault record by 6
Mike Bossy, NYI	1977-78	73	53	38	91	Raises Martin record 20%
Teemu Selanne, Win.	1992-93	84	*76	56	132	Raises Bossy record 43%

Photo: O-Pee-Chee Collection/HHOF

32

Wayne Gretzky 1982-83

Art Ross Winner Does It With Assists Only

Gretzky matches Hall-of-Famer Bill Cowley in becoming the second player to collect more assists than anyone else has points. Gretzky tops runner-up Peter Stastny's 124 points with 125 assists in winning the 1982-83 Art Ross and Hart Trophies. The Edmonton Oiler would have won or shared the Art Ross four times on assists alone during his career.

Essential Stats	Year	G	A	P	Runner-up	P	Gap
Bill Cowley, Bos.	1940-41	17	*45	*62	Five players	44	1
Wayne Gretzky, Edm.	1982-83	*71	*125	*196	Peter Stastny, Que.	124	1
Wayne Gretzky, Edm.	1984-85	*73	*135	*208	Jari Kurri, Edm.	135	–
Wayne Gretzky, Edm.	1985-86	52	*163	*215	Mario Lemieux, Pit.	141	22
Wayne Gretzky, Edm.	1986-87	*62	*121	*183	Jari Kurri, Edm.	108	13

Photo: Bruce Bennett/BBS

33

Eddie Shore 1932-33

First Defenseman To Win Hart Trophy

'The Edmonton Express' is rewarded for combined toughness and talent with the Hart Trophy–the first defenseman to earn the honor. The Boston Bruins' great records a career-high 35 points and finishes second to Frank Boucher's league-high 28 assists. Only six defensemen have been named NHL MVP, Shore wins it four times during the 1930s.

Essential Stats	Year	GP	G	A	P	Hart Runner-Up
Eddie Shore, Bos.	1932-33	48	8	27	35	Bill Cook NYR
Eddie Shore, Bos.	1934-35	48	7	26	33	Charlie Conacher, Tor.
Eddie Shore, Bos.	1935-36	45	3	16	19	Hooley Smith, Mon. M
Eddie Shore, Bos.	1937-38	48	3	14	17	Paul Thompson, Chi.

Photo: HHOF

34

Mario Lemieux 1987-88

Scoring Title Heralds Dawn of New Era

Lemieux ends Wayne Gretzky's streak of seven straight Art Ross Trophies and eight consecutive Hart Trophies with an incredible season of his own. The Pittsburgh Penguins' center becomes the second player to average two points per game (2.18) in one season with a 70-goal, 168-point performance. Gretzky averages more points per game (2.48) over a full season than Lemieux for the last time in their careers.

Essential Stats	Year	GP	G	A	P	PPG	Noteworthy
Wayne Gretzky, Edm.	1983-84	74	*87	*118	*205	*2.77	All-time NHL high
Mario Lemieux, Pit.	1987-88	77	*70	98	*168	2.18	Breakthrough year
Mario Lemieux, Pit.	1992-93	60	69	91	*160	2.67	Mario's best PPG

Photo: Bruce Bennett/BBS

Wayne Gretzky 1986-87

35

99 Overwhelming In Points Parade

No player has ever been more statistically dominating over the rest of the scoring field than Gretzky during yet another Art Ross and Hart Trophy-winning season. The Edmonton Oilers' superstar finishes 75 points ahead of Jari Kurri–a record 69 per-cent more points than the runner-up. Gretzky also records more assists than Kurri has points (121 to 108), the last time that feat is accomplished.

Essential Stats	Year	P	Runner-up	P	Gap	Pct.	Noteworthy
Wayne Gretzky, Edm.	1983-84	*205	Paul Coffey	126	79	63%	Previous high
Wayne Gretzky, Edm.	1986-87	*183	Jari Kurri	108	75	69%	All-time high
Wayne Gretzky, Edm.	1990-91	*163	Brett Hull	131	32	24%	Best since

Photo: Bruce Bennett/BBS

"No hockey player has ever dominated his era the way Wayne has, and I'm talking about any era."
–Washington GM David Poile

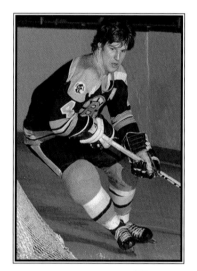

Bobby Orr 1973-74

36

Bruin Passes To Another Norris

The only reason that Orr's 90 assists aren't an NHL record is because the Boston Bruin has already broken the mark in 1970-71 with 102. His 1973-74 output represents the second-most assists ever recorded by a defenseman. The Norris Trophy winner finishes second to Boston Bruins' teammate Phil Esposito in the scoring race (145 points) with 122.

Essential Stats	Year	GP	G	A	P	Record: Defenseman Assists
Pat Stapleton, Chi.	1968-69	75	6	50	56	Pre-Orr record
Bobby Orr, Bos.	1970-71	78	37	*102	139	One of three 100-assist players
Bobby Orr, Bos.	1973-74	74	32	*90	122	4th of five assist titles
Paul Coffey, Edm.	1985-86	79	48	90	138	Best non-Orr assist total

Photo: London Life - Portnoy/HHOF

"Bobby has reached the stage of stardom, where what he does so effortlessly and continually is taken for granted."
–The Hockey News

Wayne Gretzky 1980-81

37

Beginning of Record Book Assault

Gretzky displaces two Hall of Famers from the record book in capturing the Art Ross and Hart Trophies in his second NHL season. The Edmonton Oiler tops Bobby Orr's assist mark (102) with 109 and Phil Esposito's points standard (152) with 164. Mario Lemieux is the only other player to record more than 100 assists and 164 points in one season.

Essential Stats	Year	GP	G	A	P	Noteworthy
Bobby Orr, Bos.	1970-71	78	37	*102	139	Sets assist record at age 23
Phil Esposito, Bos.	1970-71	78	*76	76	*152	Sets goal, point records at age 29
Wayne Gretzky, Edm.	1980-81	80	55	*109	*164	Sets assist, point records at 20

Photo: O-Pee-Chee Collection/HHOF

"For Wayne Gretzky, it was an unbelievable and unforgettable year. But great as it was, the odds are excellent his best is yet to come. Frightening, isn't it."
–The Hockey News

38

Bill Cowley 1943-44

Injury Ends Bruin's Record Run

"Bill Cowley established a reputation as a remarkable playmaker able to pass the puck on a dime to his wingmen."
–Hockey Hall of Fame

The Boston Bruins' center is on the verge of breaking the NHL points record (73) when a knee injury and separated shoulder sideline him for the last six weeks of the season. Cowley finishes with 71 points in only 36 games for a 1.97 points-per-game average. Only Wayne Gretzky (10 times) and Mario Lemieux (six) surpass his PPG average among players with at least 50 points in a season.

Essential Stats	Year	GP	G	A	P	PPG	Noteworthy
Herb Cain, Bos.	1943-44	48	36	46	*82	1.71	Cain's only special year
Bill Cowley, Bos.	1943-44	36	30	41	71	*1.97	MVP runner-up
Wayne Gretzky, Edm.	1980-81	80	55	*109	*164	*2.05	Will hit 2.77 PPG

Photo: HHOF

39

Dominik Hasek 1993-94

Sabre Begins His Dominance

"I was the same goalie 10 years ago, two years ago and last year. I'm playing with a lot of confidence, but I haven't changed anything."
–Dominik Hasek

Hasek takes over as a No. 1 NHL goalie in his second season with the Buffalo Sabres and doesn't disappoint. The 29-year-old, a former Czechoslovak League star, becomes the first goalie to have a goals-against average under 2.00 since Bernie Parent's 1.89 in 1973-74. The Sabres' netminder wins the first of five Vezina Trophies in six seasons.

Essential Stats	Year	GP	W	L	T	SO	GAA	Noteworthy
Tony Esposito, Chi.	1973-74	48	*31	10	6	*9	*1.77	Best of Modern Era**
Dominik Hasek, Buf.	1983-84	58	30	20	6	*7	*1.95	Best in 20 years
Ron Tugnutt, Ott.	1998-99	43	22	10	8	3	*1.79	2nd best of Modern Era

**Al Rollins also records a 1.77 GAA, in 1950-51 with Toronto

Photo: Doug MacLellan/HHOF

40

Tom Barrasso 1983-84

Schoolboy Shines In Rookie Year

"Barrasso earned the chance to play by his work in training camp games. We didn't keep him here to sit on the bench."
–Buffalo coach Scotty Bowman

Barrasso is selected fifth overall by the Buffalo Sabres in the 1993 entry draft and becomes the first goalie to make the leap straight to the NHL from high school. He finishes with a 26-12-3 record and wins both the Calder and Vezina Trophies. Only Frank Brimsek (1939), Tony Esposito (1970) and Ed Belfour (1991) have ever done that.

Essential Stats	Year	GP	W	L	T	SO	GAA	Noteworthy
Frank Brimsek, Bos.	1938-39	43	*33	9	1	*10	*1.56	Makes debut at 23
Tony Esposito, Chi.	1969-70	63	*38	17	8	*15	*2.17	Makes debut at 27
Tom Barrasso, Buf.	1983-84	42	26	12	3	2	2.84	Makes debut at 19
Ed Belfour, Chi.	1990-91	*74	*43	19	7	4	*2.47	Makes debut at 26

Photo: Bruce Bennett/BBS

Virtual Perfection

By Steve Dryden & Harry Neale

I t is the greatest NHL team never assembled. Twenty-two players chosen from the thousands who have played in the league over the past 50 years, headed up by a coach and general manager of incomparable stature.

This isn't an all-star team. It's a real team. Well, actually it's a virtual team that would be virtually unbeatable if it existed anywhere but in our imagination.

The Hockey News set out to assemble the perfect NHL team, a team whose individual players aren't necessarily perfect, but are perfectly suited to job descriptions typical to any NHL team. Even extraordinary NHL clubs aren't filled entirely with all-stars. Rather, they are filled with players who play specific roles that, taken as a whole, contribute to the smooth and organic operation of a team.

Today's clubs are generally comprised of four lines with varying responsibilities, six defensemen with disparate roles, two goalies and a few reserves. We took that essential lineup and tweaked it, adding a utility player who could fill in on defense or forward and an honorary rover to recognize the game's roots. It was customary to ice six skaters–three forwards, two defensemen and a rover–until 1911. One of the game's greatest players ever was legendary rover Cyclone Taylor, who incinerated opposition defenses early in the 20th century.

Using this template, we asked *Hockey Night in Canada* analyst Harry Neale to help us fill in the roles with players who filled those job descriptions during their NHL careers. We decided to limit ourselves to those who had played from 1950 onwards because it was almost impossible to fairly evaluate players from before then. It was hard enough considering the merits of players in the NHL's Modern Era, which was officially launched in 1943-44 with the introduction of the red line. It would be decades after that before backup goalies and fourth lines became commonplace.

That said, we do have pre-Expansion-Era players for our backup goalie and on the fourth line because they likely would have filled those roles had they played later in the century. Arguably our No. 2 goalie, Don Simmons, would have been a No. 1 goalie had he been in his prime when there were more than six teams. Simmons is a perfect example of how we picked our perfect team. He, and not Jacques Plante, is the backup to all-time No. 1 Terry Sawchuk because Simmons was primarily a No. 2 goalie throughout his NHL career (1956-69). Only twice in parts of 11 seasons with Boston, Toronto and the New York Rangers did he appear in more than 28 games. Plante, generally considered the second-best goalie ever, filled the No. 2 or No. 1A position only late in his career (1954-73).

We worked diligently to remain faithful to job descriptions in assigning players positions on our team, but we surrendered to an impulse to recognize a pair of players, in particular, who were magnificent NHLers. Dave Keon, our No. 2 center, and Jari Kurri, our No. 2 right winger, were first line players almost their full Hall of Fame careers. But because they may well have been the two best players in league history at combining offensive and defensive skills, we couldn't, in good conscience, leave them off the two-way line.

Six players were automatic choices because they were selected the best at their positions when The Hockey News selected the top 100 players in NHL history. They are Sawchuk, defensemen Bobby Orr and Doug Harvey, left winger Bobby Hull, center Wayne Gretzky and right winger Gordie Howe.

On the following pages are our choices for the Perfect NHL Team, career thumbnails and statistics, and comments from

THN's Team

The Hockey News' perfect team on paper consists of:

No. 1 Starting Goalie	Starting netminder
No. 2 Backup Goalie	Relief netminder
No. 1 Defense Pair	Dominant defenseman
	Complementary partner
No. 2 Defense Pair	Offensive defenseman
	Complementary partner
No. 3 Defense Pair	Tidy, efficient defenseman
	Physical defenseman
No. 1 Scoring Line	Premier talents
No. 2 Two-Way Line	Secondary scoring threats
No. 3 Checking Line	Shutdown specialists
No. 4 Momentum Line	Shift disturbers
Utility Player	Defenseman-forward
Rover	Sixth skater (Honorary position)

*Terry Sawchuk
The Hockey News'
All-Time No. 1 Goalie*

The Greatest NHL Team Never Assembled

Coach
Scotty Bowman, Montreal

Key Achievement
Tied with Toe Blake for most
Stanley Cups (8) as coach

General Manager
Sam Pollock, Montreal

Key Achievement
Built teams that won nine Stanley
Cups

Legend
Coach, GM and players are listed with teams that they
acheived the most prominence and most significant
team/individual achievements.

Doug
Harvey

No. 1 Starting Goalie
Terry Sawchuk, Detroit

Key Achievement
Recorded an NHL-record 103
career shutouts

No. 2 Backup Goalie
Don Simmons, Boston

Key Achievement
Replaced injured Johnny Bower to
help Toronto win Cup in 1962

No. 1 Defense Pair
Bobby Orr, Boston

Key Achievement
Only defenseman to win NHL
scoring championship

No. 1 Defense Pair
Jacques Laperriere, Montreal

Key Achievement
Won Norris Trophy and six
Stanley Cups

No. 2 Defense Pair
Doug Harvey, Montreal

Key achievement
Won Norris Trophy as NHL's best
defenseman seven times.

No. 2 Defense Pair
Gus Mortson, Toronto

Key achievement
Led league in PIMs four times
and won four Cups with Toronto

No. 3 Defense Pair
Bob Turner, Montreal

Key achievement
Unsung hero on five straight
Canadiens' Cup champs

No. 3 Defense Pair
Larry Hillman, Toronto

Key achievement
Depth defenseman for three
straight Cup champs in Toronto

No. 1 Scoring Line LW
Bobby Hull, Chicago

Key achievement
Led NHL in goals a record
seven times

No. 1 Scoring Line C
Wayne Gretzky, Edmonton

Key achievement
All-time NHL leader in goals,
assists and points

No. 1 Scoring Line RW
Gordie Howe, Detroit

Key achievement
Named to first or second all-
star team a record 21 times

No. 2 Two-Way Line LW
Bert Olmstead, Montreal

Key achievement
Led league in assists twice, won
five Cups with Habs and Leafs

No. 2 Two-Way Line C
Dave Keon, Toronto

Key achievement
Won Conn Smythe Trophy in
Toronto's upset Cup win in 1967

No. 2 Two-Way Line RW
Jari Kurri, Edmonton

Key achievement
Highest scoring NHL European
of all time

No. 3 Checking Line LW
Bob Gainey, Montreal

Key achievement
Won four straight Selke Trophies
as league's best defensive forward

No. 3 Checking Line C
Derek Sanderson, Boston

Key achievement
Provided grit and goals on two
Stanley Cup winners in Boston

No. 3 Checking Line RW
Claude Provost, Montreal

Key Achievement
Shadowed NHL's best snipers
and still scored 254 career goals

No. 4 Momentum Line LW
John Ferguson, Montreal

Key achievement
All-time NHL heavyweight champ
averaged 18 goals a season

No. 4 Momentum Line C
Billy Harris, Toronto

Key achievement
Shone in reserve role with three
straight Toronto Cup champions

No. 4 Momentum Line RW
Mike Keane, Montreal

Key achievement
Has won Stanley Cup with three
different teams

Utility Player
Jimmy Roberts, Montreal

Key achievement
Right winger-defenseman with
fire won five Cups with Montreal

Rover
Paul Coffey, Edmonton

Key achievement
Holds single-season record for
most goals by a defenseman (48)

No. 1 Starting Goalie Terry Sawchuk

Noteworthy The all-time NHL leader in shutouts (103), Sawchuk backstopped Detroit to three Cups in the 1950s, posting an incredible 0.63 GAA and four shutouts in eight starts in the 1951-52 playoffs when the Red Wings didn't lose a game. He also won a Cup with Toronto in 1967 and was inducted into the Hockey Hall of Fame in 1971 without the required three-year waiting period.

Pollock "When he was playing behind Red Kelly, Marcel Pronovost and Bob Goldham in Detroit, he was almost an unbeatable goaler. Even in 1967 when he was past his prime, he helped Toronto win a Stanley Cup. He was a guy you'd just love to have on your team."

Teams Det., Bos., Tor., LA, NYR						All-Stars	
NHL Career	GP	W	L	T	GAA	1st	2nd
1950-70 (20)	971	447	330	172	2.52	3	4
Playoffs	106	54	48	—	2.55	4 Cups	

'52 '54 '55 '67

No. 2 Backup Goalie Don Simmons

Noteworthy Simmons replaced injured starting goalie Johnny Bower during the 1961-62 playoffs and won two of three games as the Toronto Maple Leafs captured their first Stanley Cup in 13 years against Chicago. He also won a Cup with the Leafs in 1962-63, posting a 15-8-5 record and 2.50 GAA in the regular season. Before coming to Toronto, Simmons shone with the Boston Bruins in two Cup finals (1956-57, 1957-58) against the powerhouse Montreal Canadiens.

Pollock "Simmons was a righthanded goaler, and there weren't too many of them around. He would come out and challenge the shooters, and depend on blocking off the angles."

Teams Bos., Tor., NYR						All-Stars	
NHL Career	GP	W	L	T	GAA	1st	2nd
1957-69 (11)	247	101	100	40	2.93	0	0
Playoffs	24	13	11	—	2.67	2 Cups	

'62 '63

No. 1 Defense Pair Bobby Orr

Noteworthy The phenom from Parry Sound, Ont., smashed all records for defensemen and changed the way the game is played during a career cut short by injuries. He won the Norris Trophy as the NHL's best rearguard in eight of nine full seasons he played and is the only player in history to win the Hart, Art Ross, Norris and Conn Smythe Trophies in the same season (1969-70).

Pollock "Orr was without a doubt the most spectacular defenseman I ever saw play. He was the kind of player you liked even when he was playing against you. He did things so easily and you certainly had to figure out a way to nullify him if you were going to beat Boston."

Teams Bos., Chi.

NHL Career	GP	G	A	Pts.	PIM	1st	2nd
1966-78 (12)	657	270	645	915	953	8	1
Playoffs	74						

'70 '72

No. 2 Defense Pair Doug Harvey

Noteworthy Harvey started his illustrious career six years before the Norris Trophy was even awarded and still won it seven times. He anchored the blueline brigade of the Montreal Canadiens, winning six Stanley Cups during the 1950s. A clever blueliner, he seemed to know where attackers were going before even they did.

Pollock "Harvey was the best two-way defenseman I ever saw play. He would play 50 minutes a game–killing penalties, on the power play and his regular shift. There aren't too many guys you can put out there for 50 minutes game after game. He was also a great baseball and football player, and maybe the greatest athlete that ever played in Canada."

Teams Mon., NYR, Det., St.L.

NHL Career	GP	G	A	Pts.	PIM	1st	2nd
1948-69 (17)	1,113	88	452	540	1,216	10	1
Playoffs	137	8	64	72	152	6 Cups	

'53 '56 '57 '58 '59 '60

No. 3 Defense Pair Bob Turner

Noteworthy The unheralded defenseman came east out of Regina to become a valuable handyman, skating alongside such stars as Doug Harvey and Jean Beliveau on the greatest hockey dynasty of the century; the Montreal Canadiens club won five straight Stanley Cups in the late 1950s. He played only eight seasons, but his teams made the finals six times.

Neale "In his era, most teams played just four defensemen and he always seemed to be number 4-1/2 to 5. Teammates and opponents had a much higher evaluation of him than did the fans. He could play with any partner and was as comfortable playing 10 minutes a game as 22."

Teams Mon., Chi.

NHL Career	GP	G	A	Pts.	PIM	1st	2nd
1956-63 (8)	478	19	51	70	307	0	0
Playoffs	68	1	4	5	44	5 Cups	

'56 '57 '58 '59 '60

No. 1 Defense Pair Jacques Laperriere

Noteworthy A coolheaded, reliable defender, Laperriere controlled the pace of the game on six Stanley Cup champions with the Montreal Canadiens in the 1960s and early 1970s. He won the Calder Trophy in 1963-64, the Norris in 1965-66 and led the NHL with a plus-78 mark in 1972-73 before he was forced to end his career because of a serious knee injury.

Neale "Laperriere always made the safe play and rarely was out of position. He used a very long stick with a deep blade and was able to get his stick on all kinds of passes and shots that could have resulted in goals. He was the perfect partner for an offensive-minded defenseman."

Teams Mon.

NHL Career	GP	G	A	Pts.	PIM	1st	2nd
1963-74 (11)	691	40	242	282	674	2	2
Playoffs	88	9	22	31	101	6 Cups	

'65 '66 '68 '69 '71 '73

No. 2 Defense Pair Gus Mortson

Noteworthy A hardrock from Northern Ontario mining country, Mortson handled the heavy end of the job, paired with Jim Thomson on four Toronto Maple Leafs' Stanley Cup champions between 1947 and 1951. He led the NHL in penalty minutes four times—twice with the Leafs and twice with the Chicago Black Hawks, after being traded in 1952.

Neale "In an era when coaches didn't allow their wingers to stray more than 10 feet from the boards, Mortson had the knack of catching attackers with hard open-ice bodychecks. They were easy targets for him. He was mean and nasty, and not very much fun to play against."

Teams Tor., Chi., Det.

NHL Career	GP	G	A	Pts.	PIM	1st	2nd
1946-59 (13)	797	46	152	198	1,380	1	0
Playoffs	54	5	8	13	68	4 Cups	

'47 '48 '49 '51

No. 3 Defense Pair Larry Hillman

Noteworthy Hillman was a journeyman rearguard from the Kirkland Lake, Ont., hockey factory, which continually produced talent for the NHL. He played with eight teams during a 13-year NHL career. He earned four Stanley Cup rings as depth chart ace with Punch Imlach's Toronto Maple Leafs in the 1960s, traveling back and forth between the Leafs and American League Rochester Americans.

Neale "When a team had a serious injury, Hillman was the guy you could trust to step in and do a competent job. He would get in your way in the defensive zone and was so strong that when he got a hold of you, you were going to the glass for sure."

Teams Det., Bos., Tor., Minn., Mon., Phi., LA, Buf.

NHL Career	GP	G	A	Pts.	PIM	1st	2nd
1955-73 (16)	790	36	196	232	579	0	0
Playoffs	74	2	9	11	30	4 Cups	

'62 '63 '64 '67

No. 1 Scoring Line LW Bobby Hull

Noteworthy A three-time NHL point champion, The Golden Jet made life miserable for opposition goalies, scoring 50 or more goals five times in 15 seasons with the Chicago Black Hawks. He won two Hart Trophies and earned a Stanley Cup ring with the Black Hawks in the 1960-61 season.

Neale "Bobby had the hardest shot, by far, in his era and great imagination for getting himself into a position to score. And although he always had the opponent's best winger hanging all over him, he was a powerful skater with a wide stride and very dangerous coming in off the wing. If you got a piece of him, it wasn't enough to stop him."

Teams Chi., Win., Hfd.						All-Stars	
NHL Career	GP	G	A	Pts.	PIM	1st	2nd
1957-80 (16)	1,063	610	560	1,170	640	10	2
Playoffs	119	62					

'61

No. 1 Scoring Line C Wayne Gretzky

Noteworthy The all-time NHL leader in goals (894), assists (1,963) and points (2,857), The Great One led the Edmonton Oilers to four Stanley Cups in the 1980s. He holds or shares 61 NHL records, set during a brilliant 20-year career in which he won nine Hart, 10 Art Ross and two Conn Smythe Trophies. In 1,487 regular season matches, he averaged a remarkable 1.9 points per game.

Neale "Offensively, Gretzky has no peer in the history of the game. He had a great imagination and it appeared he saw the replay before the play even took place, always passing the puck to the right man. He also had a quick-release shot and an excellent book on goalies."

Teams Edm., LA, St.L., NYR						All-Stars	
NHL Career	GP	G	A	Pts.	PIM	1st	2nd
1979-99 (20)	1,487	894	1,963	2,857	577	8	7
Playoffs	208	122	260	382	66	4 Cups	

'84 '85 '87 '88

No. 1 Scoring Line RW Gordie Howe

Noteworthy The greatest player who ever lived–if you equate greatness with longevity–Howe was the oldest player to record 100 points (102) in 1968-69 at the age of 41. He retired in 1980 at 52 after winning six Hart and six Art Ross Trophies, as well as four Stanley Cups. He ranks second in all-time NHL scoring behind Wayne Gretzky.

Neale "Howe was as strong as a bull, yet so smooth he reminded you of baseball star Joe DiMaggio. He used a short stick, but with a very high lie, so that he could keep the puck close to his body. He was always circling on the ice and knew how to conserve energy. He also had very dangerous elbows and a long memory."

Teams Det., Hfd.						All-Stars	
NHL Career	GP	G	A	Pts.	PIM	1st	2nd
1946-80 (26)	1,767	801	1,049	1,850	1,685	12	9
Playoffs	157	68	92	160	220	4 Cups	

'50 '52 '54 '55

No. 2 Two-Way Line LW Bert Olmstead

Noteworthy A solid two-way player, Olmstead hated all opponents, would do anything to win and did not appreciate teammates without the same attitude. A sharp set-up man, he twice led the NHL in assists and won five Stanley Cups with Montreal and Toronto.

Pollock "Bert was a tough competitor who played for a couple of years on a line with Jean Beliveau and Bernie Geoffrion in Montreal. Then he went to Toronto and sort of stabilized that team and helped make them into Stanley Cup winners. He would really work along the boards and in the corners. If you've got three guys on a line, you need one that's really good defensively. And he was that guy."

Teams Chi., Mon., Tor.						All-Stars	
NHL Career	GP	G	A	Pts.	PIM	1st	2nd
1949-62 (13)	848	181	421	602	884	0	2
Playoffs	115	16	43	59	101	5 Cups	

'53 '56 '57 '58 '62

No. 2 Two-Way Line C Dave Keon

Noteworthy Keon ranked 17th on the NHL's all-time points list when he retired in 1982, despite spending most of his career in Toronto playing against the other club's best center. He had 11 seasons of 20 or more goals with the Leafs, won four Stanley Cups, a Calder Trophy and the Conn Smythe Trophy.

Neale "If you add up the skills needed to become a quality player, he would have the highest skill level in the most areas. For a guy who rarely threw a bodycheck, he had an awful lot of takeouts because he knew how to get the right angle on a player carrying the puck up the ice. He also had a very effective backhand shot."

Teams Tor., Hfd.						All-Stars	
NHL Career	GP	G	A	Pts.	PIM	1st	2nd
1960-82 (18)	1,296	396	590	986	117	0	2
Playoffs	92	32	36	68	6	4 Cups	

'62 '63 '64 '67

No. 2 Two-Way Line RW Jari Kurri

Noteworthy The highest scoring European ever, Kurri was a key figure in five Stanley Cup victories by the Edmonton Oilers. He scored 50 goals or more four times and finished his career with 601, the 10th highest total in the history of the NHL. He also shares the record for most playoff goals in one season (19).

Neale "Many of the years he played in Edmonton he should have won the Selke Trophy, but because he was great offensively he was never considered. He was the perfect linemate for Gretzky because he was able to think like Gretzky and his defensive ability allowed Gretzky to take offensive gambles."

Teams Edm., LA, NYR, Ana., Col.						All-Stars	
NHL Career	GP	G	A	Pts.	PIM	1st	2nd
1980-98 (18)	1,251	601	797	1,398	545	2	3
Playoffs	200	106	127	233	123	5 Cups	

'84 '85 '87 '88 '90

No. 3 Checking Line LW Bob Gainey

Noteworthy Probably the best winger in history without the puck, Gainey won four consecutive Selke Trophies as the NHL's best defensive forward. He also won the Conn Smythe Trophy in 1978-79 when he complemented his great defensive play by averaging a point a game in 16 playoff matches. Soviet Union head coach Viktor Tikhonov once called him the best hockey player in the world.

Neale "Gainey played with a physical edge and was a great skater, who had excellent defensive intuition. He always knew where he was going when the other team had the puck. Because of this he was always a threat to score, especially shorthanded."

Teams Mon.						All-Stars	
NHL Career	GP	G	A	Pts.	PIM	1st	2nd
1973-89 (16)	1,160	239	262	501	585	0	0

Playoffs

'76 '77 '78 '79 '86

No. 3 Checking Line C Derek Sanderson

Noteworthy Often in hot water because of his adventurous off-ice activities, Sanderson was a multi-talented player who had a higher skill level than most people gave him credit for. He recorded six seasons of 20 goals or more with the Boston Bruins and was a sizable contributor in the club's Stanley Cup triumphs of 1969-70 and 1971-72.

Neale "He was the Joe Namath of the NHL. Most people remember him more for his controversial off-ice activities. His main role was as a defensive center and he could really get under your skin. Yet, if the team's first or second line center went down with an injury, he could step right in and fill the void."

Teams Bos., NYR, St.L., Van., Pit.						All-Stars	
NHL Career	GP	G	A	Pts.	PIM	1st	2nd
1967-77 (10)	598	202	250	452	911	0	0
Playoffs	56	18	12	30	187	2 Cups	

'70 '72

No. 3 Checking Line RW Claude Provost

Noteworthy Provost was perhaps the most effective shadow who ever played in the NHL. He claimed Hall of Famers Bobby Hull, Frank Mahovlich and Gordie Howe as victims of his close checking, yet created excellent scoring chances and scored 254 career goals while winning nine Stanley Cups with the Montreal Canadiens.

Neale "Provost took enormous pride in shutting down premier players and was especially effective in this role at playoff time. Although he had a bow-legged, choppy skating style, he was very hard to beat in a foot race."

Teams Mon.						All-Stars	
NHL Career	GP	G	A	Pts.	PIM	1st	2nd
1955-70 (15)	1,005	254	335	589	469	1	0
Playoffs	126	25	38	63	86	9 Cups	

'56 '57 '58 '59 '60 '65 '66 '68 '69

No. 4 Momentum Line LW John Ferguson

Noteworthy The best combo of enforcer and player who ever played, the 5-11, 190-pound winger protected Montreal Canadiens' stars during an eight-year career that included five Stanley Cups. Ready to drop the gloves whenever necessary, he is considered the NHL's all-time heavyweight champ, but also averaged 18 goals a season.

Neale "In effect, he fought his way into the NHL but improved his skills considerably after getting to the big time and became a pretty effective player. He really enjoyed the role of tough guy and even before the game began opponents would start worrying about meeting up with him."

Teams Mon.						All-Stars	
NHL Career	GP	G	A	Pts.	PIM	1st	2nd
1963-71 (8)	500	145	158	303	1,214	0	0
Playoffs	85	20	18	38	260	5 Cups	

'65 '66 '68 '69 '71

No. 4 Momentum Line C Billy Harris

Noteworthy A dipsy-doodle dandy, who weighed only 155 pounds, 'Hinky' was a brilliant stickhandler who could turn defensemen inside out. He used his superb skills and hockey sense coming off the bench to help Punch Imlach's Toronto Maple Leafs win three of their four Stanley Cups in the 1960s.

Neale "There were no fourth lines in his era, yet he filled that role in the sense that he did not see a lot of ice time but could jump in on a line, when that center was having a bad night and do an excellent job. He was very elusive and when you hit him, he seemed to be going in the same direction as you, therefore you ended up just pushing him."

Teams Tor., Det., Oak., Pit.						All-Stars	
NHL Career	GP	G	A	Pts.	PIM	1st	2nd
1955-69 (13)	769	126	219	345	205	0	0
Playoffs	62	8	10	18	30	3 Cups	

'62 '63 '64

No. 4 Momentum Line RW Mike Keane

Noteworthy A fierce competitor with great leadership skills, Keane played an important role in Stanley Cup victories for three different clubs—Montreal, the Colorado Avalanche and Dallas Stars—in the 1990s. He contributed 15 points in 19 games as the Habs won an incredible 10 straight overtime games to win the Cup in 1992-93.

Neale "Keane is one of the best shotblockers in the league, even though he's a forward and has a great knack of getting between the net and the point man to take away dangerous shots. He's also a great leader."

Teams Mon., Col., NYR, Dal.						All-Stars	
NHL Career	GP	G	A	Pts.	PIM	1st	2nd
1988-present	887	139	263	402	754	0	0
Playoffs	179	30	34	64	117	3 Cups	

'93 '96 '99

Utility Player Jimmy Roberts

Noteworthy The ultimate utility player, who could play either forward or defense, Roberts always showed great determination. He played in nine Stanley Cup finals during a 14-year career with Montreal and St. Louis, winning five Cups with the Habs. The Blues claimed him in the 1967 expansion draft, but Montreal liked him so much they later traded to bring him back to the Forum.

Neale "Being able to play up front or on the blueline was extra important in his era, because most teams had only five defensemen. He wasn't just a player you used for four minutes a night and he was always especially effective in the playoffs."

Teams Mon., St.L.						All-Stars	
NHL Career	GP	G	A	Pts.	PIM	1st	2nd
1964-78 (14)	1,006	126	194	320	621	0	0

Playoffs

'65 '66 '73 '76 '77

Rover Paul Coffey

Noteworthy The all-time NHL leader in assists (1,131) and points (1,527) by a defenseman, and second in goals (396), Coffey forces opponents to defend every time he touches the puck. The three-time Norris Trophy winner had five 100-points-plus seasons with the Edmonton Oilers and Pittsburgh Penguins, winning four Stanley Cups.

Neale "Coffey is perhaps the best pure skater who has ever played and one of the few who can accelerate while coasting. He's an excellent long passer, who can put the puck on the tape from 95 feet away. He also has a knack for being able to get his powerful slapshot from the point through a maze of players to the net."

Teams Edm., Pit., LA, Det., Hfd., Phi., Chi., Car.						All-Stars	
NHL Career	GP	G	A	Pts.	PIM	1st	2nd
1980-present	1,391	396	1,131	1,527	1,772	4	4
Playoffs	194	59	137	196	264	4 Cups	

'84 '85 '87 '91

Coach Scotty Bowman

Noteworthy The winningest coach in NHL history, with 1,144 victories in 1,977 games entering the 2000-01 season, he has won a total of eight Stanley Cups with three different teams—Montreal, Pittsburgh and Detroit. Bowman is considered a master of assessing the performance of players on any given night and assigning ice time accordingly.

Pollock "Scotty probably knows what opposing players can do better than anyone else. He's an outstanding bench coach and good at managing players. When you're coaching, you've got to be able to manage players."

Teams St.L., Mon., Buf., Pit., Det.						
NHL Career	G	W	L	T	Pct.	Cups
1967-present	1,977	1,144	539	294	.653	–
Playoffs	325	206	119	—	.634	8

'73 '76 '77 '78 '79 '92 '97 '98

General Manager Sam Pollock

Noteworthy A shrewd dealer, Pollock traded depth players in the Montreal Canadiens' organization for draft picks, which he stockpiled and used to select future NHL stars such as Guy Lafleur. The Habs won nine Stanley Cups in the 14 seasons he served as GM and missed the playoffs only once, in 1969-70. During that time the Habs won an incredible 71.6 per cent of their playoff games.

Neale "Sam was excellent at finding prospects across the country. It was said he knew every player in Canada. While he was in Montreal, the club always had about four guys in the minors you knew were going to become NHL stars."

Teams Mon.						
NHL Career	G	W	L	T	Pct.	Cups
1964-78 (14)	1,068	644	248	176	.685	–
Playoffs	162	116	46	—	.716	9

'65 '66 '68 '69 '71 '73 '76 '77 '78

Summit Series 2002 Would Be Perfect Battle

In the interests of providing our perfect NHL team with some competition, we've assembled a second team and are planning a Summit Series for 2002, the 30th anniversary of the original Clash of the Titans. Six players were automatic choices because they were among the best of all-time, as chosen by The Hockey News Top 100 Selection Committee. They are Jacques Plante, Ray Bourque, Denis Potvin, Ted Lindsay, Mario Lemieux and Rocket Richard. All players are identified with the teams with which they achieved the most prominence. NHL career lengths also are listed.

No. 1 Goalie	G **Jacques Plante**, Mon. 1954-73 *All-time pioneer*	No. 2 Two-Way Line	LW **John Tonelli**, NYI 1978-92 *Post-season star*
No. 2 Goalie	G **Michel Larocque**, Mon. 1973-83 *Dryden's backup*		C **Butch Goring**, NYI 1969-85 *Key piece of dynasty*
No. 1 Defense Pair	D **Ray Bourque**, Bos. 1979-present *Five Norrises*		RW **George Armstrong**, Tor. 1952-71 *Leafs' leader*
	D **Kevin Lowe**, Edm. 1979-98 *Defensive dandy*	No. 3 Checking Line	LW **Don Marcotte**, Bos. 1969-82 *Superstar shadow*
No. 2 Defense Pair	D **Denis Potvin**, NYI 1973-88 *Supreme commander*		C **Guy Carbonneau**, Mon. 1982-00 *Playoff star*
	D **Bob Goldham**, Det. 1945-56 *Expert shotblocker*		RW **Eddie Westfall**, NYI 1961-79 *Original Islander*
No. 3 Defense Pair	D **Al Arbour**, Chi. 1953-71 *Ultimate fill-in rearguard*	No. 4 Momentum Line	LW **Tiger Williams**, Tor. 1975-88 *Prince of PIMs*
	D **Tex Evans**, Chi. 1950-63 *Made shooters pay price*		C **Red Sullivan**, NYR 1951-61 *Blue-collar Blueshirt*
No. 1 Scoring Line	LW **Ted Lindsay**, Det. 1944-65 *Tough in corners*		RW **Bill Ezinicki**, Tor. 1946-55 *Wild man on blades*
	C **Mario Lemieux**, Pit.1984-97 *Incomparable skill*	Utility Player	D/F **Lou Nanne**, Min. 1968-78 *All-purpose player*
	RW **Rocket Richard**, Mon. 1943-60 *Passion and fury*	Rover	C **Denis Savard**, Chi. 1980-97 *Sparkling performer*

The hockey world was Slava Fetisov's playground during a magnificent 22-year career. He stands beside the giant unisphere at the site of the 1964 World's Fair in New York City.

Global
Superstar

By
Mark
Brender

In the heyday of Soviet hockey, when players couldn't so much as buy a used car without the coach's consent, Slava Fetisov lived with his teammates in the Central Red Army dormitory at Archangelsk outside Moscow, cut off from all semblance of a normal life 11 months of the year. For 13 straight seasons, from his late teens until he was 30, he had no choice but to call that place home.

The dormitory was equipped with a single, much-in-demand telephone. Fetisov used that phone to call his wife in the city, his parents and friends, since actually seeing them wasn't something the captain of the most prestigious sports team in the Communist world was permitted to do. Actually there was one other phone, for use when the dorm lineup got too long. "Sometimes guys take a walk," Fetisov says. Three miles down the road.

It seems like a lifetime ago.

Fetisov carries a cell phone in his pocket now, one of those annoying musical jobs with the ring that sounds like a video game. When he cradles it in his left hand and puts it to his ear, the sparkling gold inlay of his mammoth Detroit Red Wings' Stanley Cup ring shines like a starlet's glitter dress on Oscar night.

It seems like yesterday.

So busy dealing with life's crazy bounces off the end boards, Fetisov has never had time to reflect in peace. His triumphs belong on a movie set with Clark Gable, his tragedies embedded in the gloom of an Arthur Koestler novel.

Two Olympic gold medals, two World Junior Championship golds, seven World Championship golds, a record nine World Championship first team all-star selections, nine USSR first team honors.

A dead teammate, a dead brother, government spies following his every move, a fight for freedom, a cloud of loneliness, two close friends crippled for life.

"In every station I reached my highest point, something happened to me all the time," Fetisov says. "I don't know why, but I never got too much time to celebrate anything. It's probably my destiny, how they test me all the time, how I can overcome situations like that."

He overcame it with great skating ability and an uncommon physical nastiness; by playing like a tough Ray Bourque with the leadership of a Mark Messier; by anchoring the 'Green Unit,' the most famous quintet in hockey history: Fetisov, defense partner Alexei Kasatonov, and the KLM forward line of Vladimir Krutov, Igor Larionov and Sergei Makarov; by fighting a Communist Party-run system–"one of the most anti-human systems in the world," he says–and winning.

Asked for his reaction to being selected by The Hockey News as the top European player ever, based on international and all non-NHL league play, Fetisov struggles for words. He thanks his teammates and coaches and struggles some more.

Soviet Captain No. 1 All-Time

Slava Fetisov won every team and individual award of significance in international hockey. It came as no surprise, then, that when we asked a distinguished panel of international hockey experts to pick the best player ever in non-NHL national league and international competition, Fetisov was a near-unanimous choice. The long-time captain of the Red Army club and Soviet Union national team heads up The Hockey News All-Time World Team. *(See page 151 for a story on the entire squad.)* Fetisov, born in Moscow April 20, 1958, was a sensation from his first season in the Soviet Elite League at age 18 and maintained an extraordinarily high level of play throughout his 13-year career with Red Army. He played his last international game at age 38 in the 1996 World Cup; he completed a stunning 22 seasons of triumphs by winning a pair of Stanley Cups with the Detroit Red Wings before retiring in 1998. Fetisov and Red Army/Red Wings' teammate Igor Larionov are the only two players who have won an Olympic gold medal, World Championship gold, Canada Cup title, World Junior Championship gold and Stanley Cup. Now, Fetisov has earned another honor: Status as the greatest player ever in non-NHL competition.

This is a man who refused to become a Communist Party member while captain of the national hockey team, the first to take such a stand. (He signed up when Mikhail Gorbachev became president, but quit three months later when he saw the same men running the show.) This is a man who met with Pavel Grachov, Russia's Minister of Defense, to explain why he played one game for Spartak instead of Central Army during the 1994 NHL lockout. He has had his share of big moments.

"It's a big honor, actually," Fetisov finally says. "A big honor."

What says more is his silence. He sits on a hotel lobby couch fidgeting, scratching his face. A tape recorder rolls on, taking in empty time.

❑ ❑ ❑ ❑

At 42, comfortably stylish in a tailored black suit and black shirt, Fetisov cuts an imposing figure two years removed from his final NHL playing days. Thick and broad through the chest. Squat, meaty legs. He carries the "Who's he?" presence of a man used to success. Fetisov has homes in Detroit and in New Jersey, where he is an assistant coach for the Devils. By any account, he has a life of privilege, finally, fit for the finest player Europe has ever produced.

"He was born for this game," says his former Devils' teammate, Czechoslovak star Peter Stastny. "It's hard to name the skills and qualities he had because he had them all. That's my gospel, I'm spreading it all over."

Was he as good as Bobby Orr or Doug Harvey? No. Was he better than Denis Potvin or Larry Robinson or Paul Coffey or Bourque? The Devils' director of scouting, David Conte, who was playing professionally in Europe when Fetisov broke into the Soviet Elite League, suggests flipping a coin to decide that question.

Some points to consider when comparing Fetisov to his North American peers: No NHL defenseman has won the Hart Trophy as most valuable player since Orr in 1972. Fetisov was twice named the top player in the Soviet Union and three times the top player in Europe.

As for longevity, Fetisov's 22 seasons in the Elite League and NHL are more than any of his superstar peers. Next year will be Bourque's 22nd. While it might be argued that Bourque has played at a superstar level longer than Fetisov, 13 seasons of year-round training, nine more grueling years in the NHL and more than 500 international games is bound to take its toll.

Fetisov led Soviet defensemen in league scoring in most of his 13 seasons, including a career-high 49 points in 44 games in 1983-84, but never considered offense his priority.

"I've probably never been a minus player in any tournament," Fetisov says. "In some games, probably, but to play the game right, that was my priority. I mean, I scored more than 300 goals (including NHL and international competition), but never put my defensive responsibility on the side. For me it was defense first and then if I got a chance, I could join the rush or I could jump, back door, in the high slot, stuff like that, but with minimum risk all the time...I was lucky enough to play with guys who can complement each other."

Fetisov was above all a winner, possibly the winningest hockey player in history.

From age nine when he joined the Central Army system, until age 18 when he was the seventh defenseman for the Soviet Union's bronze medal-winning 1977 World Championship team, he never lost a tournament or a league title. In his 13 years with the senior team he won 13 Soviet League titles. Central Army lost the year before he came and the year after he left. Fetisov lost only five games that mattered his entire time in the Soviet Union: To Canada and Czechoslovakia in the 1985 World Championship, to the U.S. at the 1980 Olympics and to Canada, twice, in the 1987 Canada Cup.

Fetisov was 18 when he made the Central Army team, a 6-foot-1, 220-pounder with the body of a construction worker and the agility of a soccer player. At 19, he fell victim to a mysterious disease and landed in hospital, paralyzed from the waist down. He lost 45 pounds. He saw the pity in the doctors' eyes when they told him he'd be lucky to walk again and couldn't stand it. Five months later he cried again with his first steps back on ice. No explanation for the illness was ever found.

In 1978, he won the award for best defenseman at the World Junior Championship in Montreal and the World Championship in Prague, a feat that has never been matched. Fetisov calls the gold medal-winning 3-1 victory over Czechoslovakia in Prague the tensest game he ever played, but it was his performance in Montreal that convinced the Montreal Canadiens to select him with the 201st overall pick in the 1978 NHL draft. He was the Habs' first-ever European pick. A few years later Montreal dropped Fetisov from its protected list, allowing New Jersey to draft him, 150th overall in 1983.

That WJC was also the first of many battles between Fetisov and Wayne Gretzky. Gretzky later called Fetisov the hardest defenseman to beat 1-on-1. Other opponents and former teammates talk about a sense of timing so special that it didn't conform to conventional rules. "He understands you," says former Soviet superstar teammate Sergei Makarov. "You do some move, he understands you."

Stastny, the former Quebec Nordiques' ace, remembers a play in one NHL game against Fetisov's Devils. The Devils had the puck in the corner in the offensive zone, but were about to lose it. Everybody could see it; the play was in transi-

Slava Fetisov goes up against Canadian superstar Mario Lemieux during the 1987 Canada Cup.

tion, a Nordiques' attack ready to take shape. So Fetisov, of course, cut to the front of the net, took a pass and scored.

"I would never anticipate this because you just don't see certain plays," Stastny recalls. "And when I looked I said, 'Yeah, I should have known.' That's the sense when you know you've got to help your teammate and the sense that if he's got to give it somewhere, he's going to give it right here. And he would be there."

Fetisov was named Red Army and national team captain early in 1982. At 23, he was the youngest captain ever. It was a time of turmoil for the Soviet national team. The previous year, star veteran forward Valeri Kharlamov had died in a car crash. The year before that was the shocking loss to the Americans at Lake Placid.

Fetisov's appointment as captain represented a changing of the guard and the pressure leading up to the 1984 Olympics was almost too much to bear. "I was so responsible, always responsible for the result, responsible for my teammates," he says.

Even those not privy to the inner dynamics of the Soviet machine could tell Fetisov was the anchor. "There were times you could see some discouragement," says Dave King, long-time coach of Canada's national team. "Makarov, who was a great player, Krutov, a great player, you could see them a little frustrated. And you could think, 'I've got them off their game.' You could never sense with Fetisov you've got him off his game."

Nonetheless, Fetisov felt it inside, day after day, month after month, year after year. You try winning 39 league games in a row, losing the next one and then watching as the same army generals calling the shots in Afghanistan show up at practice looking for answers. That's why the Soviets' 1984 Olympic win in Sarajevo is the highlight of Fetisov's career. It wasn't the best hockey tournament ever, but it was much-needed affirmation. In medal round games, the Soviets outscored Sweden, Canada and Czechoslovakia 16-1.

"He's leader," says Makarov, now living in San Jose. "Always, always, he's leader. He would like to be best all the time."

They had their battles, Fetisov and Makarov. Fetisov said it was always about performance, never personal. Mesmerized by that passing, we in North American thought we were watching perfection. Fetisov knew better.

"If he thinks you're wrong, he tells you, 'You're s---,' " Makarov says. "When he goes on the ice, for him it's like, 'Guys, I'm here. Hello guys, I'm here.' And that's it, he just don't care about who is around him. He always was like this."

That summer after the '84 Olympics, coach Viktor

Tikhonov began a two-month stint of four-a-day practices in preparation for the 1984 Canada Cup. During that time, the Red Army club travelled to Italy for the European Cup club team championship tournament. Following a full day of travel and being forced by Tikhonov to practise without a flood on cut-up ice at 10:15 at night on a rink used for public skating, a teammate lost an edge, fell and landed on Fetisov. The captain missed the Canada Cup with a broken leg.

The next year, in 1985, Fetisov crashed his car while driving in Moscow. His younger brother Anatoli, a promising prospect, was killed in the passenger seat. He was nine years younger than Slava; Anatoli had been like a son to him.

By the winter of 1988-89, Fetisov had enough of Tikhonov and pushed things to a head. Instead of defecting during a North American tour–including a stop in New Jersey–he returned to Moscow and quit Central Red Army. His phone was tapped, his car followed home from his army desk job. He made it back for the 1989 World Championship only because his teammates said they wouldn't play without him. When he finally received his ticket to New Jersey, he became the first Soviet to receive a visa that allowed him to come and go as he pleased, opening the floodgates for the rest to follow.

"It's probably one of my biggest victories besides my gold medals," he says. "I feel I had big enough name to accomplish something besides being champion."

In New Jersey, Fetisov lost more games in the first two months than he had the previous decade in international competition. At first he felt lost, unwelcome, mentally exhausted, lonely in the country of freedom. Though the feelings eventually subsided, his trade to Detroit in 1995 and playing with the Wings' 'Russian Five' gave him new life and, in 1997, a cherished Stanley Cup. It would bring him only the briefest joy.

Six days after the Cup victory, Fetisov was in the limousine that crashed into a tree and left teammate Vladimir

Konstantinov and Wings' trainer Sergei Mnatsakanov with brain damage. As a result of the accident, Fetisov played the next season with barely any feeling in his right leg. He could only pivot properly in one direction. He told only a few people, figuring he didn't have much reason to complain.

Chess champion Garry Kasparov once said Fetisov could be Russian president if he wanted. Asked how Fetisov is seen in Russia today, New Jersey winger Alex Mogilny said he doesn't know about that; he doesn't go home very often. That's the Russian generation gap, right there.

Fetisov wants to go back. He might build a house in Moscow some day. He fought not only for the right to be free, but the right to return under his own terms. He has already given back plenty. Sergei Samsonov, Valeri Bure, Sergei Brylin and scores of other Central Army club teenagers wore equipment that Fetisov shipped home and paid for with half his first year's salary with the Devils.

Devils' GM Lou Lamoriello doesn't believe current New Jersey players will ever be able to understand Fetisov's stature. But they'd be wise to know his story if they care about the history of their game.

"Legends," Lamoriello says, "have a way of surfacing in conversations."

They surface in other places, too. Conte remembers visiting a Koho factory in Finland to pick up his sticks before the 1976-77 season. Conte's apartment walls were bare, so he grabbed a few of the rolled-up posters they offered him. When he unraveled them at home, he found they were all of Fetisov.

The kid was 18 years old. He had yet to earn international acclaim, but that's the great thing about legends. People in the know can appreciate their talents and see them coming long before their time.

You can see in Fetisov's face that legends appreciate being remembered as well.

Fetisov's Journey To Greatness

Soviet	Team	GP	G	A	Pts.
1976-77	Red Army*	28	3	4	7
1977-78	Red Army*	35	9	18	27
1978-79	Red Army*	29	10	19	29
1979-80	Red Army*	37	10	14	24
1980-81	Red Army*	48	13	16	29
1981-82	Red Army*	46	15	26	41
1982-83	Red Army*	43	6	17	23
1983-84	Red Army*	44	19	30	49
1984-85	Red Army*	20	13	12	25
1985-86	Red Army*	40	15	19	34
1986-87	Red Army*	39	13	20	33
1987-88	Red Army*	46	18	17	35
1988-89	Red Army*	23	9	8	17

ON GOLDEN POND

Slava Fetisov's combined national-international career was golden. Here's a synopsis of team and individual honors. Included are the number of times Fetisov earned honors and the total number for which he was eligible.

Honor	Number
Soviet League Championships	13 in 13 seasons
Soviet League 1st All-Star	9 in 13 seasons
Soviet Player of the Year	2 in 13 seasons
World Championship Gold Medals	7 in 11 events
World Championship 1st All-Star	9 in 11 events
World Championship Best Defenseman	5 in 11 events
Olympic Gold Medals	2 in 3 events
European Player of the Year	3 in 11 seasons

NHL	Team	GP	G	A	Pts.
1989-90	New Jersey	72	8	34	42
1990-91	New Jersey	67	3	16	19
1991-92	New Jersey	70	3	23	26
1992-93	New Jersey	76	4	23	27
1993-94	New Jersey	52	1	4	5
1994-95	NJ/Detroit	18	3	12	15
1995-96	Detroit	69	7	35	42
1996-97	Detroit**	64	5	23	28
1997-98	Detroit**	58	2	12	14
Soviet League		478	153	220	373
Major Tournaments		157	57	102	159
NHL		546	36	192	228
*Soviet Champions	**Stanley Cup				

The Hockey News All-Time World Team has three Vladimirs, two Valeris and one Viktor. It could be no other way.

Because had they ever played together, there would have most assuredly been just one victor–this magnificent collection of players chosen by a panel of 16 international hockey experts as the best ever to play in European national and international competition. All 23 members of the international-size roster were selected because they starred in their country's top leagues and glittered in major events against European or North American competition.

Thirteen players, plus the coach and manager, are products of the powerhouse system that propelled the Soviet Union to the top of international hockey during the 1960s, '70s and '80s.

Anatoli Tarasov, the guiding influence behind the pivotal early development of Soviet hockey, is the manager and Viktor Tikhonov, the ruthless taskmaster who won eight World Championships and three Olympic golds, the coach.

On their roster is a group of players to behold, including eight from the former Czechoslovakia and two from Sweden. Tops among the Soviets is Slava Fetisov, who was selected the best European ever. Panelists were asked to rank the top three goalies, seven defensemen and 13 forwards (with no regard to forward position) on the basis of achievements in non-NHL league and international competition.

For instance, second all-star goalie Dominik Hasek, the backup to No. 1 choice Vladislav Tretiak, earned a place on the team strictly on the strength of superlative play in and for

World Beaters

'The Godfather' of Soviet hockey, Anatoli Tarasov, is also 'The Godfather' of The Hockey News All-Time World Team. It is comprised of Europeans who have performed brilliantly on the international stage. Tarasov is manager and Viktor Tikhonov the coach.

Czechoslovakia and the Czech Republic, not for anything he has done in the NHL.

As a result of this distinction, absent from the team are such present and past European-trained stars as Jaromir Jagr, Jari Kurri, Peter Stastny, Borje Salming, Teemu Selanne and Peter Forsberg. Each of them has starred in the NHL at the expense of making bigger and longer-term impacts in their home countries.

Two other players are conspicuous by their absence: Forwards Igor Larionov and Vladimir Krutov didn't make the team despite membership in the legendary 'Green Unit.' The Fab Five is represented by Fetisov, Alexei Kasatonov and Sergei Makarov. All six members of the All-Time World first team are Soviets: Tretiak, Fetisov, Valeri Vasiliev, Valeri Kharlamov, Anatoli Firsov and Alexander Maltsev.

By Denis Gibbons & Jason Paul

The Hockey News All-Time World Team

Coach
Viktor Tikhonov
Soviet Union (1971-present)

8 World gold medals
3 Olympic gold medals

Manager
Anatoli Tarasov
Soviet Union (1954-74)

9 World gold medals
3 Olympic gold medals

Legend
Listed for each player is career length (including NHL where appropriate) and most significant team/individual achievements. Abbreviations: World, World Championship; Czech., Czechoslovakia.

1st All-Star Goalie
Vladislav Tretiak
Soviet Union (1968-84)

3 European Player of Year awards
5 Soviet Player of Year awards

2nd All-Star Goalie
Dominik Hasek
Czech./Czech Rep. (1981-present)

1 Olympic gold medals
5 Czech./Czech Rep. Player of Year

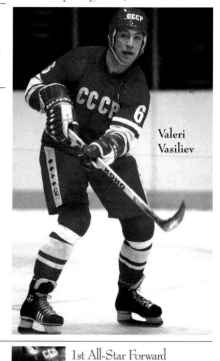

Valeri
Vasiliev

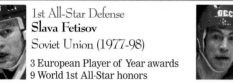

1st All-Star Defense
Slava Fetisov
Soviet Union (1977-98)

3 European Player of Year awards
9 World 1st All-Star honors

1st All-Star Defense
Valeri Vasiliev
Soviet Union (1967-82)

3 World best defenseman honors
5 World 1st All-Star honors

2nd All-Star Defense
Frantisek Pospisil
Czechoslovakia (1961-79)

2 Czech. Player of Year awards
3 World 1st All-Star honors

2nd All-Star Defense
Jan Suchy
Czechoslovakia (1963-84)

2 Czech. Player of Year awards
4 World 1st All-Star honors

3rd All-Star Defense
Alexei Kasatonov
Soviet Union (1976-97)

5 World 1st All-Star honors
1 World best defenseman honor

3rd All-Star Defense
Alexander Ragulin
Soviet Union (1958-73)

10 World gold medals
1 World best defenseman honor

1st All-Star Forward
Valery Kharlamov
Soviet Union (1967-81)

8 World gold medals
3 World 1st All-Star honors

1st All-Star Forward
Anatoli Firsov
Soviet Union (1958-74)

3 Soviet Player of Year awards
3 World best forward honors

1st All-Star Forward
Alexander Maltsev
Soviet Union (1967-83)

9 World gold medals
3 World best forward honors

2nd All-Star Forward
Vsevolod Bobrov
Soviet Union (1946-57)

2 World gold medals
3 Soviet League goal-scoring titles

2nd All-Star Forward
Sven 'Tumba' Johansson
Sweden (1951-69)

3 World gold medals
2 World best forward honors

2nd All-Star Forward
Vaclav Nedomansky
Czechoslovakia (1962-74)

3 World 1st All-Star honors
4 Czech. scoring titles

3rd All-Star Forward
Sergei Makarov
Soviet Union (1976-98)

2 European Player of Year awards
9 Soviet League scoring titles

3rd All-Star Forward
Vladimir Petrov
Soviet Union (1965-81)

9 World gold medals
3 World 1st All-Star honors

3rd All-Star Forward
Boris Mikhailov
Soviet Union (1962-81)

2 Soviet Player of Year awards
1 European Player of Year award

4th All-Star Forward
Josef Golonka
Czechoslovakia (1955-72)

3 World silver medals
1 World scoring title

4th All-Star Forward
Ivan Hlinka
Czechoslovakia (1968-85)

3 World gold medals
1 Czech. Player of Year award

4th All-Star Forward
Vladimir Martinec
Czechoslovakia (1965-85)

4 Czech. Player of Year awards
3 World gold medals

Spare Goalie
Vladimir Dzurilla
Czechoslovakia (1957-82)

3 World gold medals
2 World 1st All-Star honors

Spare Defenseman
Lennart Svedberg
Sweden (1963-72)

3 World 1st All-Star honors
1 World best defenseman honor

Spare Forward
Slava Starshinov
Soviet Union (1957-75)

9 World gold medals
1 World best forward honor

1st All-Star Goalie Vladislav Tretiak

Claim to Fame At 20, Tretiak sparkled against NHL stars in 1972. He shone again in 1981 when the Soviets embarrassed Canada 8-1 in the Canada Cup final. His acrobatic style and quick reflexes left shooters shaking their heads. Career: 1968-84
Anatoli Tarasov "First of all I liked his absolute eagerness and fanatic devotion to hockey. I also liked his uncommon abilities. He could profoundly analyze his actions. His game was thought through to the highest degree."

2nd All-Star Goalie Dominik Hasek

Claim to Fame Hasek stoned Canada in a shootout at the 1998 Olympics, then shut out Russia 1-0 for the gold medal. The five-time Czech Player of the Year foils forwards with an unorthodox style based on extraordinary agility. Career: 1981-present
Peter Stastny "His aim is to stop the puck any way he can. In Europe we had schools of goalies with different styles, but he is more free-spirited, like North American goalies. He developed himself in the style of organized chaos."

1st All-Star Defenseman Slava Fetisov

Claim to Fame At 20, he was the best defenseman at the World Championship. He won everything that mattered–Olympic, World Championship and World Junior golds, plus 13 Soviet titles, the Canada Cup and Stanley Cup. Career: 1977-98
Viktor Tikhonov "Slava was equally strong in defense and on the attack. He willingly joined the attack and had a powerful and accurate shot. He was the soul of the squad and indisputable leader of Central Red Army and the national team."

1st All-Star Defenseman Valeri Vasiliev

Claim to Fame He captained the Soviet national team to victory in the 1981 Canada Cup. A hard hitter, Vasiliev was feared by opponents, but also generated offense with pinpoint, 90-foot passes to streaking winger Alexander Maltsev. Career: 1967-82
Vladislav Tretiak "Valeri was always an example of hockey power for us. Bobby Hull once confessed that whenever he saw Vasiliev approaching, he wanted to get rid of the puck as quickly as possible."

2nd All-Star Defenseman Frantisek Pospisil

Claim to Fame The cool-headed Czechoslovakian captain led his country to three World Championship golds in the 1970s. He had excellent hockey sense and was a master of the long pass from his zone to the center red line. Career: 1961-79
Stastny "He was a kind of quarterback. He had no speed, yet he could play the fastest game because he moved the puck with precision. He was one of the best in the transition game. When you found a hole, you knew you were going to get the puck."

2nd All-Star Defenseman Jan Suchy

Claim to Fame He was jailed for almost a year following an auto fatality for which he was blamed. Small and slight, like Hall of Famer Pierre Pilote, he specialized in scoring off the trailer pass and was a talented shot-blocker. Career: 1963-84
Stastny "Suchy always was the second goalie on the ice. He was tireless and self-sacrificing. He would block slapshots with the backside of his glove, then just take his hand out, shake it a bit, put it back in the glove and just keep playing."

3rd All-Star Defenseman Alexei Kasatonov

Claim to Fame A Leningrad native, he meshed with his Moscow mates to lead all Soviets as they won the 1981 Canada Cup. A slick passer, he also sent defenders looking for their jockstraps with clever dekes and faked shots. Career: 1976-97
Igor Larionov "He was a robust fellow with ruddy cheeks and recklessness in his eyes. They don't often produce hockey masters in the 'Venice of the North.' But sometimes gifted guys do appear on the banks of the Neva, and Kasatonov was one such fellow."

3rd All-Star Defenseman Alexander Ragulin

Claim to Fame A stay-at-home giant, he anchored the Soviet blueline brigade of the 1960s, using his strength to clear the front of net without taking penalties. He had the total respect of teammates, who saw him as a man of principle. Career: 1958-73
Tarasov "Running into him can be like running into a brick wall. Yet Alexander never loses his head. He has a knack for picking off oncoming wingers. But what is really surprising is that his body-checking is really gentle."

1st All-Star Forward Valeri Kharlamov

Claim to Fame He stunned a sold-out Montreal Forum with two brilliant goals in the first meeting between the Soviets and NHL stars in 1972. He often challenged defenders to take the puck away from him, then blew right by them. Career: 1967-81
Tarasov "I want to emphasize that the bosses of Canadian professional hockey long ago recognized Valeri Kharlamov as the best forward of the 20th century. With his darting fakes and fancy stickhandling, he put the pros in embarrassing positions."

1st All-Star Forward Anatoli Firsov

Claim to Fame A lightning-quick thinker, he was the star of the great Soviet teams of the 1960s and creator of new techniques. He liked to beat defenders by dropping the puck back to his skates, then kicking it ahead to his stick. Career: 1958-74
Tarasov "He had a fantastic capacity for work at training sessions. He was constantly looking for new ways to improve his game, yet he was quite modest. He never let success go to his head. His speed, faking and camouflaged decisions made him the ideal player."

1st All-Star Forward Alexander Maltsev

Claim to Fame Maltsev appeared in more international games (313) than any other Soviet. The crafty puckhandler was adept at changing skating speeds. In a 1980 exhibition against the United States, he scored while skating backwards. Career: 1967-83
Tarasov "He was a grand master who understood creative hockey and therefore, from the first training sessions, was able to develop a common language with his linemates. He played many positions and was everywhere on the ice."

2nd All-Star Forward Vsevolod Bobrov

Claim to Fame The two-sport phenom (also soccer) captained the Soviet Union to its landmark 1954 World Championship. Bobrov was the consummate offensive force, leading the Soviet League in goals three times. Career: 1946-57
Tarasov "He was a daring, solo attacker who had a very accurate shot and effective fake moves on the goalie. He played the individual Canadian style in an era when the Soviets specialized in team play."

2nd All-Star Forward Sven Johansson

Claim to Fame Nicknamed 'Tumba,' the huge center introduced the slapshot to Sweden after studying Canadian players and had a tryout with the Boston Bruins. He was named best Swedish player of the 20th century. Career: 1951-69
Tarasov "He was often shadowed by the other team's best checker. He, himself, would start shadowing a different player on the opposition. In this way, the opponent had two players close to him and it left a Swedish player open for a pass."

2nd All-Star Forward Vaclav Nedomansky

Claim to Fame He was a powerful skater with an iron will. 'Big Ned' had a heavy wrist shot and could score from outside the blueline against surprised goaltenders. He scored 163 goals in 220 international games. Career: 1962-74
Stastny "Vaclav was an absolute idol. He was the dominant and most spectacular player in Europe at the time he played. He had great acceleration and a shot so hard that some goalies actually were afraid of him. When he shot, they just froze."

3rd All-Star Forward Sergei Makarov

Claim to Fame A brilliant stickhandler and skater, he led the Soviet League in scoring a record nine times. His bow-legged skating style and powerful legs made him very tough to knock off the puck. Career: 1976-98
Tikhonov "Makarov was a star of the top magnitude. His moves were unexpected and even seemed to be illogical or incorrect. But top hockey skill manifests itself exactly in this unpredictability of actions."

3rd All-Star Forward Vladimir Petrov

Claim to Fame A physically strong center, he used slick passes to set up wingers Kharlamov and Mikhailov on the Soviets' top line in the 1970s. He set the all-time World Championship record, averaging 3.4 points per game in 1973. Career: 1965-81
Tarasov "One of the finest points about Petrov was his ability to round out an attack. He had the uncanny gift of administering the coup de grace. He could hit the net from almost any position on the ice."

3rd All-Star Forward Boris Mikhailov

Claim to Fame The inspirational leader of the 1970s Soviets was paradoxically short on emotion and long on talent. He rallied the troops to win the 1979 Challenge Cup and drove goalies crazy, sneaking in on the off-wing to one-time passes. Career: 1962-81
Tarasov "Mikhailov had daring and plenty of ingenuity. He seemed to like to tangle with the player checking him. He skated far and wide and if he did lose the puck, he would immediately try to retrieve it."

4th All-Star Forward Josef Golonka

Claim to Fame He knelt down and kissed the ice and danced around the rink on his skates after Czechoslovakia upset the Soviets twice at the 1969 World Championship, less than a year after the Soviet invasion of Czechoslovakia. Career: 1955-72
Stastny "He was a playmaker par excellence and a very, very fierce competitor who would dig pucks out of the corner. He was outspoken, a leader by example and a player who would do anything to win."

4th All-Star Forward Ivan Hlinka

Claim to Fame A playmaking center with a deceptive shot and a huge heart, Hlinka also was an expert at using his size and strength to protect the puck and was tough to beat on faceoffs. Career: 1968-85
Stastny "Ivan was a great overall talent who was unstoppable once he reached top speed. He and defenseman Jiri Bubla had a set of signals. They would pass the puck back and forth and Bubla was usually able to find Ivan near the net to finish off the play."

4th All-Star Forward Vladimir Martinec

Claim to Fame He was one of Czechoslovakia's greatest pure finesse players of all-time and all but impossible to stop 1-on-1. He had the skills to play in the NHL, but never did because heavy body contact was not his style. Career: 1965-85
Stastny "Martinec was an icon of Czechoslovak hockey. He was incredibly intelligent, had unbelievable hands and combination-wise he was a genius playing on a line with Bohuslav Stastny and Jiri Novak, which was dominant in world tournaments."

Spare Goalie Vladimir Dzurilla

Claim to Fame The rotund refrigerator repairman cooled out Team Canada shooters 1-0 in the opening round of the 1976 Canada Cup, before losing to the same Canadians in OT in the final on Darryl Sittler's goal. Career: 1957-82
Stastny "He was born to be a goalie. He used a standup style and was aggressive in challenging shooters. He was full of confidence, an excellent communicator with his defensemen and in charge of the situation every time he was in the nets."

Spare Defenseman Lennart Svedberg

Claim to Fame A superb skater, he started his career as a forward and became a Swedish national champion with Brynas in 1964. Nicknamed '*Lill Strimma*'—'The Little Streak'—he died in an auto accident at age 28 in 1972. Career: 1963-72
Tarasov "Svedberg was the only Swedish player I really wished we had on the Soviet team. Arne Stromberg, the chief trainer of the *Tre Kronor*, concentrated his attention on physical conditioning and especially on speed skating."

Spare Forward Slava Starshinov

Claim to Fame The feisty center who re-arranged Carl Brewer's face at the 1967 World Championship sometimes played two- to three-minute shifts. He also had a knack for scoring winning goals in the dying minutes of crucial games. Career: 1957-75
Tarasov "Starshinov's courage was unique. He really shone playing right in front of the net. For it is in this 'kill zone,' where the toughest battles are fought and the defense is especially hard-hitting, that he most fully displays his qualities as a fighter."

Torch Carriers

By Mike Ulmer

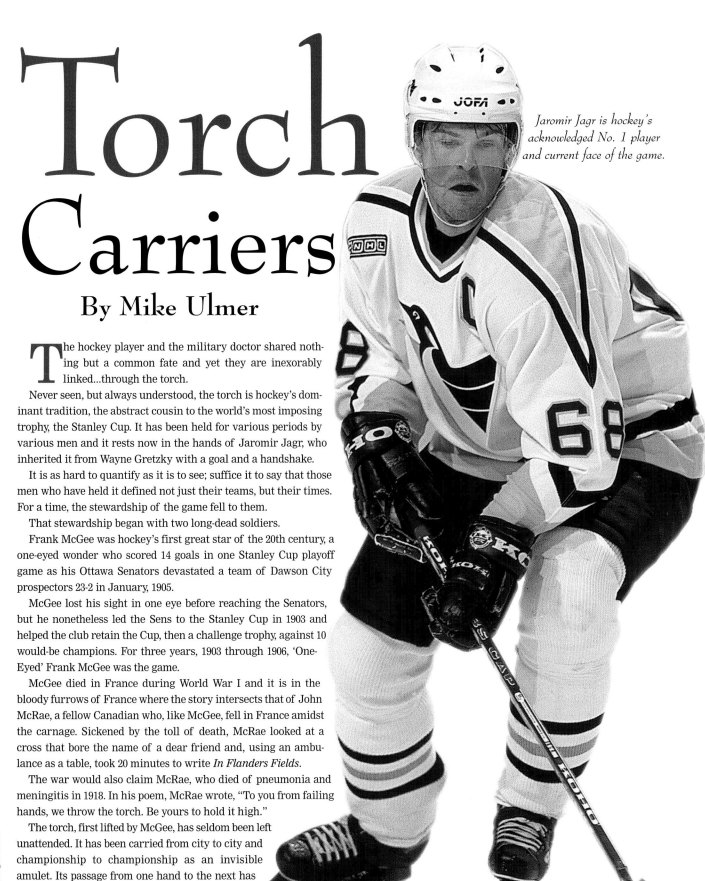

Jaromir Jagr is hockey's acknowledged No. 1 player and current face of the game.

The hockey player and the military doctor shared nothing but a common fate and yet they are inexorably linked...through the torch.

Never seen, but always understood, the torch is hockey's dominant tradition, the abstract cousin to the world's most imposing trophy, the Stanley Cup. It has been held for various periods by various men and it rests now in the hands of Jaromir Jagr, who inherited it from Wayne Gretzky with a goal and a handshake.

It is as hard to quantify as it is to see; suffice it to say that those men who have held it defined not just their teams, but their times. For a time, the stewardship of the game fell to them.

That stewardship began with two long-dead soldiers.

Frank McGee was hockey's first great star of the 20th century, a one-eyed wonder who scored 14 goals in one Stanley Cup playoff game as his Ottawa Senators devastated a team of Dawson City prospectors 23-2 in January, 1905.

McGee lost his sight in one eye before reaching the Senators, but he nonetheless led the Sens to the Stanley Cup in 1903 and helped the club retain the Cup, then a challenge trophy, against 10 would-be champions. For three years, 1903 through 1906, 'One-Eyed' Frank McGee was the game.

McGee died in France during World War I and it is in the bloody furrows of France where the story intersects that of John McRae, a fellow Canadian who, like McGee, fell in France amidst the carnage. Sickened by the toll of death, McRae looked at a cross that bore the name of a dear friend and, using an ambulance as a table, took 20 minutes to write *In Flanders Fields*.

The war would also claim McRae, who died of pneumonia and meningitis in 1918. In his poem, McRae wrote, "To you from failing hands, we throw the torch. Be yours to hold it high."

The torch, first lifted by McGee, has seldom been left unattended. It has been carried from city to city and championship to championship as an invisible amulet. Its passage from one hand to the next has never been solemnly marked, but it is as much a part of the game as rock-hard rubber and frozen water.

Rocket Richard passes the torch to Jean Beliveau during closing ceremonies for the Montreal Forum in 1996. The tradition-rich Montreal Canadiens are the unofficial 'keepers of the flame' and have John McRae's words inscribed on their dressing room walls.

Etched on the dressing room wall of the Montreal Canadiens, the words from *In Flanders Fields* recognize a legacy begun with McGee and passed to Frederic 'Cyclone' Taylor, the first star of the National Hockey Association who was breaking into the professional ranks in 1906 as McGee was undertaking his final season.

Taylor, nicknamed for his stunning skating style, scored seven goals in three games as Vancouver became the first West Coast team to claim a Stanley Cup in 1914-15. Taylor's time in the sun lasted from 1908 through 1919. As Taylor's career faded gradually into darkness, a ghost was emerging from the shadows. 'Phantom' Joe Malone was entering his halcyon days with the Quebec Bulldogs and the Montreal Canadiens.

For a decade, beginning in 1911, Malone was hockey's reigning star. He would strike for 44 goals in 20 games in 1917-18, a pace of 2.20 goals per game that will never be equalled. He scored seven goals in one game in 1920 to establish another record, but in 1923, he too saw the end coming.

"I took a look at a kid in our training camp in Grimsby, Ont.," Malone would later recall, "and I knew right then I was headed for the easy chair. He was Howie Morenz and in practice he moved past me so fast I thought I was standing still."

On and on the torch has been passed, from the glorious Morenz (1924-33) to the brutal and brilliant Boston Bruins' defenseman Eddie Shore (1929-1939), hockey's reigning volcanic presence until, after a short gap, there arrived a player whose incendiary will to win dwarfed that of even Shore and the torch.

Maurice 'Rocket' Richard (1943-59) was hockey's first 50-goal scorer; more than a half-century later, that accomplishment remains hockey's most enduring offensive standard and it is here that the

> *'To you from failing hands, we throw the torch.*
> *Be yours to hold it high.'*
> *– John McRae*

trail of the torch veers from hockey's most incandescent performer to the game's most durable and indomitable star. Gordie Howe (1948-1971) never scored 50 goals, but played 26 NHL seasons, most of them magnificent.

Howe fed directly into Hull, Bobby Hull (1959-72), the most electrifying player of the early 1960s and the first in a trio of stars whose calling card was unforgettable and unmatchable speed. Hull would revolutionize the way the puck was shot. Bobby Orr followed and re-defined a position. Orr (1966-75) was the game's first true offensive defenseman and his skating allowed him to stretch the parameters of the game to his whims.

Orr gave way to the 'Flower,' Guy Lafleur. The Canadiens' icon, cut from the same red cloth as Morenz, was the dominant player in the 1970s. After owning the game from 1974 through 1980, he too would give way, as everyone did, to Wayne Gretzky. No. 99 and his Edmonton Oilers laid claim to the 1980s; his 20-year reign (1979-1999) included the ascension of a rival king. Gretzky would extend his mantle to Pittsburgh Penguins' megastar Mario Lemieux (1987-97) with a pass for the winning goal at the 1987 Canada Cup.

Nonetheless, Gretzky remained the face of hockey.

Back woes would force Lemieux from the game, but by then, his teammate and protege, Jaromir Jagr, had claimed the mantle as the game's greatest performer. With Lemieux gone, it fell to the graying Gretzky to physically pass the torch and he did it with a handshake as Jagr ended Gretzky's final game with an overtime goal in 1999.

It is a mantle the great Pittsburgh star shows no sign of relinquishing. Like all torch-bearers, Jagr's incandescent talent and desire powers the flame.

The 13 Fabulous Faces of Hockey History

Thirteen players have carried the torch in North American hockey history. There have been times when no special player represented the game and others when careers overlapped. Only Bobby Orr and Wayne Gretzky carried the torch their entire careers.

Name	Frank McGee	Fred Taylor	Joe Malone	Howie Morenz	Eddie Shore	Maurice Richard
Period of Dominance	1903-06	1908-19	1911-22	1924-33	1929-39	1943-59
Primary Team	Ottawa Senators	Vancouver Millionaires	Montreal Canadiens	Montreal Canadiens	Boston Bruins	Montreal Canadiens
Nickname	'One-Eyed'	'Cyclone'	'Phantom Joe'	'Stratford Streak'	'Edmonton Express'	'Rocket'
Mark of Distinction	Unstoppable offensive force	Pacific Coast Association icon	NHL's first great goal-scorer	Labelled 'Babe Ruth of Hockey'	First truly dominant defenseman	Epitome of passion and fury on ice

| 1900 | '05 | '10 | '15 | '20 | '25 | '30 | '35 | '40 | '45 | '50 | '55 | '60 | '65 | '70 | '75 | '80 | '85 | '90 | '95 | 2000 |

Frank McGee 1903-06

Fred Taylor 1908-19

Joe Malone 1911-22

Howie Morenz 1924-33

Eddie Shore 1929-39

Maurice Richard 1943-59

Gordie Howe 1948-71

Bobby Hull 1959-72

Bobby Orr 1966-75

Guy Lafleur 1974-80

Wayne Gretzky 1979-99

Mario Lemieux 1987-97

Jaromir Jagr 1999

| 1900 | '05 | '10 | '15 | '20 | '25 | '30 | '35 | '40 | '45 | '50 | '55 | '60 | '65 | '70 | '75 | '80 | '85 | '90 | '95 | 2000 |

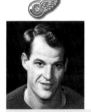      

Gordie Howe	Bobby Hull	Bobby Orr	Guy Lafleur	Wayne Gretzky	Mario Lemieux	Jaromir Jagr
1948-71	1959-72	1966-75	1974-80	1979-99	1987-97	1999-present
Detroit Red Wings	Chicago Blackhawks	Boston Bruins	Montreal Canadiens	Edmonton Oilers	Pittsburgh Penguins	Pittsburgh Penguins
'Mr. Hockey'	'The Golden Jet'		'The Flower'	'The Great One'	'Le Magnifique'	'Mario Jr.'
Most complete player in history	Charismatic scorer face of the game	Revolutionized way game was played	Speed and finesse like no other	Redefined NHL scoring standards	Best pure physical talent to ever play	Classic combo of skill and strength

Index